EMPOWERING YOUR LIFE WITH
JOY

Empowering Your Life with
JOY

Gary McClain, Ph.D. and Eve Adamson

ALPHA

A member of Penguin Group (USA) Inc.

International Standard Book Number: 1-59257-097-6
Library of Congress Catalog Card Number: 2003106911

05   04   03   8   7   6   5   4   3   2   1

Interpretation of the printing code: The rightmost number of the first series of numbers is the year of the book's printing; the rightmost number of the second series of numbers is the number of the book's printing. For example, a printing code of 03-1 shows that the first printing occurred in 2003.

Printed in the United States of America

Publisher: Marie Butler-Knight
Product Manager: Phil Kitchel
Senior Managing Editor: Jennifer Chisholm
Senior Acquisitions Editor: Randy Ladenheim-Gil
Book Producer: Lee Ann Chearney/Amaranth
Development Editor: Lynn Northrup
Senior Production Editor: Christy Wagner
Copy Editor: Nancy Wagner
Cover Designers: Doug Wilkins and Charis Santillie
Book Designer: Trina Wurst
Creative Director: Robin Lasek
Indexer: Brad Herriman
Layout/Proofreading: Angela Calvert, Megan Douglass

To our readers, who, whether they know it or not, are already—
at this moment—filled with joy!

Contents

Introduction

In the 1960s, The Beatles sang from the heart, telling the world that *love is all we need*. A hundred years earlier, poet Emily Dickinson mused that hope is the wonderful *thing with feathers*. Today, in our own lives, in times of difficulty and challenge, friends and family extol us to *keep the faith*. Faith, hope, love—are these the ingredients for joy?

And if faith, hope, and love are joy's ingredients, is the method of the recipe one simple instruction: *Pursue happiness?* After all, here in the United States our own Declaration of Independence asserts that the pursuit of happiness is among humankind's inalienable rights.

But what if we *aren't* happy? (Or happy enough ...?) The world, we all know, is not always a happy place. Is joy impossible, then? And what if faith seems too hard; hope, naive; and love, something lost or unattainable? What then? Is joy impossible then, too? Do we decide to be brave and make the best of it, putting on humor like a coat of armor to face life's harsh realities? Like Woody Allen's take on Emily's poem: "How wrong Emily Dickinson was! Hope is not 'the thing with feathers.' The thing with feathers has turned out to be my nephew. I must take him to a specialist in Zurich."

So throughout our lives, in good times and bad, we bravely attempt this recipe for joy, managing sometimes to summon a little more faith, if we can find it; a dash of hope, if we can find it; and as much love as we can. Whether the result comes out half-baked or well done, though, appears less connected to our skill with the whisk of happiness, to the quality of our intent, or to the exact proportion of joy's ingredients we find we have at hand, than to some mysterious alchemy beyond our grasp.

And that is exactly what we want you to know, to empower your life with joy. Joy exists for you right now, no matter what is happening in your life, your family, your town, or in the world. This is the best news you could possibly receive. The possibility to manifest joy is there in every moment, every situation, every breath of life—whether the conditions seem conducive to joy or not. Whether you feel up to the "work" of creating joy, or not, it is there. Waiting. Inherent. *Yours.*

We organized this book around one of humanity's brightest creations of joy, Ludwig van Beethoven's *Ninth Symphony,* which contains the famous "Ode to Joy." Many of us, when we think of Beethoven, recall that famous bust of him with that fierce expression—not particularly the rapturous look of a joyful person. Beethoven's music is often associated with fierce passion. Indeed, there is a wonderful line in the movie *Room with a View,* where actress Helena Bonham Carter's character asserts that she is discouraged by her family from playing Beethoven on the piano because it "leaves her peevish." Beethoven, the face of *joy?*

Beethoven wrote the *Ninth Symphony* at the end of his life, when he was deaf, ill, and struggling financially. Yet it is arguably one of the most magnificent pieces of music ever composed. We urge you to listen to it as you read this book. For we are all like Beethoven: passionate, flawed, sometimes fortunate in circumstance, sometimes not, always searching with the full weight of our human being to reveal the alchemy of joy.

As we finish the manuscript for this book and compose this introduction, our book producer at Amaranth, Lee Ann, called to tell us a story of joy that arose from the "Storm of the Century"—the Nor'easter snowstorm of February 2003. Editing our joy chapters as the snow fell, Lee Ann took breaks by hauling on boots, parka, and mittens and going out into her yard—a wildflower meadow in the summertime—to flop down, wave her arms, and make a snow angel. Soon, Lee Ann's yard filled with a chorus of snow angels. She ended her day thinking this a good metaphor for joy, but a better one soon came to be.

Two feet of snow fell in Lee Ann's town, and by the time Lee Ann awoke the next day, all the angels were obliterated, filled in by the falling snow. *But I still know they are there,* she thought. And that, perhaps, is enough to hold onto their joy. Still, it did not seem quite the same. Lee Ann continued editing our chapters, and over the next day or two after the storm, the temperatures rose enough that the snow started to melt rapidly. To her surprise, as she looked out the window of her home office, she saw the outline of the snow angels slowly reappear, a mighty chorus more joyful than ever.

We create joy, we lose joy, we hold onto joy even when we cannot "see" it, we rejoice when joy "reappears." The truth is this: Our human experiences are mercurial, destined to change and evolve with each passing moment—for this is human nature, but *joy is enduring.* Join us in exploring how we can all empower our lives with joy.

Acknowledgments

I want to thank all of the people in my life—friends, clients, family—who are daily reminders that joy is found everywhere but begins in our own hearts and minds, and who challenge me to be always open to the joy in my own life. And I also thank Eve for the joy of working with her on this book.

—Gary McClain, Ph.D.

Thanks to my parents for giving me the incomparable gift of a joyful childhood and to my children, Angus and Emmett, for letting me live it all over again; thanks to Gary, for his gentle, quiet brand of joy; to Lee Ann, for her joyful work ethic; and to Jim, who knows how to live joyfully in spite of himself.

—Eve Adamson

The First Movement
What Is Joy, and How Can You Have More of It?

Allegro, ma non troppo, un poco maestoso
(Quick tempo, cheerful, not too fast, a bit majestically)

Our book is organized into four movements, after the famous Beethoven's *Ninth Symphony*, the "Ode to Joy." The path through the human experience is marked by pain, loss, and sorrow, inevitably, inexorably—but also by joy! Life moves, like a symphony, through stages of different emotional tempos, but underlying that symphony is joy—not joy as fleeting moments, but joy as enduring reality.

In this first movement, the *allegro*, we explore, in a quick and cheerful tempo, the notion of joy and how it fits into our lives—or how it *could* fit, flowering more fully as we learn to live in the present moment. To embrace *all* of our experiences with joy is to embrace our humanity in a way that nurtures and grows into compassion and empathy toward all that lives. Listen along with us to the first movement of the *Ninth Symphony*. Beethoven called his symphony "the triumph song of life." Move through this symphony along with us to empower your life with expressions of joy.

Chapter 1

That Elusive Feeling

Whether we know it from within or merely by reputation, each of us has a relationship with the concept, if not the feeling, of joy. Many of us recall the bubbling feeling of joy from childhood, and know the fleeting sensation of joy as a flutter in the chest or a rush of excitement in the stomach. And then, just as suddenly as it arrived, it slips away.

Joy is elusive. It brings us pleasure, or the memory of pleasure. It is something we may seek but unlike a drink or a drug, unlike a place or a thing, we might find joy hard to apprehend at will. We can't take it, we can't go there, we can't buy it in a store. Can we even define it?

On top of its elusive nature, joy has somewhat of a questionable reputation among "serious" adults. Ask somebody how much joy he or she has in life, and you might engender a snicker, a rolling of the eyes, or some comment along the lines of, "Who has time for joy?" or "That's what happy hour is for."

We tend to associate "joy" with childhood, with frivolity, perhaps with our raucous youth, or as something for people with too much time on their hands. As adults, aren't we supposed to be serious, dedicated, hard-working, even a little bit beaten down by life?

Many of us are plagued with a deep-seated unhappiness, and even if our lives are pretty good for the most part materially, we may feel an emptiness, or wonder why we can't embrace the beautiful joy we once knew as we experienced things for the first time in youth. Even as we know that it's natural and common to experience anger, disappointment, pessimism, and frustration, how can we help but wish for something greater to balance the negativity we experience in our day-to-day lives as grown-ups in a complicated, so-called civilized society? Where is the big payoff for all our work? Where is the great happiness we've been working toward? Shouldn't we be able to have a little more joy? Is this really our destiny as fully grown humans? Is true pleasure, openness, and vulnerability in relationships, self-knowledge, and simple joy in the face of daily existence meant to be the stuff of childhood memories, things we've long left behind, even things we've never had and don't quite believe exist?

We say no ... and so this book is born.

The authors of this book, Gary and Eve, have had their own individual battles and dances with joy. As a therapist and someone who is highly sensitive to the feelings and moods of others, Gary often sees and feels the lack of joy in his patients. He can't help but be filled with sadness about what he witnesses in the world. As a natural optimist, Eve sometimes becomes frustrated at the way people around her seemingly refuse to embrace joy ... but believes everyone has the potential to move toward a more joyful life. (There she goes again!) Working together, we have compiled our experiences, thoughts, and strategies for physical, mental, and emotional revision to bring more joy into life, and we hope you will en*joy* the journey!

People need joy quite as much as clothing. Some of them need it far more.
—Margaret Collier Graham (1850–1910), American writer

Over the last couple years, we have all witnessed and experienced what anger and hatred can lead to. Yet refusing to let the pressures of daily life conquer the simple joys is really a matter of small steps, tiny changes, seemingly insignificant adjustments.

It's natural, and human, to feel disappointment, frustration, and sadness, but instead of simply accepting these feelings as reality, we believe it is important to see them instead as what they are: *feelings*. Not self-definitions. Not "the nature of things." Every one of us has the ability to look inside ourselves to see the big picture, the whole self, and that includes what inside us causes these feelings. And this is the purpose of our book. In it, we hope to lead you through a slow and gradual process of infusing your life with more, and more genuine, joyfulness. Every one of us, no matter our situation, no matter our personality, no matter our relationships, can find joy in the here and now, in who we are, what we do, and where we are going. We hope you'll join us along this joyful path.

Express Your Joy!

One important component to empowering your life with joy will be your Joy Journal. This journal is a tool to help you uncover and discover the joys in your life, and the obstacles that keep you from experiencing joy. Throughout this book, we will give you cues for writing or drawing in your journal, to help guide you in your joyful exploration of your inner self. But first, you'll need to have a Joy Journal. Choose a bound book, a spiral notebook, a ring binder filled with loose-leaf paper, a sketch pad, or any other journal that appeals to you and which lends itself to writing and, if relevant for you, drawing. As you work through this book, write in your Joy Journal about what you think, feel, and discover. Don't feel limited by our Joy Journal cues. You can write in your journal any time you feel the urge. Keep it handy so it's always available when you need it.

The Other Guy Did It!

To begin, let's look at some of the things that keep us from experiencing joy. You might be surprised to discover that some of these things are the very things we thought would *bring* us joy! First off, we want to introduce you to one of the key concepts in this book, an idea we will come back to again and again: the notion that joy, and lack of joy, is caused by the *other.*

Who is the other? Any other. And what do we think about that? We think—in fact, we strongly believe—that no one but *you* causes your joy or your pain, your sorrow or your fulfillment.

That's tough to accept for many of us, especially if we are in the habit of assuming that the negative feelings we experience are caused by or imposed by others. *He* hurt you. *She* left you. *They* made you feel worthless. *The government* is ruining things. *Your parents* messed you up. *Your boss* has foiled your life success. Is that really the way it is? Are we subject to and at the mercy of the whims and moods and actions and words of everybody around us?

As a matter of fact, we aren't—or, perhaps we should say that we *needn't be*. Are you? We'll keep on saying it: No! To find more joy in your life, one of the most important things you can do is to realize that who you are is all about you, and only you, when it comes to what you feel within. Even if you don't believe it right now, just open your mind to the possibility, because what if it *is* true? What if your emotional reality really is within you, and only within you? What if all those things other people do and say and "cause" to happen are just things, and all that matters is your reaction to those things, the part of you that dwells within you? What *if?*

If you think this is a book about how to blame others for your sadness or how to get your joy out of anywhere other than within, this isn't the book for you. But if you are ready to take a serious look at what's on the inside of the only being on earth who can bring you joy—if you are ready to take a good hard look at yourself, your attitudes, your values, your perspectives, your attachments, and your desires, and to rethink it all, then get ready, because we're here to help you.

Joy-Full Exercise: Influences and Emotions

Our lives are full of external influences: people, events, and change. Our lives are also full of feelings: sadness, happiness, contentment, despair, and many others. Make a list of three external influences on your life, and see if you can associate those influences with an overriding feeling. For instance, you might list "mother" or "father" or "husband" or "wife" or "teenage son" or "best friend Charlotte." You might list "two-hour round-trip commute," or "living in Chicago," or "money in the bank." Then, you might follow your chosen name with "comfort" or "resentment" or "pride in my accomplishments" or "jealousy" or "the sudden and uncontrollable desire to binge-eat."

Influence on My Life	Associated Emotion
_____	_____
_____	_____
_____	_____

Now, examine each of these three influences and consider, in very specific terms, whether the individual influences you listed actually cause those emotions you associate with them. Or do you and your reactions to those influences actually cause those emotions? You don't have to decide right now, just think about it.

Then, consider this: If it's you, and not them, then it's a reaction you can change to suit you.

We realize, of course, that it's one thing to say, "Others don't cause your unhappiness." It's quite another thing to get to the point of understanding how to control your own reactions to external influences like other people and events. The personal challenges to joy that you face in your own life will be different from anyone else's, but having worked professionally with hundreds of people over the years as a therapist, Gary has seen some pretty specific trends, many having to do with the kind of life we are trained to live and the game at which we are expected to succeed here in the western world in the twenty-first century.

Keeping in mind that it is our own reactions and perceptions that actually get in the way of our joy, let's look at some of the pervasive influences many of us face—things that distract us from knowing ourselves and living our lives with joy.

Material World

If we think about joy at all, many of us tend to associate it with tangible evidence of material success—a great job, a big house, attractive friends, relationships filled with grand romance, a six-figure salary, an annual foray to the South Pacific. How often have you caught yourself dreaming about at least one of these so-called signs of happiness and thinking, "If only I had _____, everything would be just *fine!*" It's all right, you can admit it. We catch ourselves doing it, too, every once in a while … thinking that joy won't come until we have this, or that, or the other …

Yet when we give it some serious thought, we know (and you probably do, too) that these signs of "success," these "happiness indicators," really have nothing to do with joy. Someone who is joyful might or might not get to be joyful in Fiji or in a 12-bedroom mansion or as a Hollywood star. Someone who is joyful might just as easily be living a simple life on a modest budget.

Studies even support the notion that material prosperity is not associated with personal happiness. One famous example is related in the popular book *Your Money or Your Life* by Joe Dominguez and Vicki Robin (Penguin Books, 1992). In it, the authors relate a study they did, sampling more than 1,000 people in the United States and Canada. They asked people to rate themselves on a happiness scale from 1 (miserable) to 5 (joyous) with 3 being "can't complain." They then correlated answers to income and were surprised to find that the average happiness score was between 2.6 and 2.8, with absolutely no correlation to income.

Not only were people habitually unhappy across the board, but also even though many of them believed that money, in the amount of "more than I have now," would make them happier, those who made $1,000 every month were actually slightly *happier* (at an average of 2.81) than those who made more than $4,000 per month (at an average of 2.63).

So if material prosperity doesn't cause joy—and we would even take that one step further to suggest that the unceasing quest for material prosperity may even *hamper* joy—then where *do* we find joy?

Joy-Full Exercise: Can Money Buy You Joy?

How much money do you think would make you more joyful in the long term? Write down a number: $_____.

Now consider this: How much money would you accept if it meant you'd never meet a partner to love and share your life with? If it meant you'd never parent or mentor a child? If it meant you could never walk by the ocean and breathe in the sea air? If it meant you would always have to work at a job you hate? If it meant you could only eat bland food? If it meant that in exchange for your financial gain someone in the world, even somebody you may never know, could never experience joy again?

Perhaps money isn't really as important as you thought it was. Remember the Lennon and McCartney song that immortalized the old saying, "money can't buy me love"? We might add "money can't buy me joy."

Joyful? You First!

Because we live in a society, and a crowded one at that, we are bound to have many different kinds of relationships with many different kinds of people. We've got our families, our friends, our co-workers, our casual acquaintances … and then there are all those people we don't know, people we see on the street, people we may never see again.

Gary lives in New York City, where people play "chicken" with each other on the sidewalk. They take their half out of the center, as they say, and then walk straight ahead as if they don't see you. It's up to you to move over. You can see the other person stiffen his shoulder for the inevitable brush, or slam, that occurs. And then, in a game only seasoned New Yorkers know how to play, each person discretely moves just enough to avoid the other. In other words, each gives in, but discretely. Each "wins," without ever quite having to admit any kind of compromise.

Whenever Gary found himself playing this game, he would be subtly annoyed for the rest of his walk, if not for the rest of the day. Playing "chicken" drained the joy out of what could be a wonderful, joyful experience: walking through perhaps the greatest city in the world! So one day, Gary decided to stop playing the game. Now, when he sees someone barreling toward him on Fifth Avenue, Gary moves over a few inches and continues with his thoughts.

But what's really going on here? Is Gary giving in? Compromising? Being *uncool*? Of course not! What Gary discovered about this subtle power play that happens every day a million times on every city block is that it generates negative energy. While the opposing pedestrian isn't *causing* Gary's negative feelings, Gary recognized his reaction to the game and decided he didn't want to play. That negative feeling was taking up brain space, and Gary has other, more important things to keep in his head. So although Gary did nothing to change someone else, he changed something he *can* control: his own reaction. And once he did so, he could once again embrace the positive aspect of each New Yorker's powerful walking energy with joy! In the same way, as each of us deals with the myriad personal influences on our lives and moods each day, we can learn to see which sources generate negative energy. Only then can we write our own prescription for joy, subtly shifting our individual perspective in ways that deflate negativity and leave more space for focusing on the things that fill us with positive feelings.

Men who are unhappy, like men who sleep badly, are always proud of the fact.
—Bertrand Russell (1872–1970), British philosopher and mathematician

Or maybe Gary's example doesn't work for you because you live in a city where people simply don't walk very much. Consider, instead, the damaging on-the-road version of this power energy scenario: road rage. Whenever Gary goes home to visit his mother, he is amazed at the road rage he witnesses. If his mother drives too slowly, she is often passed, cut off, honked at, and flipped off. Necessary? Certainly not, but such common examples of road rage are certainly a symptom of something wrong in our society. Why do we get so *angry* because the person ahead of us isn't speeding?

Gary works with clients from a variety of backgrounds, and his interactions with these clients can also shed some light on how we interact with each other. Who hasn't met someone with a bad attitude, someone who barks orders or questions, acts sullenly, or is overly critical and negative? Gary used to react in kind, feeling a bit ego-bruised by the verbal abuse, as he felt he had done nothing to deserve such treatment. Or he would find himself behaving passive-aggressively for the sake of retribution, which was not a very joyful way to go through the day. Do you find yourself reacting this way to people who infuse your environment with negativity, taking it personally, letting it fill you with negativity? Even when Gary felt he had "won," gotten the better of someone, he felt drained of energy and spiritually disheartened. Such a "win" wasn't worth it, even though, in our naturally competitive society, we often find ourselves trying to "win." Sound familiar?

Instead, Gary has discovered a better, easier, less stressful way to deal with aggressive negativity. Now, when Gary encounters clients with a negative attitude, he stops, takes a step back, and rethinks the situation from the client's point of view. Everyone has his or her own disappoint-ments, pressures, and family problems. Instead of frowning back (literally or symbolically), Gary has learned to smile (literally or symbolically!). As a therapist, empathy became Gary's greatest ally. "It looks like you are having a bad day. Do you want to talk about it?"

The results in a therapy setting are amazing, and the results in your life can be amazing, too. Clients quickly adjusted their attitudes because someone had taken the time to notice how they felt and express concern. It almost never fails, and you don't have to be a therapist to use this technique to make your day happier. It works on friends, co-workers, family, and even if the other person doesn't open up to you, you'll feel better. You'll feel your own attitude adjusting, softening, opening ... you'll be allowing joy into your heart. Sometimes, sidestepping that com-petitive impulse can reveal hidden passageways to joy.

Negative feelings and reactions to life's little problems are like small fires that quickly grow into large, uncontrollable fires when fueled by the wind of discontent and negativity. Don't add fuel. Neutralize the fire with kindness.

Joy-Full Exercise: Mirror, Mirror ...

Just how do you extinguish the fires of negativity with positive energy? Sometimes negative reactions are so automatic, we don't even realize we are engaging in them. Try this exercise the next time you feel the discom-fort of negativity creeping over your day. Take a five-minute "mirror break." Excuse yourself, find some privacy and a mirror (the nearest restroom, perhaps?), relax, and take a good hard look at yourself. Find that negativity in your face. A crinkled brow? Frown lines? Harried expression? Where is it coming from? Now ask yourself the following questions:

- Am I trying to control someone else instead of my own reaction to someone else?
- Am I withholding kindness and/or generosity?
- Am I unhappy about the lack or loss of something material?

If you answered yes to any (and it might well be all) of these ques-tions, take a moment to breathe deeply and readjust your attitude. Think or speak the following affirmation:

I can control what I have within;
the only thing I can control is what I have within;
I only need what I have within;
and what I have within is worth sharing.

Feel better yet? We know *we* do.

Joy Is a Boomerang

Gary lives in a Manhattan apartment, and just yesterday, in his building, he was on the elevator when it stopped a couple of floors below his on the way to the lobby. A man had been using a wheeled cart that the building keeps in the lobby—people use it for taking large boxes or groceries up to their apartments—and he was now returning it. Here's how Gary tells the story:

"Can I take that down for you?" Gary asked the man.

He laughed. "You must be new to the building."

"No," Gary answered. "I've lived here a few years."

The man explained that he was going to the lobby to pick up his mail, but thanked Gary for his offer.

When they got down to the lobby, Gary said, "I hope you have a nice day."

The man answered, "After meeting you, I'm sure I will."

Gary walked to the gym with increased energy. The encounter released endorphins that gave him a whole new sense of well-being. After all, New York City can be a scary and impersonal place. Encounters like this can go a long way toward remembering how wonderful its eight million inhabitants truly are!

The encounter made a difference in Gary's workout, too. He felt stronger and had more energy. This outlook was in direct contrast to the times when he had arrived at the gym frustrated, annoyed, disappointed: ready to use physical activity to express those feelings aggressively through an exhausting workout that depleted instead of restored. But this time, kindness gave Gary a noticeable increase in strength and endurance.

There is a theory in psychology called equity theory. Basically, the theory is that when we are anticipating something—for example, waiting to hear about a new job that we have applied for or news about a loved one's arrival—we will do kind things for others in anticipation that this will somehow cosmically affect our own outcome.

While it might sound superstitious, many of us nevertheless believe that doing good will come back to us in return—help your elderly neighbor carry her groceries or that new mom heft her stroller up the park entry stairs, and you might just get that promotion!

This isn't a new idea. Ancient eastern philosophy expounds upon the idea of karma. Although many of us think of karma as a universal system of punishments and rewards, karma is actually about universal balance. If you spread negativity, negativity will flow back to you. If you spread love and kindness, love and kindness will flow back to you. What you reap, you sow, to quote the old saw. Do unto others as you would have them do unto you, or, to quote Gary's father, "cast bread on the water."

Karma isn't about doing good things for people just so you can get good things yourself. By its very nature, banking good karma is a selfless act because it recognizes that the self is really just the part of a great whole. Spreading kindness and joy to others is the same as receiving kindness and joy because we are all part of a universal whole.

It is never right to do wrong or to requite wrong with wrong, or when we suffer evil to defend ourselves by doing evil in return.
—Socrates (469–399 B.C.E.), Greek philosopher

Maybe you don't believe in karma per se, or the "universal whole" business, and that's fine, too. The notion that we are all part of a greater "oneness" exists in many different cultures and religions across the world, but that doesn't mean you have to accept it. However, the theory of karma is also backed by science. Chaos theory (and we're oversimplifying, here) states that every minute event in a system (in this case, our world) has a ripple effect, an impact across the entire system. What we do affects everything else. We don't exist in a vacuum.

Plus, you've probably experienced joy's boomerang effect in the same way Gary did that day in the elevator. You feel good when you are kind, when you spread joy to someone else. It makes you feel better, lighter, happier, doesn't it? We believe this effect goes far beyond any religious/cultural conditioning that it's right to help and give to others (a concept inherent in all major world religions).

Your Joy Boomerang

Experience the joy boomerang for yourself. Do something nice for somebody today—anything at all. Then, in your Joy Journal, describe what you did, how the other person reacted, and how it made you feel. How did the act impact your day? Your energy? Your emotions? Did it encourage further acts of kindness? Did you experience a return on your investment, even if just a feeling of lightness? Do your best to describe the experience.

Joy Is Viral

Viral marketing is a term used in the business world meaning that if one person has a good experience with a product or service, or a book or a TV show, and tells someone else about it, then the product becomes a success through word of mouth without traditional marketing communications, like mass advertising. But viral marketing works both ways.

In groups of people, rumors, negative attitudes, and criticism can spread the same way. If you work in an office, you probably know exactly what we're talking about. One person spouts off about how uncaring the company is, how difficult the boss is, or how troublesome another employee is, and the bad feelings grow from there. Even group members who don't want to be pulled into the vortex may end up feeling "infected."

But the good news is that joy works the same way. One person feels it and passes it on to someone else through a simple gesture, a few positive words, a smile, or a life-affirming reaction to a potentially negative situation.

Joy-Full Exercise: Turn the Tide

Sometime today, try this out: When you encounter someone who seems to be having a bad day—a salesperson who seems preoccupied or short-tempered, a co-worker who snaps at you or ignores you—smile at him.

Not snidely, not sarcastically, but simply and sincerely. Just smile. You might be surprised at the response you get.

If Joy Is So Great, Why Don't We Have More of It?

So where's the joy? If it's so easy to stop the negativity and be positive and optimistic, why doesn't everyone do it? Because it *isn't* easy, that's why. So much of what we hear on the news and even what we experience directly seems in direct opposition to a joyful attitude, not to mention an optimistic one. At a time when financial well-being is considered so important, the economy isn't doing so well, and even in the best of times, many of us are not included in the boom. International politics are unstable at best, which worries many of us and causes others a great deal of anxiety. Many people believe they can't trust their political leaders, their religious leaders, or their community leaders.

If you feel a general weariness, a sense of disappointment, a dearth of positive role models, and an overriding cynicism, you aren't alone. Many of us have learned through the years to assume the worst, not the best. Groups are divided, and suspicion seems to be the default when it comes to dealing with people we don't know. Better safe than sorry, right?

Yet the world, our lives, are also full of things to be joyful about. Which do you focus on? You are alive. You get to see beauty every day in the world around you, sometimes right next to the ugliness. You have people you love and people who love you. You have loved people in the past, even if they aren't with you today. You can take pleasure in small things, like a stroll on a sunny day, time with friends, a moment of quiet, listening to your favorite music, or a moment of raucous laughter. Regardless of what is going on in the world, joy is never completely out of reach.

Yet somehow people continue to resist the pull of joy. Why?

Myths About Joy

Perhaps you, like many others, believe one or more of the many myths about joy. Let's look at them:

⚫ **Joy isn't cool.** There has long been a vibe in our culture that it's hip to be edgy and cynical. If someone offers you a big grin, is it cooler to grin back with abandon, or roll your eyes and mutter, "What-ever!"? If you think joy is *so* "five minutes ago," you might suffer from what we like to call terminal cool. You might look cool, you might act cool, but if you can't find the joy in a smile, in a warm moment with someone you love … if you are too cool even to embrace love … then you are missing out on the things that make our time on earth worth being here. We aren't saying you should change your whole image and become a great big goofball. In fact, we consider ourselves pretty darned cool—just not too cool to stop once in a while, look around, and think, "Wow, sometimes the world is really beautiful." Just like Louis Armstrong singing "What a Wonderful World." It's corny, but it's true!

Exuberance is better than taste.
—Gustave Flaubert (1821–1880), French novelist

⚫ **Joy makes you vulnerable.** Are you afraid that if you appear joy-ful, people might take advantage of you? First of all, being joyful doesn't necessarily correspond to *looking* joyful. As we said, we don't expect anybody to walk around with a big goofy grin all day long. And being joyful doesn't mean being a doormat. Joy won't make the grocery clerk more likely to cheat you because you look too happy to complain, and it won't make somebody more likely to push ahead of you in line or behave in an otherwise rude manner. Many people frown and avoid eye contact so they look as if they are in control, but who says they really have the advantage? (They can't *see* you!) Don't fall into the mistaken notion that only a sim-pleton could have a positive attitude in this miserable world we live in. The world is what it is, but our attitudes are made within us. They don't mirror the world, they mirror our souls. A strong inner presence not subject to the ebb and flow of the external world is what radiates to the world that you are no doormat. You are an entryway, your soul issuing an invitation to the world to experience a unique and special human being: *you!*

⚫ **Dissatisfaction is more motivating than contentment.** It's the American way, to always want more than you have, to always

16

try for a better, faster, more efficient way of doing things, to keep climbing, keep striving, keep getting ahead. Isn't joy the same as complacency? If you're happy where you are, you'll never move up, right? If Bill Gates were a joyful person would we be using Windows right now? How joyful is Oprah Winfrey or Donald Trump, Colin Powell or Hillary Clinton, Madonna or Tom Cruise, or any other really successful American icon? How joyful could Thomas Edison or Eleanor Roosevelt or Alexander Graham Bell have been? Weren't they all too busy? Weren't they always looking for more? Many of Gary's clients refuse to enjoy their accomplishments because they fear complacency, that joy will disempower them. What if they stop moving? Yet joy in the present moment, joy in accomplishments and successes, is exactly the payoff that *does* keep us moving ahead. If it isn't any fun, why bother? The more you enjoy your life, the more it's worth living, until joy becomes a fuel that can power you.

If you imagine the worst, it won't happen. You've probably considered this idea ... if you enjoy something too much, won't the fates somehow conspire to snatch it away? If the cup is half empty, you can't be disappointed when the whole drink drains away, right? Perhaps as a child, you had unhappy parents or other adult authority figures who would swoop down and take things away from you, because they were unable to allow anyone else to be happy. Perhaps you learned to protect yourself by refusing to enjoy anything. One of Gary's clients once told him that whenever he and his brothers and sisters were watching a program they enjoyed on TV, their father would walk in and change the channel. For him, this became a metaphor for experiencing life. Just when he settled into a comfortable relationship or job, this man feared that somehow, someone would change the channel. Whether you superstitiously avoid joy or do so as a protective mechanism, refusing to experience the joy that comes your way or refusing to allow yourself to experience joy results in a grayed-out version of life. When you live in the present moment, joy is full, complete, and total. It doesn't matter if a thing is taken away tomorrow if you've fully experienced it today. Give yourself permission to feel joy in each and every moment without demands, expectations, or strings attached. Just be in your joy right here, right now.

Joy-Full Exercise: Do You Have To?

What is it you believe you really *have to* do? Do you have to make a six-figure salary? Do you have to get married? Do you have to move into a bigger place? Do you have to get a new car? Do you have to make Vice President? Do you have to have children? Do you have to finally be a success in the eyes of your father, mother, in-laws, brother, sister, or whomever? Make a list of the have to's in your future, like this:

I, _____ (your name):

have to _____

have to _____

have to _____

have to _____

have to _____

have to _____

have to _____

have to _____

Try this affirmation whenever you begin to feel overwhelmed by the negativity, anxiety, or anger of the "have to's" of life. Sit, relax, close your eyes, and say these words out loud:

I am filled
with calm, acceptance, peace.
I am fearless.

Now, go back, cross out the word *have* and insert the word *want* in front of each item on your list. Read it again. How does this change the meaning for *you?*

Remembering the Big Picture

It's easy to get caught up in negativity when you become so immersed in one line of thinking or one aspect of life that you miss out on the big picture. You might be feeling overwhelmed by how much work you have, but try stepping back and looking at how successfully you are building a business that will move you ahead into the future. Perhaps a troublesome relationship has you full of anxiety or sadness, but are you learning about yourself and about someone you love?

Gary has clients who tell him that in the midst of a stressful day at work, they take a moment and glance at a photo of a partner or their children, and feel an overwhelming sense of pleasure that, while it doesn't make the stress go away, certainly gives the day, and its current demands, a more profound meaning. Or you might take a moment to consider your current success—not necessarily by society's standards, but by your own. Perhaps making money or getting a promotion or becoming well known in your field *is* important to you. If you've done it, enjoy it! Perhaps finding love is meaningful to you, and you've done it. Think about your imperfect loved ones, and consider how perfect they really are, in all their humanity. Let yourself love. Or perhaps what really matters to you is making the world a better place. Maybe part of that is traveling and visiting new places, cultures, and peoples to see what it means to be human, everywhere in the world. Stop once a day to consider how the things you do help the world, even in very small ways.

Joy is more than ecstasy and it is less than ecstasy, but finding it is simply about what you decide to do with your mind. You can look at the bad. You can look at the good. Or you can step back from it all and simply see it as what it is and feel joyful that you get to experience it all. That's the kind of joy that endures because you can experience it any time, in "good" times and "bad," in happy times and sorrowful times, in times of plenty and times of want. It is the joy of *being*.

Remember that there is also joy in being part of something outside of ourselves. If you can feel a oneness with the ebb and flow of life, you will discover the comforting rhythm of existence that murmurs and flutters and glides over the surface of the earth. Find a quiet place and focus on what ebbs and flows within you, and let yourself accept your unique and important place in the universal music of existence. Rather than fighting with each breath to stay afloat, let yourself slide into the river of being and ride the current. Everything is as it should be at this very moment, and here you are.

Joy-Full Exercise: The Right Place

Breathe in deeply and affirm: *I am in the right place at the right time.* Breathe out fully and completely and affirm: *I have a sense of oneness with the world.* Breathe in again deeply, feel your chest lift and your heart open as you affirm: Every moment of breath and life is a wonderful moment! Breathe out and smile.

Joy in the Moment: Turning Around a Bad Day

Gary found himself on a flight from hell (How's that for a negative beginning to a joyful story?) from Phoenix to New York, all six feet two inches of him stuffed into a coach seat. Hungry and thirsty, he had purchased a big bottle of water and then mistakenly left it in the boarding area, plus he just *knew* the guy next to him wanted to assert dominance over the armrest. To top it all off, surely the small child two rows ahead would begin bawling at any moment. Oh yes, Gary sat good and ready to bask in some serious negativity. He settled in for four hours of joylessness, but then again, he knew he had to write up his notes for this book ... this book about joy.

A conundrum.

So Gary decided to play a game. He pulled out his journal and began making a list of "joyful moments" as they occurred. Here are the joyful moments Gary was able to find, right smack in the middle of his "flight from hell":

- The flight attendant's genuine smile accompanying an offer of a cold beverage.
- The pleasant sense of anticipation for the glass of ice water coming Gary's way.
- The thought of going home, unlocking the apartment door, making a call to a friend.
- His anticipation of returning to interesting work and the clients who value that work.
- The colors of the rock formations as the flight passed over the mountains.

- That child two rows ahead who turned around and smiled, rather than crying and fussing.
- The chocolate-covered wafer cookie that he had hoarded in his briefcase from the last flight.
- The exaggerated expression of joy on the face of the armrest-hogging guy sitting next to him when Gary offered him the other cookie.
- The rush of joy caused by writing this very list!

Your Inner Joy

When you are in the midst of an unpleasant experience, whether it's a delayed airline flight, a tough test, or a difficult conversation, repeat this affirmation:

No matter what I experience, I have a steady, inner core of joy available whenever I choose to tap it.

Copy this affirmation at the top of a page in your Joy Journal, and use a highlighter to emphasize it visually. Take the Joy Journal with you to the next activity you have where you anticipate a less-than-joyful time of it. Keep an open mind, and under the affirmation write down each joyful emotion, thought, or action you witness or experience during the activity. Learning to look for the joy may soon become a beautiful new habit, and way of perceiving the world that adds value to every task, situation, or encounter.

Finding joy is a habit, like brushing your teeth or saying "good morning" to your co-workers or having that first cup of coffee. You get yourself dressed and looking decent every morning. Why not get yourself feeling decent, too, by getting into the joy habit?

Instead of a source of joy, Gary's airline flight could easily have been miserable indeed! It would have been the easiest thing in the world to sit and wallow in frustration and inconvenience. After a bad flight, Gary could have arrived home in a fit of self-righteous rage that would have leaked out during the long wait for luggage, as well as the longer wait for a cab. But by looking for joy, Gary arrived home feeling peaceful and relaxed. His doorman made a joke about how disheveled he looked, and they both laughed. That night, Gary slept like a happy baby, instead of tossing and turning like a toddler throwing a tantrum. He woke up full of energy and ideas. And all this happened because of a little bit of joy work.

Joy-Full Exercise: Reclaiming That Inner Child

As adults, we are taught to be responsible and rational. Yet without a little wiggle-room for a childlike appreciation of the world, being grown-up is hardly worth the price! Today, do one thing you haven't done since you were a child. Swing on the swings, eat an ice cream cone, play fetch with your dog, or skip … even if it's just down the hall where nobody can see. Remember how fun those things used to be? A good dose of childlike behavior is a great way to claim a joyful moment.

Quiz: How Much Joy Do You Have in Your Life?

Maybe you think you are pretty joyful, or maybe you know you always see the glass half empty. Or maybe you aren't sure? Take this quiz to determine how much joy you have (or choose to notice) in your life today, right now. Go through this list of situations, and circle the letter of the answer that comes closest to how you feel:

1. You are heavily multi-tasking with five or six projects going at once, and a co-worker drops another "ASAP" job on your desk. You are most likely to respond by saying:
    a. "What, I'm the only one who works here? I don't think so. Give it to somebody else, I'm not doing it!"
    b. "Okay, if this really has to get done, then I guess I'll have to fit it in on top of all the other urgent things I have to do … somehow." (Follow with a deep sigh.)
    c. "I'll do what I can if you find somebody to help me do it, because I'm not doing it alone."
    d. "I'm glad we've got so much going on today! However, I'll need to do some prioritizing. I'll start by making a list. Maybe a co-worker can collaborate on this with me, if necessary."

2. You walk into the kitchen to have your first cup of coffee, and your partner is sitting at the table, hidden behind the newspaper. Your first response is likely to be:

   a. "Apparently the morning news is more important than I am!" (Slam some stuff around.)

   b. "It sure was nice when we used to sit and talk over breakfast. Oh well, I guess that stage of our relationship is over."

   c. You say nothing and sullenly wait for your partner to say something first. You will *make* your partner notice you through abject silence!

   d. "Good morning! Did you sleep well? Any interesting news this morning?"

3. The waitperson at the lunch counter grunts and tosses your check into the puddle of coffee left behind after sloppily refilling your cup. What are you likely to say?

   a. "Get back and clean this up!"

   b. "Okay, I can see right now exactly how the rest of my day is going to go."

   c. "You'll have to do better than that if you expect a tip."

   d. "Looks a bit hectic in here. I hope your day gets better!" (Sincere smile.)

4. Your evening plans to have dinner with old friends are cancelled when a rainstorm makes driving hazardous and they decide not to make the trip across town. When they break the news, how do you respond, in your own mind?

   a. "That's just irritating. It's rain, what's the big deal?"

   b. "I know it's raining, but I wonder if that's just an excuse to get out of spending the evening with me."

   c. "Well, that's just rude. Who needs friends like that? I think I'll just happen to be busy the next time they call."

   d. "I'm glad they're not taking any undue risks in this weather, and now I can spend a nice evening by myself in front of the fireplace reading or watching television!"

5. You ask your child, or a niece, nephew, or neighbor child, what he or she did at school today. The child launches into a convoluted story that is obviously going to take a while. How do you respond?

   a. Interrupting: "Short version, please!"

   b. "Uh huh. Uh huh." (Said with an eye-roll and a pained half-smile—oh the things you endure!)

   c. "How interesting. Why don't you go tell your sister or brother about it. I'm sure somebody else will be glad to hear the *rest* of the story."

   d. "Really? What was that like? And then what happened?"

6. It's Friday evening and you realize you haven't made any plans for the weekend. What's your first thought?

   a. "And here I thought I actually had friends. Apparently not, as nobody has bothered to call me!"

   b. "Gosh, I try and try, and if I don't always take the lead, I'm ignored."

   c. "I'll make sure I get on top of my schedule better next weekend."

   d. "Maybe I'll make a few calls. I also want to get some exercise in. And it would be great to visit my mom for an afternoon."

7. It's your birthday and, yes, your friends have thrown you a party, cooked your favorite meal, even made a cake. What would be your typical response?

   a. "Don't remind me! I hate birthdays!"

   b. "I can't believe I've reached ____ years old and this is the first time anybody has ever bothered to throw me a party."

   c. "This was a nice idea, everyone, but I wish you would have consulted me first. I'm really busy. Can we do this another time?"

   d. "Thank you! I'm really touched! Shall I pour the wine?"

8. You and a friend decide to meet and see a movie. You are ahead of schedule so your friend suggests you arrive early and take a half-hour walk around the mall before entering the theater.
    a. "Walking is a pain. Besides, it can be so crowded there, and I really didn't have this extra time to waste."
    b. "You know I can't keep up with you. Sometimes I feel like you want to make me feel inferior."
    c. "Do you think we should? Maybe we'll run into someone we'd rather avoid, and I'm not sure it is safe at the mall anyway in the evening."
    d. "Fantastic idea! We can use the time to talk and to get some exercise before the movie starts and we're sitting for two hours. And we can check out the sales on walking shoes, too!"

9. On the drive to work, a car comes out of nowhere on the highway and cuts you off. How do you react?
    a. "You %$#!@!#$%$&$@!!!"
    b. "Oh no! Is that guy trying to kill me? What if he has a gun? What if he's crazy? I'd better slow way down and drop back! Don't make eye contact … don't make eye contact … "
    c. Accelerate, tail the guy for a while, then pass him and cut *him* off. That will teach him a lesson!
    d. "Looks like that guy's in a hurry. I'm glad I hit my brakes when I did. Now, let's see, back to planning what I need to do at work today … "

10. You are invited to attend a forum on racism in your community as one of many representatives from all different backgrounds. The goal is to find a way to reach out to each other, in response to hate crimes in your area.
    a. "Oh, I don't think so. I'm not wasting time getting all touchy-feely with a bunch of people I don't know. Besides, *I'm* not committing any hate crimes."
    b. "This problem is way too big. People will always hate and be violent, and trying to fix it is just futile and depressing."

    c. "How is it being organized? Who's behind it? Do they know what they're doing? Has this been approved by the Chamber of Commerce? If I can't be on the board, I'm not really interested."

    d. "Sure, I'll check it out and see what I think. I'd like to help if there's something I can do. And I'd like to hear what some of the other people have to say."

We hope simply taking this test has helped you to see how much joy you have (or don't have) in your life. Now let's see what your answers reveal.

And Your Answers ...

Go back through the list and count the number of A, B, C, and D answers. Which letter did you circle the most? See how you did and what kind of obstacles might be hampering your quest for more joy.

If you chose mostly a answers, you let life engage you, but instead of finding the joy, you tend to get angry and frustrated by the negative things you perceive. It's tough to let go of anger, and anger may not seem like a habit, but a knee-jerk reaction of irritation and frustration actually is largely a matter of habit. The trick is to catch yourself before you automatically *react* (notice we didn't say *act*) in anger. Spend some time thinking about your triggers. What frustrates you? What irritates you? Chances are, you often become angry over things you can't control. Even the things you can't control aren't best controlled in an angry frame of mind. As you read through the rest of this book, keep in mind that anger, irritation, and frustration tend to be your areas of vulnerability. We'll often address this kind of reaction and give you lots of different strategies for handling it. In the meantime, though, what can you do today?

Joy-Full Exercise: Anger Antidote

The next time you start to feel your blood boil, try this four-step anti-anger strategy:

1. Immediately remove yourself from the situation (or, do so as soon as possible) without actually saying one single word out loud to whomever or whatever is angering you.

2. Grab a piece of paper—or a computer keyboard—and start writing. You don't necessarily have to write about what happened, just write about how you feel. Get all your feelings down in written words, no matter how irrational they sound. Let it all out.

3. Take 10 slow, deep breaths. Yes, 10.

4. Now, go back and read over your notes. See if you can analyze, with a clearer head, whether or not your anger is directed at things you can't control. Think about how you might let that anger go so it stops clouding your thinking regarding the things you might be able to change to improve the situation.

If you chose mostly b answers, you might not call yourself a defeatist, exactly, but you might feel like life is often out of your control. You are sad, or disappointed, or let down ... or all of these things at once. Maybe you've had some bad experiences in life. We all have, but admittedly, some of us have had more than our fair share of tragedy. Life isn't always sunshine and roses, and we certainly don't mean to sound like it should be! On the contrary, life is also sadness, disappointment, and tragedy. However, joy is not equivalent to a long string of good luck. Joy is the ability to see the hope within the tragedy—the proverbial silver lining. It isn't empty-headed optimism, either. It's simply an insistence on living in the present moment and letting yourself experience and move past whatever happens without letting it touch your inner core, where the true, beautiful you lies untouched by the tumult of the external world. But what can you do right now to mitigate your disappointment and sorrow?

Joy-Full Exercise: Sadness Solutions

Feeling disappointed? Defeated? Overwhelmed by life? Depressed? It's perfectly understandable. The next time a wave of disappointment or sadness hits you, try this exercise to help you put your feelings in perspective. Take a moment to yourself, sit down, relax, take a few deep, slow breaths, and speak these words:

My feelings come and go. I can watch them come, I can feel them, and I can let them go. They are not me.

If you chose mostly c answers, you probably consider yourself a strong, assertive person, but you are probably also under a lot of stress. Why? Because in all your strength and drive, you have taken on more than you need to take on. You sometimes mistake the things you can control for the things that are not under your own control, and in your quest for total control over your environment, you risk the loss of spontaneity, adventure, freedom, and even self-knowledge. Our society values people with a lot of control (read: power). Yet real power comes from understanding exactly what you can and can't control. Which is which? That's easy. You *can* control what you do, what you say, what you think, how you act and react to the world around you. You *can't* control what others do, what others say, what others think, and how others act and react. Sure, you may be able to influence people's actions, even thoughts. But you can't control them, and recognizing that can take a lot of stress off your burdened shoulders. Try living the next hour from this perspective, that you can only control yourself, and see how far it gets you. If your actions, thoughts, and words are in accordance with your beliefs and goals, you'll go far ... and chances are, others will follow. But how do you get to the place where you can see this? Throughout this book, we'll talk a lot about the nature of control and putting control issues in perspective, but try the following exercise today.

Joy-Full Exercise: Control Freak? *You?*

If you try to control everything and everybody around you, life can get pretty stressful. Give yourself a break! The next time you begin to feel that overwhelming urge to jump in and take over, stop for a moment and answer two questions before you make a move: "What is my job in this situation?" and "Is this part of my job description?"

Your job could be anything from CEO to junior editor to teenage baby-sitter, or in a non-employment-related context, "supportive friend" or "team member" or "life partner" or "helpful neighbor" or even "evolving human." Now look at what it is you are trying to control. Is this your job? Is this something you can really control? A mother can control her mode of discipline for her children but can't control what they think about how she disciplines. A junior editor can control her quality of work but can't control the boss's opinion of her work or anyone else's. An evolving human can control his or her own work on self-improvement but can't "help" a spouse or friend become something he or she doesn't want to become. If you recognize that your impulse to control is aimed at something that isn't part of your job description, make a conscious and deliberate decision to *let it go.* Refocus on what you really should be doing at the moment.

If you chose mostly d answers, we'd say you're a pretty joyful sort. You are open and spontaneous, flexible and ready to have fun, and you roll with life's changes in a generally good humor. That doesn't mean you won't sometimes get angry or sad, frustrated or anxious, or feel the urge to control people and things you can't really control, but you have access to your inner, joyful core, and that's a beautiful thing! Keep accessing your joy because the more you plumb its depths, the deeper and wider and more magnificent your joy becomes.

So why bother to be joyful? Being joyful makes life more vivid. It helps you to develop your spirit. It adds richness and texture to your life. It helps to deepen your relationships, define your life purpose, and clarify your goals. Being joyful helps you to feel more energized. It even makes you look better! It helps you to let go of anxiety and embrace every moment. In other words, joy makes every day worth living.

What hunger is in relation to food, zest is in relation to life.
—Bertrand Russell (1872–1970), British philosopher and mathematician

And you can find it, no matter who you are, where you live, what you do, or how you approach life. Joy is accessible to anyone and everyone, without denying any situation, without defying any feeling, without neglecting to notice anything real about the world. Joy does not equal "good times" or "happiness." Joy is the essence of embracing life in all its fullness, multiplicity, diversity, and ultimately, in all its great and powerful unity—and then, letting it go.

So join us in our quest for more joy, and you, too, can empower your life!

Chapter 2

Defining Joy

Imagine the earth as a globe spinning in front of you. See all the continents of the world, all the oceans and seas, even the large lakes and wide rivers. Imagine running your hands over the detailed topography of mountains and plains, deserts and glaciers. Imagine the expanses of stone, ice, sand, and scrub, the fields of corn and wheat planted in rows that run for miles, the vast rolling hills covered with wildflowers, or the hush of a million pine trees blanketing the mountains.

And now, imagine that across this globe, you were to chart the locations of all the people. Imagine that each tiny being on the face of the earth is a little spark, an almost microscopic silver star. America would be covered with hundreds of millions of stars, clustered in the cities and along the coastlines, spread in smaller, wider groups across the continent's wide expanse. Canada would be sprinkled with stars, and so would Alaska. Stars would glitter like a river down Mexico and through Central America, spreading into a great sea all over South America. They would sparkle like a handful of ice chips toward the poles and shimmer like a galaxy all over Africa. Imagine the stars spread over every country of Europe, the sheer magnitude of stars in India and Asia and the Middle East, the stars all over Australia and the islands of the South Pacific, the twinkles here and there along the vast expanse of Siberia.

It's a beautiful thought, our Earth glistening and decorated with stars. But what if we added another layer to our imaginary globe? What if we added a grid of joy?

Constructing Our Grid of Joy

We like the idea of building a grid of joy over the planet. The very thought fills us with joy. It might seem a simple task, at first, but let's look deeper.

The first goal, of course, would be how to define joy. Would we know it when we saw it? Which stars would sparkle with joy, and which ones would lay dim and untwinkling? How would we know? Would joy change from moment to moment? Would it flow in waves over the planet? Would there be a pattern? Would some countries have more joy and some have less?

Perhaps our definition would be different than yours. Can humanity come to a consensus that joy is, say, an inner state? A spiritual state? A physical state? Is joy the same as happiness? As being well liked? Is joy being free of material concerns? Free of stress? Or is joy having power? Enlightenment? Is joy the same as love?

While joy is a personal matter for each individual, we can certainly find joyful trends and certain universal joys. Perhaps we can agree that joy is an inner state that can be affected by the external world. Perhaps we can agree that joy can involve the spiritual, as well as the physical, and can be boosted by being well liked or free of stress. Perhaps we can even agree that while they are similar, joy is not the same as happiness.

Let's consider the question in a little more detail before we settle on any one definition. What is joy? Let's take a closer look at our globe.

Joy-Full Exercise: Sending Joy Around the World

Find a globe or a world map or even an atlas. Spin the globe or flip through the pages of the atlas. What are your preconceptions about the people that live in countries other than your own? Choose a country or a region that you find you have certain preconceptions about, and take a moment to close your eyes and imagine sending joyful blessings to the people who live there. Let your joy open your heart and dissolve your preconceptions.

Joy Per Continent

People are people, right? Yet culture is also culture, and the world is covered with many different cultures and cultural attitudes. Some of these attitudes are bound to influence our sense of what joy really is, and although we would argue that joy is joy wherever you go, every country, every city, every neighborhood, every family, and every individual has a different way of getting there.

Here in America, we are often stereotyped by our international neighbors as a decadent, power-hungry nation out for world domination. Sure, many of us work long hours and brag about it. Some of us never take a vacation, and it's easy to forget how to relax. Stress-related illness runs rampant in our country, and many people are alarmed by the growing presence of violence in American life—from a tendency toward frustration and rudeness in everyday communications to ever-present violence in movies, on television, and in many of the video games our kids play, to road rage, guns in schools, and drug-related crime. Where is the joy?

Yet the concept of joy is at the heart of our nation's founding: "life, liberty, and the pursuit of happiness."

Our forefathers meant for us to live in a society where we were free to live as we pleased as long as we did not impinge on the rights of others. That didn't necessarily mean that we weren't supposed to work hard; our ancestors worked long hours under extremely hard conditions. But it did imply choice. They envisioned a future where people would choose how they spent their time and whom they spent it with. They wanted us to be able to follow our joy in whatever direction it led, through spiritual pursuits, recreation interests, or family events. They hoped that we would follow occupational paths that allowed us to express our values.

While Americans can arguably be criticized for working long hours with infrequent and short vacations, we also have a wide range of opportunities for the social, recreational, cultural, and spiritual pursuits that our founders had in mind. We have, in a word, freedom.

This brings us back to what we said in Chapter 1: Joy takes work. It doesn't mean just deciding to think more joyfully and trying to spread more joy to others. It also means taking a look at the components of your life and seeking how you can claim "life, liberty, and the pursuit of happiness" in your own life.

When it comes to the world, we all tend to characterize and even stereotype other cultures in a certain way (accurate or not), and we might feel that the grass is always greener on the other side of the border. Europeans take month-long vacations, drink wine with every meal, and take two hours for lunch, so they must get more joy out of life, right? Asians eat simply and healthfully and all practice Zen, right? In Mexico and South America, life is all about fiestas and siestas, right?

Of *course* these stereotypes are just as misleading as the "power-hungry American" stereotypes. For example, when Gary was recently in Tokyo, he was impressed by the clean functionality and beauty of the art, architecture, and design, but the frenzied rush hours and the wild nightlife certainly seemed anything but "Zenlike."

Yet we can learn a lot about how to find joy by looking at different cultures and the way other people live their lives, whether we look with a more open mind toward our eccentric next door neighbor or consider how joyful life might be in a tiny peasant town in Bhutan, where the average annual income won't pay some Americans' monthly mortgages, food comes from the local community's resources, and everybody knows everybody else.

Joy, American Style

Bucking the stereotype, a movement begun here in America in the 1970s, continues to grow with gathering strength toward greater simplicity and less materialism. This trend is transforming the face of corporate America. More and more people quit their high-powered jobs in favor of working at home, starting their own businesses, or moving to smaller towns in an effort to live more simply on less money—all to make room for more joy in their lives and in their families. Although many of those who work long hours truly do find joy in their careers, those who don't are ever more likely to say, "This isn't working for me," and change their life plans at any time in their lives, from their 20s to their 70s.

The happy ending is our national belief.
—Mary McCarthy (1912–1989), American writer

Even as we struggle to attain it, we in America specialize in the pursuit of happiness, in stress management, in self-improvement, in activism, in the continued quest to learn and grow and understand our world so we can make it better. The "decadent Westerner" stereotype might be true in some ways; sure—every culture has its decadent side, and every culture has its share of people who haven't figured out how to find joy in life. Yet we Americans do what we do in a big way, and when we find joy, we hold on!

Although we think happiness is different than joy, we think that joy is part of the *pursuit* of happiness. Joy is in the journey, in the daily discoveries of the miracles of life around us, in the inner glow we get from really living our lives. We Americans think joy is deeply connected to freedom and our ability to feel and think and say and believe whatever makes sense for us.

Yet despite our love of our own culture and our pride in our country, Americans also find joy in learning about other cultures and borrowing from their philosophies, whether French fashion or Asian theology or South American music. So let's take a look at ideas of joy from a few other cultures, to expand our own personal repertoires of joy.

An Eastern Perspective on Joy

Many Asian cultures are rooted in a tradition in which joy comes out of embracing simplicity and disassociating oneself from the material world. As Gary discovered on his trip to Tokyo, the Asian *philosophy* isn't always in keeping with the Asian *lifestyle*, but of course, that describes every culture.

Let's take a look at that philosophy, from the perspective of our quest for more ways to incorporate joy in our lives. Specifically, let's look at Zen Buddhism, a philosophy and a way of thinking which many Americans embrace as in keeping with their own values.

Zen Buddhism is just one of many sects of Buddhism that have evolved all over Asia since Bodhidharma, a sort of Buddhist "missionary," first traveled from India (where Siddhartha Gautama, the original "Buddha," lived) to China in about 475 B.C.E., to spread the word. Chinese art depicts Bodhidharma as a rather extreme-looking bearded man with bulging eyes, due to a legend that Bodhidharma was so devoted to staying awake in meditation that he cut off his own eyelids. (We don't advocate such a practice in the pursuit of joy, by the way!)

Bodhidharma is generally credited with bringing Buddhism, and also tea, to China, and although he had very few followers during his lifetime, his influence reverberates all over Asia to this day.

Although Zen itself fully flowered in Japan many centuries later, the teachings of Siddhartha Gautama remain at its heart. While this first Buddha preached nonattachment to attain inner peace and freedom from suffering, as Buddhism evolved, many latter buddhas (a buddha is anyone who has attained enlightenment, or entered that transformative state of truly recognizing the ultimate nature of the universe) were able to discover the joy in this life and how to live in the world while remaining unattached to it, walking lightly on the earth, offering a life of service to humankind, and preaching the virtues of nonviolence and the cultivation of inner joy. Even the Dalai Lama, Tibet's human incarnation of Buddhist ideals, recently wrote a well-received and immensely popular book called *The Art of Happiness* (see the resources section at the end of this book for more information on the many wonderful works penned by the Dalai Lama).

Can't Let Go?

To be human is to hold on to things, or so it sometimes seems. Each of us has certain things to which we are particularly attached—children, pets, life partners, our houses, our cars, our computers, our bank accounts. What are your attachments ... the things you can't imagine living without, the things you would find it incredibly difficult to give up? Don't worry, we aren't telling you you have to give up anything. Instead, write in your Joy Journal about the things to which you feel the most attached. What are they, specifically? How do you feel about them? What do they mean in your life?

Consider, for example, Hotai (Putai in China), the laughing Buddha (the fat smiling bald fellow so often represented in statuary all over Asia). This Buddha, far from the gaunt ascetic figures of Asian holy men, represented prosperity, good health, happiness, longevity, and family. While these hardly seem in keeping with the notions of non-attachment and separation from worldly ideals, Hotai embodies the classic fusion of self-mastery and enlightenment with ideas already inherent in China, such as prosperity and family.

This Buddhist "Santa Claus" experienced joy through laughter, and an entire sect of Buddhism is devoted to laughing meditation. Hotai usually carries or wears a cloth sack and sometimes carries a bar of gold. He is often surrounded by children. He was also known for predicting the weather with amazing accuracy, illustrating how much he must have paid attention to the natural world around him. This buddha illustrates how we can walk lightly on the earth and still appreciate its joys by laughing, loving others, sharing our wealth, and becoming a part of the natural world around us.

Zen Buddhism, more specifically, is the practice of zazen, or sitting meditation, and sometimes of kinhin, or walking meditation, for the purpose of training the mind to let go of thoughts, impressions, and feelings—not to banish them, but to see them, acknowledge them, and rather than engaging them or deceiving oneself that they make up the sum of reality, to let them go. Zen Buddhism teaches us to live in constant pursuit of truth, to see the self beyond thought, the self beyond emotion, even the self beyond intellect. Once our minds achieve one-pointedness, all we will see is unity and the way in which each one of us is a transitory wave in a great sea, as we recognize how each one of us and every part of us is an integral part of that sea.

Westerners tend to put a premium on individuality and may shy away from the idea that we are a faceless part of some generic universal idea. We want to be who we are! We want to stand out, be famous, be remembered, be *individuals!* Yet it is a common misapprehension of the nature of Zen to believe that our individuality is an illusion. Individuality is real, yet it is transitory. You are you right now, manifesting in the present time, but you will not be you forever. The essential you, however—that inner part of you that is connected to the universal flow of energy, the brilliant light that is universal awareness—that does not die, that simply is. We come to our lives as individuals and we live this way for a while, but what is essentially *us* is not this body with these particular sexual organs, this person with this particular job or hair color or personality or dazzling smile or big feet. According to Zen Buddhism you are not your external features, just as you are not what happens to you or even what you think or feel. Yet for now, for this precious time on earth that each of us has, you get to be those things.

And yet life sometimes involves suffering. Life can be painful. During these times, and even during times of joy and abundance, remembering that inner light that connects you to the universal sea can be an immense comfort and can shore you up in times of need.

That inner place can bring you joy because it is made out of joy, and it can help you to let go of the things that don't last—all the many other things that don't last, beautiful and precious as they might be—because when it comes right down to reality, you can't hold on to things forever, and nothing really belongs to us except that inner light that *is* us.

We think such a philosophy is a glorious gift from our Eastern neighbors, and it fills us with joy to think that humans, in all our fallibility, were able to see this thousands and thousands of years ago and pass it down so that we can hold it within us today.

Joy-Full Exercise: Culture Shock

Think about your last trip or vacation, whether it was to a nearby city or a continent on the other side of the world. How were people different? Today, see if you can incorporate one thing into your day from the culture, people, or customs of the place you last visited—or just do one thing to remind yourself of your trip. It can be something serious or something fun. You've been trekking through the Himalayas of India and Tibet? Meditate with your mala beads or twirl your Tibetan prayer wheel. You just came back from Mexico? Make a traditional Oaxacan mole for dinner. From Europe? Find a way to incorporate some aspect of European fashion chic into your wardrobe. From camping in a nearby U.S. National Park? Research wildlife on the Internet or make s'mores for dessert tonight! Use your imagination, and let it be a fun reminder of other places and fond memories.

A European Perspective on Joy

Ah, Europe—long vacations, short workdays, wine with every meal, freedom from sexual repression, affordable medical care, a really *chic* fashion sense. What's not to love?

Americans often view Europeans as possessors of a carefree existence, and many Europeans are indeed horrified at our work-obsessed existence. Of course, everyone, no matter where they live, can experience worry, anxiety, stress, depression, and a lack of joy. Residence in Europe doesn't exempt anybody from stress, and in fact, according to the World Health Organization (WHO), more people per capita commit suicide in Europe and (surprisingly) Australia and New Zealand than in the United States (Mexico, Central America, and South America have the lowest suicide rates).

Yet once again, although many people in Europe may be unhappy just like anywhere else, Europeans have developed a societal attitude that emphasizes leisure in a way Americans find difficult to comprehend. We can learn something from our European neighbors about how to squeeze the juice out of life and learn how to enjoy it, moment by moment. In 1972, the Council of European Ministers announced the prelude to Beethoven's "Ode to Joy" as the anthem of the European Union.

Whenever Gary travels to Spain, he marvels at the way everyone hits the cafes after work and dines at 9 or 10 P.M. The pace is inexorably slower and more relaxed. On a recent trip to Italy, Gary experienced this altered pace as well, along with a distinct surprise, concern, even disgust for the "workaholic" American way.

When Gary journeyed to Italy, he spent the weekend wandering the city because he didn't know anyone. On Saturday evening, he had dinner alone at the hotel and, like any self-respecting American, he brought along his laptop computer and the report he had to finish. The waiters were respectful but horrified as they helplessly tried to find a spot for Gary's wine glass amongst the papers, folders, and wires. Later, most people showed up for a 6 o'clock meeting between 6:30 and 7. Gary couldn't believe it … until he realized that's the European way. What's the hurry? The work will get done. Slow down, put the work away, enjoy the wine, watch the people, soak in the scenery, *be there*.

On a trip to Denmark, Gary stayed in a hotel that naturally featured a sauna and massage, but he felt uncomfortable jumping into these touchy-feely modalities and missed out on his chance to experience these hallmarks of Scandinavian culture. In Germany (known for precision and meticulous attention to detail), Gary's clients asked him, in wonderment, if it could possibly be true that Americans have such short vacations and sometimes neglect to take vacations at all. The German company Gary worked with told him that, for example, meetings could not be scheduled in August because that's the month everyone is on vacation. The *month!*

Across the pond in England, Gary recalls a long lunch with clients. Guess who kept looking at his watch? Finally, the clients asked Gary who, exactly, was going to reprimand him for being late to wherever he had to go next.

Europeans seem to have embraced an existence less constrained by time. They tend to have a worldview about politics, religion, sex, and all the other hot-button issues that is tempered by centuries of history and experience. We Americans are children by comparison! After first-hand experience of the horrors of war and conflict, contemporary Europeans emphasize the importance of nurturing union and joy. Every European may not live by the Dionysian philosophy of "Eat, drink, and be merry for tomorrow we may die" (a phrase originally from the Bible as an example of how *not* to behave), but we certainly believe Europeans generally know exactly how to eat well and drink well.

Cooking is an art form in Europe unsurpassed across the world, and European wine culture is an ancient and venerable art as well. Europeans do tend to drink wine, more often but in much smaller amounts than we do in America, and their food is much more often freshly prepared from whole foods rather than commercially packaged. Europeans have lower rates of heart disease and cancer than we do in America, probably a result of a combination of factors: the healthy food, the moderate wine consumption, the low-stress existence, and the connection to family.

How often do we in America forget to pay attention to the time, decide not to hurry, and instead, spend long hours savoring our food, our drink, and good conversation with our families? Do we ever enjoy a European-style afternoon lounging in a café discussing poetry or lingering over a multi-course meal of food prepared from the freshest possible ingredients? Just the thought makes us relax and fills us with joyful anticipation.

Every culture has its own priorities, its preferences, its wonders, and traveling to other cultures—either in reality or even through books and the Internet—is a fun way to experience the world. You're sure to pick up some joyful tips and broaden your horizons at the same time. Consider it research for the construction of that global grid of joy!

But what about you, right now, there at home? As we mentioned earlier in this chapter, what constitutes joy may differ by culture, but it also most certainly differs by individual. The things that bring us joy may not bring you joy. An afternoon of coffee and poetry may sound like sheer torture to you, but a night of salsa dancing or an early morning run down a mountain path or skydiving or simply giving someone you love a long hug may sound like pure joy to you. (Those all sound pretty good to us, too, actually …)

We all have our own opinions and ideas and personalities, even as we all have the capacity for happiness, sadness, boredom, passion, and every other emotion. To best understand how to empower *your* life with joy, let's examine more closely who you are right now. Only in consciously determining what brings you joy and what probably won't, can you craft a plan for infusing your own life with color.

O world, I cannot hold thee close enough!
—Edna St. Vincent Millay (1892–1950), American poet

Quiz: How Do You Define Joy?

Remember those pop quizzes your teachers used to pull on you, the ones where you walk in to the class and suddenly find yourself facing a test you didn't expect? This short quiz is *nothing* like that! You don't even have to take it (but we hope you will), and best of all, there are no right or wrong answers, only *your* answers.

The point of this quiz is to start you thinking in more specific terms about your own personal definition of joy, and to help you consider other wider definitions you might not have thought about before. Write down the first answers that come to you, and if nothing comes at first, spend a few joyful moments mulling it over.

1. List five words you associate with the concept of joy:

_____

_____

_____

_____

_____

2. Let's consider some different ways to define joy. Fill in the following sentences in any way you like. Even though some of them might seem almost the same, see if you can come up with different (but still accurate for you) answers:

Joy is:

_____

Joy means:

_____

Joy is like:

_____

Joy is about:

_____

Joy is not:

_____

I feel joyful when I think of:

_____

Doing _____ makes me feel joyful.

When I was a child, I thought joy was:

_____

As an adult, I now think joy is more about:

_____

I would like to feel more joyful about:

_____

All in all, I think my personal definition of joy would have to be:

_____

3. What could happen to make you feel joyful right now at this moment?

_____

4. What could you do to make someone else feel joyful right now?

   _____

5. What could you put into practice in your life, without the help of anyone else, that would bring you the most possible joy?

   _____

6. What could you do for someone else that would bring them the most joy possible?

   _____

7. What people, places, or things exist in your life, *right now,* to fill you with joy?

   _____

   _____

   _____

   _____

   _____

8. What kinds of people, places, or things interfere with your feelings of joy?

   _____

   _____

   _____

   _____

   _____

9. When you feel joy, do you also feel guilty about enjoying yourself, or do you assume that if it's good, it can't last?

   _____

10. When you feel joy, what physical "symptoms" do you also experience?

    _____

    _____

    _____

    _____

Now, take a moment to look back over your answers. Do you define joy as a feeling from inside, or as the direct result of external circumstances ... or both? Do the things that make you joyful fall into predictable categories, like attention from other people, material possessions, or situations without stress like vacations from work? What kind of things stand in the way of joy? Guilt? Anxiety? Workload?

Get a picture in your mind of what brings you joy—we're sure you have a list, but we mean a more general picture. If joy is the absence of certain negative energies in your life, see if you can redefine joy in positive terms: what things would *happen* (as opposed to what things would have to *stop happening*) for you to feel more joy? Envision your "joy categories"—secure finances, loving relationships, self-esteem, more connection to spirit, etc., and picture these conditions surrounding you. Let this be your visualization of your joy profile.

As you read through this book, keep your personal joy profile in mind, to best utilize the information as we look in more detail at joy and how to find it. Also be aware that joy can probably be found and apprehended in many ways you never really considered before. Keep your mind open and ready to embrace joy at every opportunity, even in places you never thought you'd find it.

Now that you've got a clearer idea of your own views about joy, let's look a little more closely at some of the things you might have put on your lists.

Happy All the Time?

In your profile, did you say that you wished you could be happy? As we talk about joy throughout this book, we want to make it clear that by joy we do *not* mean happiness. One dictionary we have defines "happiness" as "characterized by good fortune." And sure, good fortune can bring you joy. Sometimes the definitions of "joy" and "happiness" can co-exist: You can be happy and joyful at the same time, but you can be happy without being joyful, joyful without being happy. The same dictionary defines "joy" as "a feeling of pleasure or happiness," and the word "feeling" is the empowering key we envision to creating joy in your life.

Joy, to us, and for our purposes in this book, is a *feeling* you can induce when you need it. But it is also more than a feeling. The state of joy can exist within you as an accessible inner core. Happiness comes and goes according to circumstances, but joy isn't *what* happens to you. Joy is in the way you *react* to what happens. Joy is a constant empowering strength that can center and guide you through all of life's ups and downs.

Believing joy is the same as happiness may lead to a state of frustration or the thought that joy will be unattainable for you. Don't we all struggle for happiness? And what if we can't find it, or have it *every* day? What if we ... *(gulp) aren't happy?*

Joy isn't about being happy all the time—nobody can expect to be happy all the time, nor should they. Life is rich and full of color, and its texture of highs and lows and in-betweens helps us to recognize and distinguish happiness and joy when we find them. For although happiness might be fleeting or elusive, joy is at the heart of every experience, every day.

Joy, though, isn't about giggly, ecstatic optimism, nor is it gushing about the silver lining to that black cloud hanging up there in the sky. Joy doesn't mean you won't sometimes be afraid or experience loss, personal tragedy, failure, betrayal, disappointment, or any of a thousand different things that can *happen* to anybody. Joy remains possible when happiness seems unattainable. The potential for joy exists at every moment for every person, and that's what makes joy so powerful, so beautiful, and so human.

Happiness is the ability to recognize it.
—Carolyn Wells (1869–1942), American writer

Would you want to feel happy all the time? Probably not. To be human, we need to experience sadness and loss, disappointment and sorrow and fear. We also need to experience love and hope, passion and contentment, and sometimes, great happiness. When we are in a state of emotional extremity, we may *long* for a steady and constant (numbing?) sense of general happiness, even if it means ignorance is bliss. But this isn't a book about how to be happy or how to dull the pain of tragedy with a "happy pill."

Joy is something entirely different. To us, joy is an inner knowing, a sense of the big picture, the ability to feel pain and sorrow but to see it for what it is … a passing state, and one of many that will come and go in this great ocean of universal being. Joy is finding beauty in ugliness while still recognizing the ugliness. Joy is acknowledging both pain and the growth it inspires. Joy is courageous and won't be thwarted. Joy is empathetic, sometimes cheerful and sometimes quietly serene, but joy always recognizes humanity and the common bond we all share. It is the soul's rescue crew. It is the spark of the human spirit.

Oh, to Be Desired

Maybe you put on your list that you want to be loved or even to be desired. For some people, nothing offers a greater high than being desirable, in demand, wanted, being the one everybody *pines for*. Whether that means you are desirable as an object of beauty, as a source of power, as a great wit, being desired can be addictive.

Maybe you are a performer and live for the applause, or maybe you quietly spend your evenings anonymously on the Internet in chat rooms because you like the attention you get from strangers who want to get to know you. Maybe you love to visit your mother because she dotes on you, or maybe you crave time with your young children because they think you are the greatest person they have ever met.

The desire to be desired is a powerful one, and while being wanted by others—in any of a number of capacities—can definitely induce a sense of pleasure, it can also become an obsession. Like any desire, if you let it control you, it can take over. Maybe you are spending way *too* much time in those chat rooms, or maybe you date obsessively without settling down with one person because you crave the excitement and adoration you receive when relationships are new. Maybe you have become obsessed with your appearance, with looking young or handsome or beautiful or sexy, all to get that thrill of turning heads on the street. If you feel like the "rush" of being desirable is something you can't live without—like an addiction—then you have allowed your desire to be desired to take over, and this will result in the antithesis of joy.

Yet that doesn't mean you can't feel joy at the attentions of others. Human relationships are one important key to finding your inner joy. The trick is to see desire for what it is. Humans are social animals, and we don't like to be lonely. We have lots of ideas and fantasies about what kind of people we think we need in our lives.

American culture is all about icons. We pick certain people our culture decides are desirable in the *right now,* and we raise them up and worship them. The rest of us struggle to try to be a little bit like those icons—be they pop singers or supermodels or box office superstars or CEOs of Fortune 500 companies or computer whizzes or billionaires (or the ones who fit in several of those categories). Some people get to be fifteen-minute icons by virtue of reality show contests!

We all have fantasies and ideas of the "perfect" people—who we should be *more* like and who could make our lives better. Yet so much of this longing, this desire to be desirable, this desire to desire others, is based on that thin veil that is the external. Trying to be your own personal version of icon for the world, or trying to be somebody else's "perfect person" won't bring you joy, even if it distracts you from an inner feeling of emptiness for a while.

What will bring you joy? Desiring your own inner being—finding it, knowing it, loving it, and letting it shine. Being *you* in all your wonderful unique quirkiness is part of the great joy of getting to live a human life in an individual, unique human body. The journey into *you* is enlightening, fulfilling, self-actualizing, and quite honestly, a whole lotta fun.

And ironically, one of the lovely side effects of knowing yourself and making yourself better while ignoring what others think you *should* be, just happens to be that you become much more attractive and desirable to others. The difference, then, is in the focus and the design of the journey: be your best self, not somebody else's best self, and you'll be desirable to others, more comfortable in your own skin, and more beautifully brimming with joy.

Your Fortune 500

Each of us experiences good fortune and bad fortune. Today we'd like you to start a list of 500 things for which you are fortunate. Yes, 500! And no, you don't have to finish it today. Just start it as a special appendix section in your Joy Journal—be sure to leave plenty of room! Begin your list with 10 people, places, and things you know, have or have experienced that have made your life better or more joyful. Try to add 10 more every day until you reach 500. Work on your list whenever you have a free moment or need a boost. When you reach 500, keep your list handy, in your wallet or on your refrigerator, so you can refer to it often.

Money Money Money Money

Chances are, somewhere on your joy list you had at least something related to money. Bill Gates notwithstanding, who couldn't use a few more bucks at the end of each month? Many of us spend a lot of time worrying about money, and worry can certainly impede our access to joy.

Most Americans feel they would be happier if they made more money, and having enough money to get by without worrying certainly can alleviate a certain degree of life stress, we won't deny it. Even though most people typically spend about what they make (or a little more), somewhere for each person there is a line dividing "not making it" and "getting by."

Many of us even fantasize about fabulous wealth—winning the lottery, being a billionaire without having to journey to the top, inheriting huge sums, finally quitting that job, traveling around the world, driving the most luxurious car, living in a mansion with a staff, shopping at will, never worrying about money again. Ah, the joy ... or would it really be such a joy?

Actually, although money does offer certain opportunities for joy-inducing activities, it does not in itself infuse anybody's life with happiness or joy. Joyless folks won't suddenly be gifted with joy along with a heftier paycheck or a sudden inheritance, and those who have access to their inner joy will be joyful in lean times as well as in times of plenty.

On the other hand—isn't there always another hand?—the simple fact is that our culture runs on money and not having enough to get by on the basic necessities is certainly stressful. In many cases, the answer to removing the *financial barrier* to joy is to get control over your money by knowing exactly how much you have and spending less than you earn (easier said than done, we know, and this subject is a book in itself).

Notice that we say money can be a barrier to joy. We don't consider it a means to joy. Having money simply alleviates worry, but a state of nonworry is not the same as a joyful state. Money is a means, not an end. Having enough money to buy things and do things can be fun, and having financial freedom can make joy seem more accessible, but because joy must spring from within to be authentic and lasting, money can never engender joy. Money is decidedly external in the same way blond hair or a six-pack abdomen are external. (No, those won't engender joy, either.)

However, money and joy are connected in another way. Consider what you *do to make money*. Now we are on to something. If you feel your job drains the joy from your life, yet you feel chained to it because you "need the money," you are facing a serious barrier that may take some effort to get over. If you feel your job is a source of joy in your life, then what you do to earn money might also be an important way to keep you in touch with joy.

A job or career that fulfills you, improves the world in some way, and makes you feel worthwhile and important can be a great place to help you fulfill your human potential. A job is much more than a source of income. It is a defining force in your life.

Have you ever noticed that people tend to ask, "What do you do?" instead of "Where do you work?" or "What is your job?" Jobs are what we do, and what we do is directly related to the way we interact with the world around us.

We'll talk more about your work and your joy in a later chapter, but for now, just keep this in mind (And this has nothing to do with money): *You are what you do.*

The joy of a spirit is the measure of its power.
—Ninon de Lenclose (1620–1705), French society figure

Be a Light Unto Yourself

We love to quote the words the Buddha supposedly said on his deathbed. When all is said and done, after we pore over and comb through our lists of what we need to bring us joy, of all the things we want and crave and desire, joy comes down to one thing: the light within.

Buddha, who found enlightenment during his lifetime, saw the foolishness of seeking the external in finding joy. He was rich, he lived a privileged life, then he gave it all up. He also saw the foolishness of extreme asceticism—in fact, he saw the foolishness of all extremes. Buddha preached moderation in all things, and finally, that all we need, everything we are, everything that will bring us a deep, enduring sense of joy is within us. If we are a light unto ourselves, then our paths will

49

be forever lit, our steps will be forever light, and our hearts will be forever infused with joy.

So once again, take a look at your list, your "joy profile." Look at what you think you want, what you think you need, and then perhaps you may find yourself reconsidering. Or maybe you won't! And that's fine, too. The process of inner knowing and empowering your life with joy is just that: a process. As we work through that process together, getting to know ourselves and further defining the paths of our lives, each of us will continue to hone and reshape our own definitions of joy. Your joy is what you make of it. Let's search it out together.

Chapter 3

Expressions of Joy

Joy isn't a theory. Joy is a reality of the human experience, and the evidence decorates history and every culture across the globe.

Why do people create art? Why do they build towering structures, stately monuments, magnificent sculptures? Why splash color across a canvas or spin clay on a wheel? What is the purpose of a fountain, a kite, a stained-glass window, a prayer flag, a magnificent transitory Tibetan sand mandala? Why celebrate holidays, why grow flowers, why give flowers, why write or play or sing or dance to music, why create candy sticks and chocolate truffles, why craft a fine artisan wine, or bake and frost a birthday cake, or simmer a soup on the stove all day long? Why spend even three seconds blowing into a pinwheel or a bubble wand?

Our answer is *joy*.

As humankind strives to create the embodiment of joy, giving it form and substance in the tangible world, that evidence stands as testament to the possibility of apprehending the joy in each of us. Perusing humankind's joyful creations does more than inspire us, although it can certainly do that. It can also urge us toward the loving kindness and creatively empathetic spirit that could help us to further our evolution toward our best destiny. Joy is a process, and the joy of humankind has evolved across millennia.

Let's take a peek at just a small handful of the joyful works, thoughts, artifacts, and evidence that, while the human experience may have its dark side, it is also full of brilliant light. We can almost hear the celestial music of the spheres. Joy to the world!

Joy in Art and Architecture

Color and form, image and texture, light and shadow. Whether these qualities spread across a sheet of drawing paper, build in layers on a canvas, or decorate ancient scrolls, tapestries, or cave walls, art has no immediate utilitarian purpose. Yet for thousands of years humans have created art, and we imagine they will continue to do so for thousands of years to come.

What is it within us that urges us to create the beautiful, to defy the darkness, to imitate what we see and how we perceive the world around us? Art—that re-seeing through the glass of the soul—means many things to many people. Consider the many styles, forms, and media through which art has manifested itself over the centuries, and you'll see how fantastically joyful the artist can be.

Of course, art often also reflects the darkness of the soul and of the world, as that darkness becomes a part of each individual artist's reality. Yet joy remains present and is part of that ability to feel that darkness and release it, transform it, live it, and let it go. It is part of that very urge to create. If the artist moves to paint, to sculpt, to draw, to build, then there is hope and light. There is an answer, and there is that joyful impetus to live and be and leave a mark on the world.

Painting the Soul

Consider Leonardo da Vinci (1452–1519), one of the great masters of Renaissance painting. Da Vinci was a painter, sculptor, architect, and an engineer. His great joy in the technical workings of different structures, from the human body to hydraulics and optics, set the ideological groundwork for many modern scientific developments. Da Vinci loved knowledge and spent his life in pursuit of it. He infused his art with his technical skill but also—or at the same time—with his joy at the complexity and diversity of the world and its phenomena.

Although many of da Vinci's works are famous, perhaps the most famous painting in the world is the *Mona Lisa*. Thousands have speculated on the meaning behind the *Mona Lisa*'s knowing smile. Artists have studied the lifelike figure, the luminous hands and face, and the masterful brushstrokes for centuries. The *Mona Lisa* is neither a ravishing beauty nor engaged in any kind of war, love scene, death, birth, or any other triumphant or dramatic human moment; nevertheless, she radiates a quiet, confident joy. Perhaps she knew how famous she would become. Perhaps she knew what great skill went into her making. Perhaps she knew that she would someday be a testament to human creativity and the quest for greatness.

Both Leonardo da Vinci's Renaissance painting the Mona Lisa *and Henri Matisse's Fauvist painting* The Gypsy *show the face of joy.*

But then consider *The Gypsy* by Henri Matisse (1869–1954), a French Fauvist painter and one of the great masters of color and the emotional expression of form. The face of Matisse's gypsy isn't realistic, luminous in the same high-Renaissance way, or even very clear, especially when viewed next to the *Mona Lisa*. Yet these two subjects share something similar in their smiles—some sense of the joy of the moment in which they were captured. Matisse's form is in itself joyful, capturing color and movement in a pure, natural, almost childlike way. We can't help but feel joyful whenever we browse the works of Matisse.

What I dream of is an art of balance, of purity and serenity devoid of troubling or depressing subject matter ... a soothing, calming influence on the mind, rather like a good armchair which provides relaxation from physical fatigue.
—Henri Matisse (1869–1954), French painter

We feel the same way about other modernist painters like Paul Klee with his bright colors, Wassily Kandinsky's joyful geometrics, the tranquil beauty and stained-glass appeal of Mondrian, Marc Chagall's ebullient floating characters, Paul Gauguin's exotic beautiful forms, Pablo Picasso and his bold interpretations, or Van Gogh with his swirling colors and bright intense landscapes. Most of us have seen a print of Van Gogh's *The Starry Night*, or his famous sunflowers, if not the original paintings.

Although Vincent Van Gogh (1853–1890) experienced much pain, loss, and suffering in his life, he was also bound to his art in such a way that even in the face of mental illness, perhaps a direct result of an epileptic disorder, painting was Van Gogh's primary solace and source of peace, tranquillity ... and joy. While being treated in an asylum at St. Rhemy, Van Gogh painted his best-known work, *The Starry Night*, during a period of recovery. This painting's deep serene color, peaceful evening cityscape, and joyfully celebratory movement of nature in harmony with the universe's bright lights helped to propel Van Gogh to the status of one of the greatest of the modern artists.

More contemporary examples of artists with difficult lives and joyful art include Keith Haring and some of the other contemporary artists who have died from AIDS. Even when these people knew they were sick, they continued to paint works of art that epitomized the joy of the present moment. Knowing they had limited time left, these artists were able to express their great realization that every single moment of life can be infused with the joy of being alive and awake in the now.

Of course, modern art is only one small piece of the joy that is the history of the art of human experience. For those who prefer a homey kind of folk art, consider P. Buckley Moss, who overcame a learning disability to become one of America's most popular and beloved folk artists with more than 15,000 images in print, or any of hundreds of other folk artists who paint or sculpt images of rural America.

Van Gogh's The Starry Night *captures the motion and mood of joy, transcending the artist's personal pain in a celebration of the heavens' glow.*

Thousands of great artists span human history—Titian, Rembrandt, Michelangelo, Rodin, Dali—and long before them, the creators of the art of Greek sculpture. From the *Venus de Milo* to various depictions of gods, goddesses, wars, deaths, and triumphs, the great Greek artists often cast figures into dramatic situations but always brought forth the human form at its most beautiful. The Greeks delighted in the body, in beauty, and in the glorious manifestations of physical form. While Greek vases and other pottery were often likely to portray battle scenes, they were just as likely to portray scenes of love, marriage, and the joyful frolicking of nymphs and satyrs.

Famous Venuses. Venus of Willendorf *(left) and* Venus de Milo *(right) celebrate the joy of the female body.*

The *Venus of Willendorf,* perhaps a fertility goddess, perhaps a fertility charm, was the first recognizable human image on record—perhaps the first piece of true art. Her full-figured, hair-plaited, faceless, pregnant form is an archetype for many women whose bodies become vessels for the joy of creation. We love the idea of a prehistorical goddess-worshipping culture fueled by the joy of creation.

Forward from that early time we can marvel at the magnificent totems of certain Native American cultures, the Zen-inspired art of Japan, the beauty of Tibetan mandalas, centuries of aboriginal art from Australia, New Zealand, and the islands of the South Pacific, the primitive art of Africa, the ancient folk art of rural Siberia, ancient images from the Incas, the Mayans, and the Aztecs. Everywhere around the world, humans create, and we see that as among the profoundest expressions of joy.

Joy-Full Exercise: Express Your Creativity

Are you in touch with your own creativity? Take a piece of paper and a regular pencil and spend about five minutes looking at an ordinary object—something you see very day. Examine its shape, its color, its lights and shadows. Examine its textures and curves, lines and corners. Try to *see* the object for the first time. Then, without watching your hand, pencil, or paper, imitate that shape, color, light, and shadow—translate what you see from eyes through hand and pencil to paper. Don't be afraid to try again … and again. You might be surprised at what comes out of that plain old pencil!

Monuments to Joy

Architecture is another art form that reaches toward the sky in an expression of joy. From the memory of our beloved Twin Towers of the World Trade Center in New York City to the fountains of Rome or even of Kansas City, to the St. Louis arch and the Art Deco district of Miami to the beautiful buildings designed by Frank Lloyd Wright, to the colored-glass Westin Hotel in downtown Manhattan to the ornate old houses known as the "painted ladies" in San Francisco. To mysterious, metaphysical expressions of wonder such as Stonehenge, the Egyptian Pyramids, the Parthenon, Vatican City, Monte Alban, the Taj Mahal, and the Great Wall of China—a defensive fortification but at the same time, a testament to the presence of humanity upon the face of the Earth and the only humanmade structure visible from space—architecture is an expression of the joy inherent in our being. It speaks to the universe that we are here!

Entire blocks can be architectural monuments to joy, and most people who have spent an evening strolling around New York's Times Square with the fantastic lights, towering lighted animated screens, and colorful people know just what we mean. Or maybe you get more joy from sitting meditating in an ornate Viennese cathedral or from a walking meditation in the famous Kyoto gardens of Japan or touring a medieval castle in the French Loire Valley or exploring Mayan ruins in Mesoamerica or going eye to eye with the great Egyptian Sphinx.

Architecture is more than utilitarian, although it is exactly that as well. Many forms of architecture stand as monuments to spiritual traditions, great people, or philosophical ideals. The Washington Monument points to the sky as if to say, "We know something is up there, and we can't wait to find out what it is!" The Eiffel Tower, the Statue of Liberty, the leaning tower of Pisa ... these great structures demonstrate how far we will go to create something big, something beautiful, something fantastic to make our mark on the world. See what comes out of the human brain and through the human hand? See what is borne out of the desire to create, to express our joy, to make the most out of the time we have? Long after we are gone, others will say, "Just look at what they left behind!" We've been saying it for centuries about our human brothers and sisters before us.

So many artists and architects help make our lives more joyful that we could never list them all, and we're sure you have your favorites, too. Or perhaps you never considered yourself a fan of art.

Most cities, university towns, and other small towns have some kind of museum. Whether you live near a large art museum or a tiny local folk art gallery, a city with famous architecture or a tiny town with a handful of hidden old houses full of history, a leisurely stroll through the artistic creations of your region is a fun way to spend an hour or two ... or more! Rather than spending this weekend doing the same things you always do, consider taking some time out to survey the works of joy from the artists in your town or from ages past. Which pieces seem joyful to you? Which buildings say something more than, "Somebody lives here?" Which express the artist's joy, and which fill you with joy when you look at them?

Joy-Full Exercise: Virtual Art Tour

No local access to museums? Fortunately, with the Internet, you have access to the exhibits and works in major museums all over the world. Here are a few to check out that we often enjoy:

- The Louvre in Paris: www.louvre.org/louvrea.htm
- The National Gallery in London: www.nationalgallery.org.uk
- The Tate Gallery in London: www.tate.org.uk/home/default.htm
- The Metropolitan Museum of Art in Manhattan: www.moma.org
- The Guggenheim Museum: www.guggenheim.org
- Smithsonian Institute: www.si.edu
- The Baltimore Museum of Art: www.artbma.org
- Art Institute of Chicago: www.artic.edu/aic
- Seattle Art Museum: www.seattleartmuseum.org
- Museum of Fine Arts in Boston: boston.com/mfa/chinese
- National Palace Museum of Tapai in Taiwan: www.npm.gov.tw/english/index-e.htm

Bring a notepad with you to the museum, neighborhood, or gallery (or keep notes while perusing websites) and note the artist's names you admire. Make a few notes about the piece, the building, or whatever and how it made you feel. Did you like the colors? The forms? How realistic were the images, or how expressionistic, impressionistic, abstract? Do you find you prefer sculptures or art of a certain genre such as folk art, western art, African headpieces, Asian jade, Mayan artifacts? What else can you learn about the forms you enjoy?

You might even be inspired to create your own art when you get home—paint with watercolors, sculpt with clay, draw portraits or still life, or create your own original masterpieces with found objects. Experiencing the art of others can be an inspiring way to tap your inner creativity, a process that becomes a great source of joy for many, whether they consider themselves "true artists" or joyful dabblers.

Music of the Spheres

For many people, nothing expresses joy more perfectly than music. From the first moment a human tapped out a rhythm on a stretched animal skin, music has arisen from within the human psyche. For centuries, music passed from generation to generation without ever being written down or recorded. Often used as a device to help remember religious texts, music was sometimes utilitarian but also evolved as an art form in itself.

From the resonant Gregorian chants of the Middle Ages to Indian sitar music, music reflects humankind's striving toward perfection. Its mathematical precision coupled with its intuitive access to emotion make music a mystery to some, but almost everyone enjoys some kind of music. Maybe you like jazz or opera or country music, alternative or heavy metal or the music of nineteenth-century France. Do you prefer an *a capella* barbershop quartet, a swing band heavy on the brass, or an acoustic guitar in a smoky bar? Whatever your style, listening to music and letting it speak to you is more than a way to relax and unwind. It is a way to access joy.

Music, the greatest good that mortals know,
And all of heaven we have below.
—Joseph Addison (1672–1719), English poet

Many musicians tap their inner joy for their compositions much the way visual artists do—even when they have experienced tragedy, sadness, or depression, the greatest musicians still feel compelled to create. The ability to release pain and happiness together into music is a great gift. Consider Teddy Pendergrass, a Philadelphia-based R&B artist who became paralyzed after a 1982 car accident. After much physical and emotional therapy, he began to record again, and his 1988 album titled *Joy* is a poignant expression of the joy he found during his recovery.

Gospel and soul music snatch joy vigorously from within and proclaim it to the world. Opera, as it tells the story of the human condition, is full of sorrow and despair, love and ecstasy and desire, and finally, joy. Even pop music is full of the contemporary youthful experience of joy as well as the difficulty of growing up in the world as it is today. Music is, essentially, about feeling, and about what we find within our souls to express to the world, whether we are singing or playing or composing or simply listening with mindful attention.

Of all the joyful songs that have ever been written—hymns, carols, symphonies, ballads, arias, chants, concertos, television commercial jingles—we can think of no better testament to joy than the symphony on which this book is structured: Beethoven's *Symphony No. 9 in D Minor*.

In the final movement of this symphony, inspired by Friedrich von Schiller's poem, "Ode to Joy," Beethoven introduced choral voices into a symphony for the first time. The entire symphony was so new, so dramatic and emotionally evocative, that when it was first performed at Vienna's Kaertnertor Theater in 1824, some of the players wept. Composer Richard Wagner said of Beethoven's most famous symphony, "It is wonderful how the master makes the arrival of the human voice and tongue a positive necessity, by this awe-inspiring recitative of the bass strings; almost breaking the bounds of absolute music already, it stems the tumult of the other instruments with its eloquence, insisting on decision, and passes at last into a songlike theme whose simple stately flow bears with it, one by one, the other instruments, until it swells into a mighty flood."

Yet Beethoven wrote his famous "Ode to Joy" during an incredibly painful period of his life, when several of his most devoted patrons and dearest friends had died or become estranged and he had become almost totally deaf. During this period, Beethoven's diary reveals many moments of despair coupled with a turning toward spirituality for hope and strength, according to Patrick Kavanaugh's book, *Spiritual Moments with the Great Composers* (Zondervan Publishing House, 1995). After that grand performance of his symphony, the deaf composer, who stood next to the conductor to help direct the tempo, had no idea that the audience had erupted into wild applause until one of the singers turned the disoriented Beethoven around to see the emotional audience.

What spurred the man who had written in his diary, "Oh God give me the strength to overcome myself; nothing must hold me to this life," to write such a symphony that composers and music lovers would revere for decades to come? How could this poor, deaf, abandoned man access such deep and magnificent joy, translating it into a perfect piece of music?

…that each leap forward there is a new delight, without either effort or appearance of repetition; the magical blossoming, so to speak, of a tree whose leaves burst forth simultaneously.

—Claude Debussy (1862–1918), French composer, on *Beethoven's Ninth Symphony*

Somewhere within, Beethoven—like so many other artists, composers, writers, philosophers, humans—had found that inner core of joy and tapped it, channeling it through his creative gift. Many of us have heard the popular hymn adapted from Beethoven's symphony, "Joyful, Joyful, We Adore Thee," with words composed and added by the poet Henry Van Dyke.

Whether you know Beethoven's *Ninth Symphony* by heart or have never listened to it before, we encourage you to listen to it again with full consciousness and attention. Not enough time for the whole thing at once? Listen to the final movement, the "Ode to Joy." See how closely you can focus on the notes and listen mindfully to the flow of chords, the many threads, the glorious and ground-breaking chorus. Can you feel Beethoven's emotional state? Does it speak to you? Does it light your own inner emotional fire?

And maybe it doesn't—maybe this kind of music just doesn't speak to you, and that's fine! But surely some kind of music inspires you, moves you, fills you with hope and inspiration and empathy toward humanity. What kind of music is it? Whatever it is, don't forget to bring it into your life. A day without music is a day with less joy than it could have had.

Even five minutes each day listening to a single song with full mindfulness trains your mind and your heart to listen, to appreciate, to rejoice, just as humans have listened, appreciated, and rejoiced in music from that time thousands and thousands of years ago when we first discovered that sound was more than whatever we happened to hear—sound could be shaped into something beautiful, something joyful and real and reflective of the soul.

Joy-Full Exercise: Got Rhythm?

What makes a piece of music? Melody? Lyrics? Rhythm? All these factors can be integral to whatever makes music *music,* but right now, consider the *beat*—perhaps the most primitive and basic of musical elements. Find your favorite song, on a CD or tape or MP3 file, and play it. As you play it, tap your foot or your hand or fingers or even a pencil on a desk to the underlying rhythm of the song from start to finish. This exercise is meditative and helps to hone your concentration, as well as heightening your appreciation for an aspect of your favorite song you might not have paid much attention to before. This exercise is also more difficult for some people than for others, but even if you aren't rhythmically inclined, give it a few tries. Feel the song and its beat inside you without thinking about it too much, and tap, tap, tap-tap-tap your way through the music. See, you've got rhythm after all!

The Philosophy of Joy

Philosophers throughout the ages, from Plato to Aristotle, Kant to Nietzsche, Lao Tzu to Confucius to the Dalai Lama, Thomas Aquinas to David Hume to Paul Tillich, have speculated on the nature of joy, of happiness, of the meaning of life. Although we could write a whole book on the philosophical inquiry into joy, let's just take a look at one major western and one major eastern philosopher, each with very specific and curiously similar approaches to the question of finding satisfaction, happiness, and joy in life.

Aristotle's Virtues and Vices

Aristotle lived from 384–322 B.C.E. in Greece. He studied under Plato at the Academy in Athens and wrote on many subjects, including ethics, which he believed were the key to happiness. Aristotle believed that morality was the middle ground between the extremes of deficiency and excess in any category of personal qualities, and only in pursuit of these ethics of moderation could one attain self-actualization and the resultant state of happiness.

For instance, the moral virtue of courage was the mean between cowardice (deficiency) and rashness (excess). High-mindedness was the middle ground between being too humble (deficiency) and too vain (excess). Civility stands between surliness and obsequiousness; sincerity, between cynicism and boastfulness; modesty, between shamelessness and shyness.

To Aristotle, the most important virtue was high-mindedness, which he saw as respect for the self and others. Aristotle promoted autonomy of will, tying together each virtue in an overall context of right action so that any one virtue wouldn't be out of proportion to or taken out of context from the others.

Patanjali's Eightfold Path

While he merely recorded and organized wisdom from centuries before him, the Indian philosopher Patanjali, who probably lived about the second century C.E., believed that following an Eightfold Path would center and focus the body, mind, and spirit in such a way as to best promote the path of enlightenment and ultimately lead to eternal access to universal joy.

Patanjali's Eightfold Path isn't unlike Aristotle's philosophy, in that it encouraged (much like the Buddhist path for right living that came after it) moderation, the middle road, and an effort at self-actualization. Patanjali's Eightfold Path includes the following parts:

1. Moral restraint, consisting of nonviolence, truthfulness, not stealing, chastity, and lack of greed.

2. Discipline, consisting of personal purity, contentment with one's situation and self, denial of overindulgence and luxury, study of the self and of the spiritual path, and devotion to divinity.

3. The practice of yoga postures to master the body.

4. The practice of breathing exercises, to master the flow of life energy in and out of the body.

5. The practice of sense withdrawal, to fully understand the illusive nature of sense impressions.

6. The practice of concentration, to train the mind.

7. The practice of meditation, to help the mind-body comprehend ultimate truth.

8. The final apprehension of ultimate understanding resulting in ecstatic union with the divine, or enlightenment.

Not truth, but faith it is what keeps the world alive.
—Edna St. Vincent Millay (1892–1950), American poet and writer

Seeking the Face of Divinity

Religion may be as old as the first human gaze upward toward the stars, and its influence on human culture is immeasurable. Religions have evolved and spread all over the world, and their theologies, though differing on many key points, also have much in common.

Many people derive great joy from the practice of religion, but we believe that religion itself isn't a cause of joy—it is a mode through which to experience and express joy. Religion is a cultural construction set up by societies, and it works well for many, but it is external.

Spirituality, on the other hand, is what religion works with, but spirituality doesn't require religion, although it may well benefit from religion. Inherently spiritual beings, humans have found thousands of creative ways to explore and express their spirituality. Why do we do it?

When we neglect our spiritual sides, we lose balance. To become fully realized as humans, we need to nurture and strengthen our physical, intellectual, emotional, and spiritual aspects, but in a world that values intelligence and beauty, it's easy to neglect the spiritual side.

Yet those who do maintain and nurture their spiritual lives often find they have greater access to their inner joy. Caring for the whole self makes joy more accessible.

Plus, we find the implements and modes of religion and spiritual practice to be filled with evidence of joy. Let's look at some of these spiritual paraphernalia, practices, and art forms, and consider the joy that goes into using these instruments of the spirit:

- Tibetan prayer wheels are beautiful barrels made of wood or metal, mounted on sticks, which are either handheld or designed to sit on a table, and often are carved with prayers and decorated with other carvings, beads, and jewels. Inside the barrel is a strip of paper with thousands of prayers written on it, wrapped around the spindle. When the prayer spins the prayer stick in the air, the Tibetan Buddhists believe each rotation releases every prayer on the paper into the air, drastically increasing the efficiency of mantra repetition (a mantra is a short prayer, phrase, or word the meditator repeats for focus, concentration, and communion with the universal spirit). Prayer sticks, prayer flags, gongs, and bells enhance meditation and point the mind toward a single focus.

- The Tibetan singing bowl is a heavy metal bowl with a striker. During meditation, one can strike the bowl like a gong or run the striker around the edge of the bowl exerting a slight pressure to create a resonating tone.

- Rosaries, mala beads, and other "prayer-counting" jewelry are a part of many religions in which practitioners repeat prayers. Buddhist and yoga mantra meditation shares much in common with the Catholic-based repetition of Hail Marys and Our Fathers, and both religions use handheld beads to keep track of those prayers, the fingers moving along to each bead with the repetition of each successive prayer.

- Many religions use icons, symbols, statues, and charms to help orient them toward divine energy or to get the things they need. Gary has an African fertility charm, a bold design with colored beads, with a distinct energy about it. Fertility charms are just one of many sorts of small objects people have carried, worn, or set on altars throughout the centuries to represent their hopes, their needs, and their quest.

- Altars are joyful expressions of spirituality, whether they are based on models from tribal Africa, contemporary Hinduism, Zen Buddhism, traditional Catholicism, or a New Age spirituality that encompasses aspects of all of these. An altar contains images, symbols, and tools for meditation, prayer, and honoring of the divine according to individual beliefs, and we find them beautiful and personalized transitory expressions of spiritual joy.

- The crucifix, that ultimate symbol of Christianity, looks like a symbol of despair and loss, but for this religion, it actually symbolizes ultimate joy because of Christ's resurrection on Easter. The cross symbolizes the divine triumph over death and the ultimate joy in the knowledge that the soul is beloved and has a place in heaven.

- Gregorian chants use many voices to induce certain vibrations and even create the effect of overtones and echoes the monks don't actually sing. A meditative/prayer technique, Gregorian chant is a beautiful and powerful mode of access to the divine.

- Singing is a joyful communion with the universe that appears in some form or another in most major religions, whether it takes the form of organized hymn singing, ritualized chanting, or even responsive readings set to certain melodies.

Your Spiritual Toolbox

In your Joy Journal, write about the spiritual implements or practices that mean the most to you. Which ones do you use? Why do they work for you? Or if you aren't much for spiritual practices, which ones sound interesting? Might you try working a Tibetan singing bowl? Listening to a recording of Gregorian chants? Meditating? Make a list of ways you could incorporate more attention to your spiritual side into your life using the tools of spirit so joyfully invented by other people just like you on that great quest for meaning and the joy that comes with it.

- Whirling and ecstatic dancing are traditional aspects of Sufism, a mystical sect of Islam, as well as many primitive religions. By whirling or dancing wildly, the body loses its control, and the spirit is allowed to reign supreme for a short while. This type of meditation is far from the peaceful sitting meditation of Zen, but its goal is the same: union with the divine.

- Cathedrals, synagogues, and mosques, with their magnificent murals, carvings, statues, stained-glass windows, towering spires, and magnificent architecture stand as monuments to the human quest toward the divine. The architecture of religious structures is an entire study in itself—this art form has traditionally provided artists with a means to express their most joyful and ecstatic creative designs in a utilitarian monument to spirit.

- Meditation, whether in the form of prayer, mantra meditation, counting meditation, walking meditation, or mindfulness meditation, is a conscious spiritual practice designed to train the mind and body toward stillness and, eventually, toward the ultimate recognition that we are all part of the same divine spirit—that we are one with God, or Goddess, or the universe, or nature, or however you choose to interpret the unity of all things. This simple practice of focus disciplines the mind until it is able to break free of attachments to transitory things and finally see truth. That truth is rooted in joy because everything that distracts us from or tempts us away from the joy within falls away in the face of that truth. One of our favorite spiritual practices, we think meditation is an important key to accessing joy.

There are so many expressions of joy and so little space in a chapter! Yet part of the joy of exploring the history of joy is in the very exploration, so we hope you will use this chapter as a springboard for your own discovery of the expressions of joy in world culture and throughout history. What better topic is there to research in the library, on the Internet, or in the bookstore, than the history of joy in art, architecture, music, philosophy, and spirituality? Consider it an investment in the fortification of your own repertoire of joy.

The Second Movement
Creating Joy in Mind, Body, and Soul

Molto vivace
(Lively, brisk, quick, and bright)

In the second movement of Beethoven's symphonic exploration of joy, the words he uses to describe it, *molto vivace,*
say it all, in any language: *full of life.* In this section, we take
a look at joy through the lens of our own bodies, minds, and
spirits.

How do we reveal, nurture, and quicken the joy of our
essential selves through our experiences while alive here on
earth: the joy of our physical health and well-being, the joy of
our thoughts and feelings, the joy of our inner spiritual core?
How do we make our hearts unfold like flowers, as the words
of the "Ode to Joy" extol?

Our purpose here is aptly reflected in these beautiful, joyous words from Oprah Winfrey: "Every time you suppress
some part of yourself ... you are in essence ignoring the
owner's manual your creator gave you and destroying your
design. What I know for sure is this: You are built not to
shrink down to less, but to blossom into more. To be more
splendid. To be more extraordinary. To use every moment to
fill yourself up."

Chapter 4

How to Strengthen Your
Joyful Body

Take a good look at your body. What do you see? A miracle? Because that's what your body is! No matter what body shape or type happens to be in fashion this year, the human body in all its many colors, shapes, sizes, and abilities is an amazing and fantastic living machine, intricately wired with a nervous system far exceeding any computer and animated with spirit that gives each of us our unique energy, light, and *self*.

The very notion of a human body is a joyful notion, but when it comes to your body, are you filled with joy? Chances are you consider your body imperfect. Most of us have certain physical qualities we would change if we could. Maybe you wish you were thinner or stronger or a different shape. But consider this: You get to live your life in this amazing body. What you do with it can be either a source of joy or a source of negativity. How do we keep the body in check, in its rightful place, working well and feeling good, supporting our spirit and existing *in balance*?

True joy is a holistic, mind/body/spirit state of being. When you balance your whole self, you gain better and more immediate access to joy. You become more fully able to experience joy. But that means putting your body in its place—caring for it, not neglecting it, not obsessing over it. Suddenly, that doesn't sound so easy …

A true holistic balanced state happens when the physical body is strong and healthy; the mind is calm, quick, and free from debilitating stress; the emotions are confident and secure; and the spirit is nurtured and allowed to express itself. The student of joy must nurture the whole by giving equal time, attention, and care to each of these essential parts of the whole. Only then can joy blossom, unimpeded by the barriers of disease, stress, anxiety, attachment, desire, and despair that come from spiritual emptiness.

Wow, you might think, *that's some job!* Indeed, yet this job is fun—it is the job of *you.* To help you along, let's start with that most obvious aspect of the self—the physical body. It's what we see when we look in the mirror, what we show to the world. It is the vehicle of our spirit, and it deserves some proper attention.

Beautiful You

You might think that in a culture obsessed with youth and beauty, nurturing the physical self is a natural impulse. We all want to be beautiful, right? So why don't we do what it takes? And why can't we stop when we've done enough?

Many of us find moderation difficult when it comes to the way we treat our bodies. We eat too much, even to the detriment of our health! We smoke or drink too much or take drugs to make us forget uncomfortable or painful emotions. Sometimes we become addicted to these substances and find it extremely difficult to get back into balance.

Restraint is the better part of beauty.
—Frances Gray Patton (1906–), American writer

Ironically, the search for joy often leads to abuse of our bodies in a misplaced quest for pleasure of the body alone. These practices often lead to a temporary euphoria—but the resultant crash, the recognition of the loss of self-control, can make us feel like we've lost our beauty. When beauty lies on the surface, it easily slips away.

Although moderation is the key to balancing the whole self, we may associate hedonistic excess with joy rather than self-restraint and discipline. It can be lots of fun for a short time to eat too much, drink too much, have sex with anyone who strikes our fancy, or take drugs. You don't want to bring down the party, right?

It's easy to think that practicing moderation will make us somehow less than beautiful or glamorous or exciting. How easy it is to discard moderation if we focus on our external selves. Sure, we might diet and exercise excessively to the ultimate detriment—not enhancement—of our health. We may feel beautiful for a moment, but what happens when the pounds come back on or we get busy and stop going to exercise class? What happens when we look ourselves eye to eye in the mirror and see below our physical outer self to the soul beneath?

Let's consider, first of all, how we feel about our physical bodies, and then let's look at some key ways we can begin to treat our bodies in a way that will bring out better health and greater balance ... and of course, in the end, a more confident sense of ourselves and the strengths and light within each of us. (*Psst*, guess what: It's that light that makes you beautiful!)

Beauty Is ...

Beauty means different things to different people, and although we all know we are *supposed* to think beauty is only skin deep, each of us has our own private definition. Think about the people you believe are truly beautiful and in your Joy Journal, explore what makes these people beautiful. Is it really the hair, the body, the complexion? Or is it something else, an internal glow, a confidence, a sense of joy, accomplishment, power, success ... what makes beauty for you? Finally, how do you imagine you could become more beautiful? Lose weight? Grow your hair? Gain confidence? Try to pin down the ephemeral nature of beauty as you see it. Don't be ashamed of your answers, just try to write your version of the truth because, as the great poet John Keats once said "Beauty is truth, truth beauty."

Quiz: What's Your Body Image?

How do you really feel about your body? Let's look into that question with a brief quiz. Pick your best answer for each of the following questions.

1. When you look in the mirror every morning, your first gut reaction is most like:
   a. "What a mess ... but I'm kind of cute in the morning!"
   b. "Yikes, I've got a lot of primping time ahead of me this morning!"
   c. You don't look in the mirror much, you just wash and go. You're sure you look fine.
   d. You try not to look in the mirror much because it's too depressing.

2. How do you feel about your favorite feature?
   a. My best feature is responsible for making me pretty much a hottie!
   b. My best feature is a product of something I've done to myself, such as a great lipstick, teeth whitener, face lift, a perm or bleach, implants, power lifting, one hundred daily sit-ups or squats, or liposuction, for example.
   c. All my features are acceptable.
   d. Some features are better than others, but they could *all* stand improvement.

3. Do you consider yourself "in shape" or "fit"?
   a. Yes, staying in shape is a big priority for me. I work hard to stay looking great.
   b. I'd better be, considering I go to the gym at least five times a week and follow a strict toning/weight-lifting and/or cardio regimen plus a regimented diet.
   c. I like to move and I don't tire easily. I have a good energy level, although I'm not a big athlete.
   d. My shape is fine for sitting in an easy chair; I do not like or need to exercise much.

4. How do you feel about your body?

    a. I'm proud of my body.

    b. I work hard for my body.

    c. I think my body is fine, but I don't focus on it all that much.

    d. It stresses me out to think about my body.

5. Most people have a few bad habits. How do you feel about yours?

    a. I care a lot about what other people think of me. My habits are geared around activities that boost my self-esteem with others and help me feel better about myself. For example, I like to shop for new clothes, and I enjoy social drinking— some people call me the life of the party. That's not too bad, right?

    b. I care a lot about my physical appearance. My habits are geared toward eating in a particular way, such as trying every new diet that comes along or signing up for every new exercise class craze or buying every new diet supplement or exercise contraption that comes on the market. Sometimes I feel like I have a compulsive disorder, but I'm not sure I should admit it to anyone, or if I have, I'm still struggling with overcoming it.

    c. I bite my nails and spit them across the room when nobody is looking, or crack my knuckles occasionally, but nobody minds much. I guess my bad habits are pretty minor things. Maybe I drink too much coffee under pressure. But on the whole I think I'm pretty balanced.

    d. I feel like my life is out of control, no matter how hard I try. Everything seems overwhelming! My desk is a mess, I'm frequently running behind, I often have to eat on the run or make bad food choices because I need what's convenient. I don't have time to exercise; I barely have time to shower in the morning. Help!

6. How do you feel about food?

    a. I'm interested in gourmet food, fine wine, the "right" mixed drinks, whatever is in. I use food to make me look cool.

    b. I am usually on some kind of pretty strict diet plan, like one that is low-calorie or low-carb or vegetarian.

    c. I eat to live but I don't live to eat. I like a little bit of everything, and I like to try new tastes when I encounter them.

    d. Sometimes I think I *use* food rather than eat it. Sometimes I eat too much at one sitting and then I decide not to eat much at all, or I eat for emotional comfort when I'm not even hungry. Sometimes I eat out of boredom or because I'm depressed or anxious. I eat a lot of junk food, especially carbohydrates like sugar and white flour.

7. How often do you exercise, and what do you do?

    a. I go to the gym or run in the city where I can be seen in trendy workout clothes.

    b. I exercise hard and often. Some people tell me I exercise too much. Could I have an exercise addiction?

    c. I get a little exercise every day but it's usually something like walking, biking, or hiking that I enjoy anyway.

    d. I hate exercise. Sometimes I force myself to do it, but it's never fun.

8. How do you feel about sex?

    a. I love the attention I get from being sexually desirable.

    b. Sex is all about the game—the manipulation, the intrigue, the image you put out there. Then again, I have a hard time maintaining a long-term relationship.

    c. I enjoy sex a lot—who doesn't?—but I don't think about it constantly.

    d. Sex can be pleasurable but many aspects of it make me uncomfortable.

9. How much sleep do you get?

    a. I catch up on the weekends when I can sleep in. I'm often tired during the week.

    b. I often have trouble sleeping, but I get by on not very much sleep.

    c. I sleep somewhere between six to eight hours per night. I usually feel rested during the day.

    d. Not nearly enough! I'm tired all the time, and I'm sure I suffer from sleep deprivation!

10. If you could sum up your physical self in one sentence, it would be closest to which of the following:

    a. I look good on the outside, but sometimes I think I neglect other aspects of myself.

    b. Sometimes I feel exhausted trying to maintain my body, hair, skin, etc., but I feel compelled to do it.

    c. I feel pretty good about the physical aspect of me.

    d. Nothing about my body is like I wish it could be. But I've learned to live with it.

We hope simply taking this test has helped you to think in more specific terms about the physical side of yourself. Now let's see what your answers reveal.

And Your Answers ...

Count up how many a, b, c, and d answers you have, then decide which category fits the physical you the best. Read every category for which you had three or more answers, because many people have aspects of several of the following types:

If you chose mostly a answers, you look good and you know it. Sure, you have some faults, but in general you are enjoying your good looks and good shape. You have many friends, and are probably outgoing and the life of the party. However, the way you take care of your body is sometimes based more on how you look and on the attention you get from others than on finding inner balance and better health. You might diet or exercise too stringently to stay overly slim. You might not get enough sleep because you spend so much time socializing. You might forget to take time for your inner self because your outer self is such a hit!

As you work through this book, keep in mind that how you look is only one aspect of your physical body and that your physical body is only one aspect of you. You may know how to have a really good time, but what happens when you get home at the end of a long night and sit by yourself for a while? Remember to keep your physical appearance in perspective. It's great to work hard to stay in good shape, but good health is more than looking cute in a tight pair of jeans.

Plenty of glamorous people get sick because they neglect their health in ways that don't immediately impact that stunning first impression. Remember that getting enough sleep, eating healthy foods, exercising moderately, and spending some time in quiet reflection each day are also important for keeping you looking and feeling good for years to come. Meditation can help you to keep all these aspects of your physical life in perspective, so spend a little time alone each day, quiet, breathing, and contemplating the complete you. You might be amazed at the fantastic changes in your life that can come about from five minutes of quiet meditation every morning or evening.

If you answered mostly b answers, you keep very close tabs on your physical self—so much so that you might be flirting with compulsive behavior and/or addictions. Staying in shape is one thing, but constantly obsessing about the size of your thighs or that little wrinkle on your forehead is quite another. Looking good is a fringe benefit of good health, but the stress and even the abuse you may suffer as a result of minute and constant attention to your appearance will drain your health and your joy rather than adding to it.

We would never suggest you adopt bad health habits, and we applaud people who eat sensibly and exercise. We are also not telling you to stop coloring your hair or using wrinkle cream or wearing makeup or lifting weights for greater muscle definition. However, excessive dieting, exercise addiction, or obsession with appearance aren't about health. If you require help with your compulsions, please seek a qualified counselor. Or if you think you can get a handle on this yourself, take a good, long, honest look at your life and your feelings about your body.

Appearance obsession is often based in low self-esteem and attachment to the external. Meditation is an excellent stress-reducing exercise that can help you get your feelings about your body into perspective and can also help you get a handle on moderation. You might have trouble practicing moderate eating, moderate exercise, and even moderate thought, but meditation can help you to step back from your body and see the ways in which body obsession is hindering you from experiencing true inner joy. The rush of losing another pound or temporarily conquering a wrinkle is nothing compared to the infusion of serenity you can get from real physical health and genuine love and appreciation for who you are ... who you *really* are ... inside.

If you answered mostly c answers, you have a pretty balanced perspective on your physical self. You practice good health habits but you don't obsess about them, and you enjoy life in a way that is physical and healthy but doesn't focus solely on that aspect. Somehow you have managed to escape the cultural obsession with appearance, and while you certainly enjoy looking and feeling good, your life isn't *about* that. Good for you!

Are there ways you can bring yourself even more into balance? Sure there are! You might not give much thought to exercise or the food you eat, but greater mindfulness in these areas, which are great potential sources of joy, could enhance your life experience. Mindfulness is a mental technique of total awareness and attention to the present moment. Try eating a meal this way. Savor every bite, noticing the color, texture, and flavor of the food. Let the meal be a sensual experience.

The same goes for exercise. When you walk or run or ride your bike, pay attention to the beauty of the world around you, the way your body moves, the way the air feels. If you immerse yourself in the present moment more often, you will learn to truly experience the joy of being alive in a way you may never have appreciated before.

If you answered mostly d answers, you already know you have some self-esteem issues that are keeping you from making the most of your daily existence. Some of us get so overextended in our daily lives and experience stress so chronically that the structure of our lives begins to break down. Some of us are particularly vulnerable to stress due to issues in our past that have made us less confident, and some people are simply more sensitive and need to protect themselves from the extreme and constant stimulation of contemporary life.

Whichever of these categories sounds most like you, you *can* get more control over your daily existence. Believe us, it's true! As recovering out-of-controllers ourselves, we know that you can do it. It's so easy to feel overwhelmed by everything you have to do, and it's even easier to let self-care plummet to the end of your list. However, if you let your physical body go unattended, the emotions, the mind, and the spirit are soon to follow. The more stress invades your life, the more disorganized and out of control you will feel. Step one? Make physical health a priority. This will help all the other pieces fall into place.

We know what you're thinking. Something like, *I don't have time to exercise!* or *Food is my only comfort!* or *I have to take care of other people first!* or *I am more of an intellectual person, that's my strength!* Yes, yes, we've used all those excuses before as well. But the simple fact is that until you get control over your health, nothing else will work as well as it could. You are out of balance, and you know you are out of balance. Your awareness of your less-than-ideal physical state is your first and greatest strength. Now all you have to do is change it, one small step at a time. If you change one thing per week and stick to that one small thing with fervor, you can gradually adjust your health. Maybe this week you will eat an extra serving of vegetables each day. Maybe you will take a 30-minute walk each day before work. Maybe you will go to bed 30 minutes earlier. Maybe you will take five minutes to breathe and think after work before talking to anyone. Whatever thing you pick, commit to it. Don't let anyone dissuade you. This is a priority; this is acting to rescue your life. You can do it!

And next week, now that your first new habit has become a habit, add another one. Tiny steps can equal a great journey. Just watch how your life begins to transform itself. Just watch what kind of person you can become if you do it just a little bit at a time. And of course, keep reading this book because we'll have lots more ideas and inspiration to keep you going. You *are* worthy of joy, and you *do* have joy within you. You've just got to get some things out of the way so you can find it.

The Joy of Movement

Human bodies are made for movement. In a world where telecommunication is the primary method of interaction, it's easy to forget to move very much during the course of a long work day, but what we lose when we forget to move is access to a tremendous source of joy: the physical joy of action.

Some of us see exercise as a necessary evil or a tiresome chore, and some of us neglect it altogether, but our physical bodies can't achieve optimal functioning unless we stay active. Whether you take a yoga class or run around the block or bike through the canyons, movement will make you healthier ... and happier. In *Self* magazine's 2003 body-image poll, 75 percent of women surveyed who are happier with their bodies than they were 5 years before say it is because they have gotten in shape. One of the best things about exercise is that it changes you quickly. Even before you lose any weight or gain much muscle, you will feel better about yourself and have more energy. In one week you'll feel the difference.

Exercise and application produce order in our affairs-health of body, cheerfulness of mind, and these make us precious to our friends.
—Thomas Jefferson (1743–1826), third president of the United States

Science actually has an explanation for why exercise makes us feel so good. Exercise releases certain brain chemicals—namely, serotonin, dopamine, norepinephrine, and endorphins. These chemicals affect our moods in a positive way, reducing stress, anxiety, and depression and boosting feelings of well-being, self-esteem, and confidence. These chemicals also help bolster the immune system so you might be more likely to avoid catching that cold everybody is passing around. Just like chronic stress releases chemicals that can eventually make us feel stressed most of the time, the chemicals released during exercise eventually makes us feel good most of the time!

For example, cardio aficionados know all about the "runner's high," that euphoric feeling that comes after about 20 minutes of running or doing other aerobic activity like vigorous cycling, dancing, or exercising on a stair-climber or elliptical trainer. This feeling is a direct result of the release of beta-endorphins in the body, the same endorphins your body uses to deal with pain during an injury. A daily dose of this feel-good chemical is a real mood-booster.

Exercise also boosts self-esteem because it makes you stronger, calmer, better able to deal with stress, and more effective at anger management. Several recent studies have demonstrated that exercise is just as effective as anti-depressant medication in combating depression, and exercise may also reduce aggressive reactions. Studies have also linked exercise to enhanced memory, quicker reaction time, and a treatment for a variety of anxiety disorders.

The muscle-building benefits of exercise, particularly of weight-lifting, not only make you stronger, tighter, and better defined (you'll see a whole new you in the mirror if you lift weights regularly, we promise!), but the added muscle actually helps you lose extra fat because the more muscle you have, the higher your metabolism. Don't worry about getting all bulked-up unless you are training for that. Weight lifting pulls everything in and gives you back the shape you were born to have.

Exercises such as walking and weight-lifting put physical stress on bones, combating bone loss, improving cardiovascular health, helping to rid the body of excess weight, and increasing energy. People who exercise are more likely to crave healthy foods than junk food, and they even tend to sleep better at night!

Exercise is important for people of all ages and abilities. More and more kids today are overweight, but families who exercise or play sports together not only get healthier together and share a joint commitment to good health but may also develop closer relationships, better trust, and improved communication, not to mention all the great memories logged for future reminiscing.

Getting fit is a political act. You are taking charge of your life.
—Jane Fonda (1937–), American actor and fitness advocate

We can't stress enough the physical, as well as the mental, emotional, and spiritual benefits of exercise. Movement brings the body back to a place of balance. People who get back into the habit of exercise (and it is a habit) get more done during the day, more than making up for the time spent exercising.

All you need is about 30 minutes on most days. That's all! Try a walk in the fresh air, a short jaunt at the gym, and add a few weight-lifting sessions each week. Not sure how to find your way around a gym, what to do with those weights, which machines to try? Not sure how fast to walk or how much to do at first?

First, see your doctor to get advice on how to start and to make sure you are healthy enough to begin an exercise program. If you have a particular health condition, ask your doctor what kind of exercise would be best for you. Then, consider what you think you might actually enjoy.

Don't focus on the part where you imagine yourself straining or sweating or physically exerting yourself in an unpleasant way. That's not fun! Exercise should be enjoyable and it shouldn't hurt, so keep that in mind.

We love the gym because it is one-stop shopping for exercise and the trainers will set up a program for you and show you how to use all the equipment. Many gyms also offer classes, from dancing and kickboxing to yoga and tai chi. Or explore one of these movement options on your own with books and videos or with non-gym-affiliated classes offered by local experts. Maybe you would like to take up ballet or karate or jazzercise or the ancient art of Samurai sword fighting or belly dancing.

Others much prefer outside time and are happy to walk or run around their neighborhoods or a local park or natural area ... bring the dog! Join a sports league if you are athletically inclined, or join a runner's club, a hiking group, a Latin dancing society. Find something you love to do and commit to it! If you aren't exercising and you add it to your life, your life will improve.

Think you'll need a reminder? A little inspiration? Copy the following list and post it where you'll see it every day:

Exercise is a joy because it ...

- Helps normalize weight.
- Increases energy.
- Improves sleep quality.
- Helps you move with more grace.
- Increases body confidence.
- Boosts self-esteem.
- Builds and maintains healthy bones, muscles, and joints.
- Makes you sexier!
- Increases your chances of living longer.
- Improves your mood.
- Reduces risk of heart disease and high blood pressure.
- Helps you to feel more joyful about your life.

Food, Glorious Food

We love food! And we don't feel guilty about it ... much. But food is a tricky business these days. Most of us have access to much more food than we need, and much of that food is pretty sparse when it comes to nutrition. Then again, it tastes so good!

And food should taste good. We should be able to enjoy our food, and many people do. Yet the joy of eating escapes many Americans who fall victim to eating disorders and food obsession. So what's the problem? Why does eating fill us with such dread, such guilt, such obsessive-compulsive behavior? The French eat what they like, drink a little wine with every meal, and enjoy far fewer diet-related health problems than we do.

We suspect that part of the problem is the American tendency to do everything up *big*. We supersize our fast food (do you really need a whole gallon of cola and a bucket of fries?), we finish giant restaurant portions, we flock to all-you-can-eat buffets and actually take them at their word. All the processed and refined foods we eat wreak havoc on our body chemistry, jacking up insulin levels and blood cholesterol levels, making us hungrier and hungrier, fatter and fatter, more and more prone to colon cancer, cardiovascular disease, diabetes, and a host of other health problems.

Why do we do it to ourselves? In many cases, we simply get way too attached to the taste of food! Food can become an addiction like a drug, and the more we experience the pleasure, the more we want it, especially when we notice the way it dulls pain, temporarily relieves depression (*very* temporarily), or calms anxiety. We become food-conflicted and begin to use food just like a drug. It's legal, right? It's cheap. It's fun. Who is it hurting?

Everything you see, I owe to spaghetti.
—Sophia Loren (1934–), Italian actor

You, that's who! When it comes to joy, food can be a double-edged ... fork? The temporary joy of eating something really good can quickly turn sour when eating turns to bingeing or even just plain guilt at a few bites of something we think we shouldn't be eating. We fear eating too much, yet we can't stop doing it. Or we starve ourselves, binge and purge, or fall prey to any of a number of other eating disorders. Meanwhile, most of us just keep getting fatter. Yikes!

Whether you eat to dull your feelings, quell your boredom, socialize with friends, or appease a food-pushing relative (or all of the above), you can normalize your relationship with food and regain a true reality-based joy in eating once again.

If you don't have a clue about how to eat right, consider a visit with a dietitian, who can help you map out a sensible plan. Or visit the website of the United States Department of Agriculture, where they explain their Food Guide Pyramid for healthy eating. Check it out at www.nal.usda.gov:8001/py/pmap.htm.

If you *do* know what you should be eating but simply have a hard time doing it, we have one word for you: *moderation.*

The world is filled with fad diets, deprivation diets, only-this or only-that diets. We all know we should eat more fruits and vegetables, lean protein, and calcium sources, drink plenty of water, and avoid excesses of sugar and saturated fat, right? But that doesn't mean you can't ever enjoy rich foods.

Making healthy food choices most of the time and so-called "decadent" food choices once in a while equals a balanced diet. Finally, keep your portion sizes moderate, and you can eat just about anything.

This isn't a book about nutrition. It's a book about joy, but we sincerely believe that food, enjoyed mindfully and in moderation, can be a great source of pleasure and satisfaction. Eating too much most of the time will eventually compromise your health and dull your tastebuds. Using food for emotional fulfillment keeps you from addressing the real issues in your life. But paying attention to every bite you eat, making every bite count, and focusing on the experience of eating good, healthy food is what joyful eating is all about. Slow down. Relax. Taste. Chew. Refine that palate. Appreciate the best things in life: organic foods, fresh foods, and home-cooked foods, especially in the good company of family and friends. Now that's what eating is supposed to be all about!

Joy-Full Exercise: Field Trip!

Have you ever been to a health food store? If you haven't, you've got a treat in store for you! Take a trip to a local health food store, a farmer's

market, or some other organic food market and pick up some fresh produce, natural cheese, and other foods that look interesting. Shake up
your dinner tonight with something new. You might also pick up a natural foods cookbook with simple recipes. Bring your partner or children
into the kitchen with you to help you cook dinner. See if you can tell the
difference between a salad or a soup made with organic vegetables versus the kind you normally eat. Keep preparation and the meal itself light
and fun, delegating jobs according to skills and preferences, and talking
about things everyone enjoys, and you'll cover all the necessary elements
of a joyful meal: healthy food, human interaction, and, we hope, a good
dose of laughter, which we all know is excellent for digestion!

Sleep Your Way to Better Health

Finally, for goodness sake, will you please just go to bed? Chances are,
about half of you reading this book are sleep-deprived, and that's no
insignificant issue. Sleep deprivation may be responsible for much more
than fatigue. It may indeed be a significant barrier to a successful and
satisfied life.

According to the National Sleep Foundation's 2002 sleep poll, which
compared mood and sleep deprivation for the first time, researchers
found a direct correlation between sleep and behavior. Those who typically slept for seven to eight hours each night reported heightened daytime alertness and a sense of peace, life satisfaction, and energy. Those
who typically slept for shorter periods reported not only daytime sleepi-
ness but also negative moods such as anger, stress, and pessimism!

Dream It!

Your Joy Journal can serve as a dream journal, too. Keep it by your bed, and
every morning record the images you remember from your dreams. Images
and themes that recur could be subconscious methods for your life, answers to
your problems, guidance along your life path. Or maybe you will simply find
some interesting, quirky, amusing stories among your dreams. Either way,
keeping a dream journal is both fun and therapeutic. Let your dreams guide
you.

Over the long haul, sleep deprivation can lead to chronic depression,
anxiety, irritability, rage, loss of concentration, clumsiness, and even

despair. Simply making sure you get seven to eight hours of sleep each night can, all on its own, make you feel dramatically better about yourself and your life. Did you think it could ever be that easy?

Many of us think we really don't have enough time to sleep for more than five or six hours each night, but the truth is, we don't have time for sleep deprivation, which causes millions to drive drowsy, underperform at work, and behave irrationally. If you are concerned with finding more joy in your life, don't let sleep deprivation get in your way. Turn off the television, jettison the after-dinner coffee, and hit the hay.

Even employers are beginning to recognize the benefits, such as increased alertness and productivity, of adequate sleep. Some companies even provide "nap rooms" for their employees! For all kinds of interesting sleep facts, strategies, and inspiration for why we should all curl up for a snooze, check out the National Sleep Foundation's website at www.sleepfoundation.org/PressArchives/NSAWtheme.html.

Joy-Full Exercise: Winding Down

For those who have trouble falling asleep, creating a personal sleep strategy may be the answer. Many a recovering insomniac has benefited from a pre-bedtime routine coupled with a consistent bedtime each evening. Make a list of your own winding-down routine, and follow it every evening straight into dreamland. Here are some items you might consider for your list:

- Go to bed and get up at the same time every night. Allow yourself eight hours. Yes, eight. All at once.
- Let dinner be your lightest meal.
- An hour before bedtime, stop eating, drinking alcohol or caffeine, working, and exercising. Instead, listen to music, read a book, or chat with your partner or a friend.
- Don't focus on problems after 9 P.M. Compartmentalize those for the morning.
- Meditate, pray, or simply relax quietly while deep breathing for 10 minutes right before bed.
- Sleep in a dark room without a television or radio playing.

May your dreams lead you along the road to deeper joy!

Now that you've addressed your physical body, let's move on to the rest of you. Keep reading to learn more about how to find joy of the mind amidst all that mental clatter!

Chapter 5

How to Nourish Your Joyful Mind

Is joy all in your head? In a way, it is. Or at least, it begins there. The way you choose to focus your mind can have a major impact on the way joy manifests itself in your life. Joy germinates in the mind and spreads into every corner of your life like a flowering vine, making good physical maintenance possible and giving you the space and ambition to cultivate spirit. When your thinking springs from a place of joy, the rest of your life becomes lighter, easier, more pleasurable.

Best of all, a joyful mind is easy to apprehend with some regular techniques and a little practice. The joyful mind may come more easily to some than others, but anyone can apprehend it. It's just a matter of instituting some healthy mental habits!

In the same way, mental patterns that undermine joy are also a matter of habit. Low self-esteem, control issues, attachment issues, envy, resentments, stress, and personal agendas can all stand in the way of the purposeful creation of joy. How wonderful it is to find yourself leaping effortlessly over these barriers that stand in the way of so many! Just as your body moves more easily when you get exercise and build your muscle strength, so your mind will find joy an effortless condition when it is similarly strengthened through regular maintenance. So let's work out that mind muscle!

The Physiology of Joy

To better understand the nuts and bolts of the joyful mind, let's get technical for just a moment. Researchers have long known that certain areas of the brain are indeed centers of joyful feelings, just as certain areas are associated with feelings of sadness. The brain's limbic system—the part of the human brain that evolved first and is, therefore, the most ancient and, some might say, primal—is the center of emotional responses. These basic emotions helped humans survive early in their development. Joy, pleasure, fear, and other strong emotions helped us determine how to react in extreme situations. That feels good? Do it more! That hurts? Run away! The limbic system is very basic but serves as the primitive response system for instincts to fight or flee, pursue or surrender.

The particular areas of the brain that regulate these emotions are the amygdala and the hypothalamus. Purposeful stimulation of the amygdale in conscious people has resulted in euphoric feelings, and certain areas of the hypothalamus, when stimulated, elicit feelings of pleasure.

But basic emotions don't tell the whole story. The more advanced frontal lobe of the cerebral cortex helps us interpret our strong emotions, and only when these two areas of the brain work together do we find we are in the throes of an actual thought process: That feels good. I like that. I want more, or, I'm going to try to do it more often!

Furthermore, scientists have linked activity in the left brain hemisphere with positive emotions like joy and a sense of well-being, while feelings of anger and depression seem to be linked with activity in the right brain. No, you aren't doomed to be depressive if you are left-handed (each side of the body is governed by the opposite brain hemisphere), but one study showed that children with more left-brain activity behaved in a more gleeful manner and laughed more during play compared to children with more right-brain activity, who behaved in a more reserved manner.

Write it on your heart that every day is the best day of the year.
—Ralph Waldo Emerson (1803–1882), American philosopher and poet

Remember in Chapter 4 when we told you about the feel-good chemicals our bodies release when we exercise? These neuropeptides, such as serotonin, dopamine, and endorphins, also help deliver positive feelings like pleasure and contentment, while insufficient delivery of these chemicals can sometimes result in depression. These chemicals originate in your brain's limbic system but are also produced in other parts of your body, including your heart, your kidneys, and elsewhere.

But what does all this mean for you, the person seeking more joy in life? We want you to remember that your body and your mind are inextricably connected. Studies show that putting your body into certain postures, like those that open up the chest area, or hugging someone, or even forcing a smile onto your face, actually trigger the release of "joy chemicals" into your body. Certain yoga poses are designed to expand the front of the body, releasing the energy center behind the heart and opening the body to emotions and love. These poses can actually make you *feel* more open and loving.

Everything you do affects the chemicals that affect how you think, and conversely, everything you think affects the chemicals that affect how you feel. You are truly a mind-body and you have, therefore, many tools at your disposal for adjusting your own mental and physical states.

Joy-Full Exercise: Releasing Your Heart Chakra

Chakras are energy centers in the body and a foundation of Eastern medicine. Acupuncture, acupressure, shiatsu massage, and many other Asian healing techniques use the chakras and the meridians that flow between them like rivers of energy.

This simple exercise is designed to open the heart center of the body and release emotions, encouraging openness and joy. A blocked heart center is like an energy dam. Emotions can get blocked and "stuck." An open heart chakra allows you to experience your emotions freely without holding on to them, so they become part of your experience and then pass away when appropriate.

This exercise encourages the free flow of energy through the heart chakra by actually opening the front of your body:

1. Stand with your feet together, arms at your sides.
2. Inhale deeply as you raise your arms up over your head.

3. Tighten your abdominal muscles and look up, so that your back is just slightly arched but firmly supported by your abdominal muscles.
4. Spread your fingers and reach toward the ceiling.
5. Slowly lower your arms to either side until they are outstretched and parallel to the floor. Keep your palms open and fingers energized. Breathe!
6. Visualize your chest opening and releasing stored emotions and negative feelings with each breath. Feel your inner joy stirring and flowing through your body. Imagine breathing in and out from your heart.
7. Relax by slowly lowering your arms as you straighten up.
8. Rest for a moment, breathing normally, and feel the difference in your body. Notice and allow yourself to experience any emotions that came to the surface during this exercise.

Love and Work

Before we get into the mental tools for fine-tuning your joyful responses, let's look at your basic joy needs. Assuming you've met your needs for food and shelter, let's look at how you can best construct your life, mentally, to facilitate a more joyful existence.

When asked what was required for happiness, Sigmund Freud once said, "All that matters is love and work." Much as we may quibble with certain Freudian assertions, we have to agree with this one. Well, maybe love and work aren't *all* that matter, but if you have people to love who also love you (family, friends, children, a partner), and if you have work that is meaningful and fulfilling (this could also be a hobby or other pursuit beyond your regular day job), you have indeed laid the foundation for a life infused with joy.

If you wish to be happy for an hour, get drunk.
If you wish to be happy for three days, get married.
If you wish to be happy for the rest of your life, plant a garden.
—Anonymous

Although we will talk more in later chapters about your relationships with others and the work you choose, keep in mind that the lack of fulfilling work or the lack of positive human interaction can be far greater obstacles to joy than those things we so often feel are more important: money, marriage, prestige, power. While you might find it difficult to make more money, you already have people in your life to love (not necessarily soul mates or objects of romantic love, but fulfilling, loving relationships of any kind). While you might not have the most impressive job title, you can spend time doing something that is meaningful to you, even if it is constructing an elaborate model train in your basement or writing in your journal or growing vegetables in your backyard.

While many of us already have loving relationships and fulfilling work, we might still let other mental barriers prohibit us from feeling the joy and satisfaction we could feel, but putting these basic joy needs into place makes the rest of the job a whole lot easier.

Whom Do You Love?

Lots of us complain that we have "nobody to love," but we all know that's not really true. Regardless of who may love us back to what degree, we all have people we love, and reflecting on the important people in our lives can, all on its own, result in a joyful moment. In your Joy Journal, make a list of all the people you love. Don't worry about how any of these people feel about you. That doesn't matter. What matters right now is how you feel. Anyone who can allow love to flow from them onto anyone at all has access to joy. So how about it? Who do you love? (Yes, pets count, too! Put them on that list!)

Great Expectations

Have you ever noticed how a sense of inner satisfaction can be relative? You can feel wonderfully content, and then a simple change in your thought process can throw you into a state of anxiety. What happens when our minds shift us into a less-than-joyful state? It's all a matter of great expectations.

We all expect things, whether small ("I expect my co-worker to answer my e-mail today") or big ("I expect my parents to treat me like an adult"). Expectations are part of our everyday thought process—it's a natural human quality to expect things. The more we learn, the more we can guess about what will happen in the world, and some say that the more we expect things to happen, the better prepared we will be for when they do happen.

But sometimes we confuse expectation with hope or with despair: "I expect this date to go well" is a confident revision of "I hope this date will go well." "I expect nobody will like my idea" is a pessimistic revision of "I hope they like my idea."

It's also easy to think that refusing to expect something is the same as expecting the worst. Nothing could be further from the truth! If you *don't* expect someone to treat you with respect, it doesn't mean you *do* expect that person to treat you disrespectfully. It simply means that you go through life open to possibilities for growth and surprise. It means you trust the universe to provide you with the tools for creating your own life. If someone does treat you with respect, how wonderful! If someone doesn't, then what a learning experience!

When you expect nothing, the world becomes a wonderland of surprises. Moving through life free of expectation and willing to live without the need to hold on to what you encounter sets you free to find joy in every moment. Yet most of us continue to expect, and what you expect can profoundly affect how you perceive your life. We hold on to expectations, just like attachments, with our minds, and this tight mental grasp we have is directly opposed to the joyful feeling of letting things unfold.

Life's under no obligation to give us what we expect.
—Margaret Mitchell (1909–1949), American writer

For example, imagine you won the lottery, with a jackpot of $1,000,000. A million dollars! You weren't expecting the money, and yet, suddenly, you have a million dollars! You feel overwhelmed with joy! A million dollars! You immediately begin to plan all the things you will do with your million dollars.

Then, you receive a letter in the mail stating that five other people also picked the winning number. Suddenly, instead of a million dollars, you realize you will be receiving $200,000 ... *before taxes*. Suddenly, all your expectations are foiled. Had someone just given you $200,000 in the first place, you would have been very happy about it, but suddenly,

$200,000 seems like a disappointment. See what expectations can do to your thinking?

Consciousness is incredibly elastic. You can mold it into whatever you want. It isn't set, it isn't made of stone, it isn't even genetic. Some things that affect consciousness might be set, might be genetic, but your consciousness—the state of your mind and what you make of it—are completely within your own control.

Even more importantly, your consciousness is the *only* thing within your control. You can't control what other people do or think or say—not really. But you *can* control the shape and texture and environment of your own consciousness. You might think you can't, if you are in the habit of self-doubt, but you can do it. Anyone can, with conviction and practice.

Joy-Full Exercise: Expectation Affirmation

It's so easy to expect things in life. Most of us do it all day long! You expect to hear from someone, you expect a positive response to a project, you expect a check in the mail. What would happen if you really did let go of all those expectations?

This week, do your best to remain conscious of your expectations. Whenever you find yourself expecting something, make a mental note: I am expecting _____. Put your expectation into words, which can help put it into perspective. It's one thing to have an inner feeling of expectation that seems right and justified. It may be another to voice it and consider how it sounds:

I expect to get a compliment for how great I look today.

I expect my friend to say how much she appreciates my great advice.

Hey, I expect a little sympathy here!

Then, follow up that recognition with a simple affirmation, in which you put actual words to your expectation. Think this or say it out loud:

I release my expectation that _____. Instead, I choose to relish the present moment exactly the way it is.

Replacing your expectation with a conscious note to appreciate things as they are fills you with a new appreciation for your own inner resources. Why rely on something that might or might not happen when everything you need, you have within? If you get in the habit of noting and processing your expectations in this way, they will soon become self-conscious and finally, you will be able to start releasing them … and that's a very freeing feeling!

Mastering the Flow State

"Flow" is the term psychologists use to describe that state of mind characterized by total absorption in a task. Artists, writers, athletes, cooks can all tell you about flow, but anyone can achieve this centered mental space. You've probably experienced it before. Flow is that feeling of being so absorbed in what you are doing that you don't notice the passage of time, you don't notice distractions, you may not even hear people when they speak to you. Your mind has become one with your task.

Finding flow and dwelling in it for a while is a gratifying experience, and the regular immersion into a flow state can help bring a state of joy close to the surface, where it is easily accessible. Flow trains the mind to block out its typical chatter. It is anti-multi-tasking. It is complete oneness with what you are *doing*.

How do you achieve flow? Back in the beginning of this chapter, we talked about the importance of fulfilling work in order to lay the groundwork for a life filled with joy. That work needn't be the work you do to earn money. It could also be a hobby, like art, music, collecting, building, or sports. Finding this key activity—the thing about which you are passionate, the thing that fascinates you—is your inroad to the joy of absorption.

Joy-Full Exercise: Go with the Flow

Flow is a sort of working meditation, and because you are doing something you enjoy, flow can be a lot easier, and require a lot less discipline, than typical sitting meditation. Yet flow still trains the mind to focus, so the regular immersion in the flow state has many of the same benefits of regular meditation!

But some people find that flow "just happens" and find it difficult to induce this state. Try this exercise to help you induce a state of flow.

Freewriting is a technique many teachers of beginning writers use to help them find ideas or get started on essays, but you can use freewriting to achieve flow. You needn't be a writer, or even particularly masterful at the finer points of grammar, to freewrite. All you need is your Joy Journal (or you can use your computer).

Set aside 15 to 30 minutes for this exercise. Find a quiet place where you won't be disturbed. Unplug the phone, and turn off televisions, radios, cell phones, and any other distracting devices. Request that family members give you privacy during this exercise, or practice when no one else is home.

Sit in a comfortable, well-lit spot with a pen you like to use. Open your Joy Journal to a blank page. What you will do in this exercise is write randomly and persistently until you achieve the flow state. Before you start, you may find it helpful to be aware of a few things. This exercise is difficult at first. Just like sitting meditation, you will probably encounter resistance when you begin—resistance from your own mind! You won't know what to write, or you will go back and judge your own writing, or you will feel frustrated that you can't keep writing. In regular sitting meditation, meditators often initially encounter mental chatter, stray distracting itches, and the mind wandering away to other things, straying from focus. Because flow is a form of meditation, it, too, is challenging until you become more practiced at it.

When you encounter these distractions, be aware that they are normal and all part of the process. To get to the point of flow, you must push through these distractions and persevere past your mental resistance. Write, and write, and write, and keep writing, no matter how uninteresting you think the writing is. Quality of the writing is not the point in the beginning of this exercise, although eventually that may evolve. Just keep writing.

You will know the flow state when you hit it: Suddenly you will lose a conscious feeling of writing and your thoughts will begin to flow out of you. You may have trouble writing fast enough to keep pace with your thoughts as they flow from brain to page. The actual physical writing or typing will almost disappear. You won't be aware of your surroundings, and your mind will stop wandering to other things. You will be totally focused on the task.

Even if you only achieve a minute or two of flow, this is enough to acquaint you—or reacquaint you—with the feeling. As you learn how to induce flow by practicing this exercise often, you will more easily be able to slip purposefully into the flow state in your other activities, whether that means making dinner, writing a report, drawing a picture of your cat, or building a bookshelf.

Now check the clock, grab your pen or seat yourself at your keyboard and begin writing. Write anything that comes to mind, even "I am free-writing right now and I'm not sure what to write." Keep writing and writing and writing. Keep on writing until the writing dissolves and you are your own thoughts coming out in words. Welcome to the flow state!

All good writing is swimming under water and holding your breath.
—F. Scott Fitzgerald (1896–1940), American novelist

The Joy of Mindfulness

Mindfulness is a state of being acutely aware of everything in your present moment: what is happening around you, what your senses experience, how you interact with others, even what you are thinking. Mindfulness is *nowness* and pure being. It is also an amazing tool for accessing joy.

Mindfulness is another variation of meditation that trains the mind toward focus and teaches you to quiet the mental chatter with which so many of us are constantly afflicted, but mindfulness gives the joy seeker even more benefits than mental control. Many of the obstacles to joy that we face in our mental lives have to do with a fixation on the past (regrets, longings, memories, attachments) or the future (expectations, hopes, dreams, goals for how we think we "should" be).

When we become completely absorbed in the experience of the present moment, then the *now* becomes our entire awareness. The details of the now flow in and out, come and go. They are decoration for the present moment, but they are not the meaning of it. The regular practice of mindfulness is a great way to reset priorities and put things into perspective: What we hold is not ours to hold. It is simply ours to experience for a while.

The power of mindfulness is its ability to dissolve—in one fell swoop—every one of these obstacles. Here's how:

- **Low self-esteem.** This barrier to joy can undermine our daily lives in innumerable ways. Yet because mindfulness focuses on the present moment, memories of past issues that undermine our inner confidence are irrelevant. It doesn't matter what anyone ever told you about yourself, and it doesn't matter what you've ever done or not done in the past. Right now, in the present moment, you simply are who you are.

- **Control issues.** Mindfulness involves simple observation. You see, hear, smell, taste, touch, and contemplate your immediate environment. When practicing mindfulness, control is irrelevant. You don't control, you simply observe. In the same way, you are not controlled because you are impassive. You experience but remain unattached to what you experience, so the only thing you control is your own perception.

- **Attachment issues.** We are attached to so many things! Our loved ones, our possessions, our money, even our physical bodies, our lives, our very existence! Mindfulness helps us to take one step back from our attachments and see them for what they are: impermanent. The recognition that all the things we love are indeed ours to love, just not ours to possess, is a recognition that can set us free and fill us with a sudden, deep, unexpected joy.

- **Envy.** It's a horrible feeling, that sense that we aren't as good as someone else or that someone else has something—looks, personality, charisma, prosperity, luck—that we don't have. Yet through mindfulness we can understand the unreal nature of envy: You are you, and that's the end of it. What's the point of wanting what someone else has, or what you *think* someone else has? None of us really *has* anything. Each of us is unique, yet each of us is also part of one great ocean of oneness. Mindfulness puts envy in its place: It isn't based in anything that lasts or really matters.

- **Resentments.** Resentments are, quite simply, negative attitudes about past events—attachments. We hold on to something that happened before and don't allow ourselves to let it go. But why are we holding on? When we become mindful, we recognize resentments as hooks into the past that drag great weights behind us. They hinder our experience of now. When we step back and see resentments in this light, it's easy to cut that line and let the weight fall away into the past where it belongs.

99

⬮ **Stress.** Stress happens when we become overwhelmed with our lives. It is a physical reaction to too much stimuli. When we have too much to do in the future, too much to worry about from the past, too much to keep in our heads right now, then the present moment is obliterated in a sea of anxious striving. Yet when we practice mindfulness, the sea grows calm. Again, we can see all those little hooks and lines in a great tangle over the surface of the sea, and we can let our lines go—if only for a few moments. Mindfulness won't result in shirking of responsibility. We won't suddenly forget all the items on our to-do list. But we will see them for what they are: not life-altering tidal waves of worry, but simply as items on our to-do list.

The practice of mindfulness is simple. When you first try it, you might want to practice under controlled conditions: a quiet room, privacy, and time. Eventually, however, you should be able to practice mindfulness anywhere: while driving down the highway, sitting at your desk at work, having a conversation with a friend, or eating a sandwich.

Mindfulness doesn't involve any fancy techniques or equipment. All it takes is mind: breathe, see, hear, feel. Let yourself take it all in with each inhale and let it all go with each exhale. Experience it all, but don't hold on. Stand back, and let it all go. Only then will the experience of your life truly become a part of your existence.

Until we understand the assumptions in which we are drenched, we cannot know ourselves.
—Adrienne Rich (1929–), American poet

Joy-Full Exercise: Please Release Me ...

Mindfulness isn't easy, especially when you first try it, but we love a special technique that can make it easier: the release! As you practice mindfulness, you will be tuned in not only to your surroundings but to your own thoughts and feelings as well. When you feel yourself attaching to a thought with worry, anxiety, possessiveness, or desire, think or speak the release and re-orient your mind. For example, you might say or think:

I release my desire for control over my partner. I control my own perceptions.

I release my envy of anyone else. I am me.

I release my attachment to my physical appearance. I will focus on what makes me feel healthy.

I release my worry over my financial situation. I will handle my money objectively.

I release my obsession about my weight. I am beautiful in any incarnation.

I release my perceived need to be perfect. I am already perfect.

I release the need to re-create the past. The past is over and I now dwell in the present.

These are just examples. Learn to craft your own responses to your mindfulness challenges, then immediately return to the present moment and savor it in all its luscious reality and truth, for right now is all you really know and all that really exists. The past, the future are shadows. Letting the rest go makes a lot more room for joy in what really is.

Joy Tools

While seeking out human relationships, finding work, and practicing both flow and mindfulness are all excellent ways to train the mind to better experience the joy of existence, we've got a few more tricks in our big black bag of joy. These joy tools are simple strategies and easy mental adjustments to help you fine-tune your mind muscle as it gets in better and better shape. With the regular use of these joy tools, you'll find joy not only easy to come by, but also practically knocking on your door.

Your Inner Cheerleader

Do you ever feel like you are talking to yourself? Actually, we spend most of the day doing just that, even when we don't realize it. We interpret situations and tell ourselves how to feel and how to respond to them. It's as if each one of us has our own internal "mini me" pulling the levers and the strings of the selves we present to the world. This is called "self-talk."

We learn self-talk at an early age. Much of what we tell ourselves sounds a lot like what our parents used to tell us, and depending on what that was, our self-talk may have a generally positive tone or a more negative tone. If your parents always told you that you could accomplish anything, your inner self may often tell you, when you doubt: "You can *do* this!" Then again, if your parents told you that you could do anything, but when you tried something, you were likely to hear, "That was a bad decision! How could you do that?" then you are likely to second guess your decisions as an adult. You talk to yourself in the way others have talked to you in the past, often without thinking about it. That includes teachers, friends, and other relatives.

As we mature and develop our own abilities to make decisions and judgments, we can learn to keep the attitudes that help us and discard the ones that don't. However, many of us retain self-talk we can't seem to escape.

Everybody has a *theme*. You talk to somebody a while, and you realize they have one particular thing that rules them.

—Meg Wolitzer (twentieth century), American writer

The great thing about self-talk is that you can recognize the nature of yours and adjust it to suit your needs. Listen in on the conversations you hold with yourself in your own head. In what ways do you support your own efforts to grow and develop by reinforcing yourself with positive thoughts? In what ways do you undermine your own best efforts, expecting the worst or playing back what you've heard others say, even if you knew at the time that it wasn't true?

Let your self-talk be your inner cheerleader, inspiring you to achieve your best in every aspect of your life, with these subtle inner adjustments:

- Train your self-talk to accentuate the positive. Banish criticism in favor of praise. "The situation may be difficult, but I am doing my best!" "I am coping with the situation and I am fine."

- Keep your sense of humor and the playful spirit of childhood. Let yourself smile. Positive-parent yourself: "You can do anything if you put your mind to it!" "You are so smart!" "I am so proud of you!"

- Focus on the big picture rather than the details. "I've been in a situation like this before, and it turned out fine." "I solved this before and I can solve it this time." "What I learn from this situation is what really matters in the scheme of things."

- Keep your distance. Let go. "I can accept this situation." "What others say, says as much about them as anything else." "I will look for the positive change or outcome to this situation." "The best solution changes only my point of view and actions, so best to impact or influence the action of others—but I cannot force people to change, nor should that be my aim."

- Begin your day on a positive note. First thing in the morning, tell yourself that this is going to be a good day. If you let it be a good day, it will be. It's all in how you look at it. "Today I wish only all good things to all sentient beings."

Affirmations

We've already given you lots of affirmations in this book, but we're bound to give you more, because we love them. They really work! Affirmations are a tool for training the mind to see things in an effective way, a way that can help you to achieve what you need and be who you are. Affirmations keep you centered. You can write them down or repeat them out loud like mantras. You can use them during meditation or as personal themes. Collect positive quotes (like the ones in this book), or write down things you hear that speak to you and summarize how you feel or how you would like to feel. You can even write your own! Let affirmations help you, and you'll find they can bring you much joy.

Joy-Full Exercise: Affirmation Station

Like the character Stuart Smalley of *Saturday Night Live* fame, you may keep your affirmations simple and few: I am good enough, I am smart enough, and doggone it, people *like* me! On the other hand, your affirmations can be as creative as you are! Why not try writing a few of your own?

To help you out, we'll provide you with some starting points. You fill in the rest of the affirmation in a way that works for you. Remember to keep your language positive. Avoid words like *should, could,* and *ought.*

Avoid if/then thinking and self-deprecating language. Instead, focus on the language of joy: positive, inspirational, imagistic, and life-affirming. Finish the following affirmations, then use the ones you like often:

- I am a _____ person.
- Today I will let myself _____.
- I am good at _____.
- I love the way the world is _____.
- I am successful because I _____.
- I am beautiful because I _____.
- I am alive and awake right now, and my life _____.
- My inner self is _____.

Now, make up some of your own!

- _____.
- _____.
- _____.
- _____.
- _____.
- _____.

Spinning Class

One of the keys to positive self-talk as well as affirmations is putting the right "spin" on what we say, both to others and to ourselves, as well as what we think and how we react to the people and events in our lives. Your interpretation of a situation results in your emotional response, so spin the interpretation and you'll get a more joyful response!

You can consciously spin just about any response you have to anthing in the world. Say you were walking through a shopping mall and saw a friend, who rushed passed you and didn't say a word. What would be your initial response? And how could you spin your interpretation of the situation so that it didn't become a barrier to your enjoyment of your day?

When in doubt, we always default to a position of nonattached mindfulness. Rather than assuming your friend's reaction had anything to do with you, rather than expecting her to greet you and being disappointed when she didn't, rather than holding on to your feelings of rejection at being what you perceive as "snubbed," instead, spin your interpretation: Notice what happened, but without assuming, consider that maybe she didn't see you or that she must have a lot going on. Maybe, out of empathy, you will give her a call later—not to accuse, just to listen. Then, let it go.

In her book *Awakening Loving-Kindness* (Shambhala, 1996), Buddhist nun Pema Chödrön evokes the Zen koan of the woman who is always running from tigers—angry thoughts, people, feelings, situations. Over the years she gets good at running far and fast, but the tigers seem to gain ground nonetheless. Eventually, the woman, much like Robert Redford and Paul Newman in the movie *Butch Cassidy and the Sundance Kid*, finds herself hanging onto a cliff ledge wondering what to do next. She sees tigers circling above and below. There is no where else to run! Meanwhile as she sees that a tiny mouse is busy eating the vines that hold the ledge secure, she also finds her eye falling upon a bunch of luscious wild strawberries. What does the woman do? She reaches for a berry and tastes its full, delicious beauty—filled with the joy of the moment.

What Pema Chödrön illustrates in this story is our ability, at any moment, in any circumstance, to view the possibility of joy in the moment and embrace it, without preconception of the final outcome. We *all* have tigers above and below and little mice fraying the secure lines that hold our worlds together. Understanding this gives us compassion not only for our own situation, but for the lives of others as well. How much more successful life is when we decide to choose the "spin" that creates joy in the present moment—the only moment of life we can experience *right now*.

In the same way, you can "spin" your responses to the world around you from grasping and holding, worrying and wondering, to become responses of observation, acceptance, and release to joy. Now doesn't that feel better?

Joy-Full Exercise: Let It Be

You can put a lot of effort into spinning, or you can put in just a little with a simple phrase that reminds you when to redirect your interpretation of an event. Our favorite phrase is: Let it be.

Use "Let it be" whenever you feel yourself reacting or attaching to something. Someone insulted you? "Let it be." It's raining? "Let it be." You embarrassed yourself in front of your co-workers or friends? Consider that embarrassment isn't a required response, and as you consider alternative reactions, say, "Let it be." Things are as they are and you are who you are, and everybody else is who they are, and that's the way it is; so rather than investing anxiety into something that is what it is, you might as well "Let it be."

Empathy

Empathy is the identification with the feelings of others, and feeling empathy for others is one of the most profound ways to bring both poignancy and joy into our lives. We all know what it is like to watch someone else experience something and to say, "I know just how that feels!" This is empathy, and listening to it and acting on it can help to make the most self-centered among us escape our own minds for a while in order to identify with another human being.

Many religions believe that only in forgetting ourselves and serving others can we achieve happiness. Empathy allows us to find that place within ourselves that seeks to serve others, bolstering the human race as a whole rather than becoming so focused on ourselves that we can no longer see the universal nature, and fate, of all humankind.

In the Native American creation myth of the Blackfoot tribe, Blackfoot First Woman was among the first people ever created. Blackfoot First Woman stepped forward and asked the creator if humans were immortal, and the creator admitted he hadn't considered the question. So Blackfoot First Woman proclaimed that she would throw a stone into the lake. If it floated, humans would be immortal. If it sank, humans would die, and once they were dead, they would never live again. Surrounded by her fellow humans, Blackfoot First Woman cast the stone into the lake, and of course, it sank. The humans looked at each other, and for the first time, they recognized that each of them had something profound in common: each of their lives would eventually end. And so, not only was the human race born, but so also was the human condition and the empathy each of us has within us.

We love this story because it illustrates how empathy could be present from the very beginning of the creation of humans. We are who we are because we are *all* who we are, and while each of us is unique, each of us is also part of a whole.

> She did not talk to people as if they were strange hard shells she had to crack open to get inside. She talked as if she were already in the shell. In their very shell.
> —Marita Bonner (1899–1971), American writer and playwright

Empathy connects us with others and deepens our relationships. It doesn't mean commiserating about problems or taking on other people's burdens at the expense of functioning well ourselves, but it does mean that we open ourselves and allow ourselves to feel what others feel. That is a powerful gift, and it can change our lives, illuminating our own conception of who we are and what we experience.

Empathy leads to the spectacular realization that you are not only an amazing individual, but that you are also part of a community, and community is another joyful part of life as a human.

Joy-Full Exercise: Community Service

But how do you access your inner empathy? Consciously, of course! Make a plan for how you can help to bring more joy into the life of one other person each day. Decide each morning how you will do it: Will you help someone in an unexpected way? Listen to someone who needs to talk? Say something nice to your neighbor? Smile at passersby as you walk down the street? Will you call your sister to say hello, or offer to buy a friend a cup of coffee? Letting empathy grace each day in a small way will fill you … and somebody else, too … with joy.

We've reveled in the joys of the physical body. We've plumbed the depths of the joyful mind. But the self is more than mind and body. It is also spirit! Read on to learn how to help your spiritual side carry its weight in the long and joyful journey toward self-awareness.

Chapter 6

How to Nurture Your Blissful Soul

Look in the mirror ... and then close your eyes. Are you still
there? You can't see yourself, but of course you know you
are standing in front of the mirror. Your mind tells you that.

Now, try to turn off your thoughts. Are you still there?

As you strive for a balance of body and mind, remember
that spirit is the third piece of the puzzle. Spirit means different
things to different people, but we like to think of it as your
essence: *who you are,* apart from your physical body, apart
from the emotions that swell in your heart or the thoughts that
skitter through your mind. Spirit isn't your physical body. It
isn't your intellect. It isn't your emotions. It is the inner you,
the core you, the you that is you no matter how your weight
changes, your hair changes, your education level changes, your
mood changes. You can be excited or bored, tall or short,
employed or unemployed, married or single, male or female,
young or old ... but you are still *you.*

Joy comes from knowing and being who you are, and *who
you are* is much more than that familiar reflection in the mirror, the information on your resume, or how your spouse or
parents or best friends describe you. Who you are is a complex,

multi-faceted, fascinating source of ever-changing parts, and part of nurturing spirit is taking the time and energy to explore those parts and discover the unfolding story of yourself.

The Buddha, on his deathbed, is quoted as saying to his disciples, "Be a light unto yourself." One of the basic precepts of yoga philosophy is self-study. Judeo-Christian wisdom also promotes self-awareness. This journey into the self helps to put reality into perspective and makes that heretofore elusive sense of joy suddenly and magnificently accessible. Knowing your spirit feels good.

> Our own life is the instrument with which we experiment with the truth.
> —Thich Nhat Hanh (1926–), Vietnamese Buddhist monk

Although we hear more and more about spirit these days (even *Oprah* has a "Remembering Your Spirit" segment), many people continue to neglect their spiritual sides, even wondering if a spirit exists. But cultivating spiritual joy is extremely important for creating joy in your life. Spiritual joy means becoming familiar with your internal compass, remaining open to the intuitive messages the universe has to offer you, proactively seeking self-knowledge through internal exploration, and finding and defining a life purpose to give your life a deeper and more satisfying meaning.

Spiritual joy doesn't have to mean going to church or praying every night before bed. But it does mean spending time in the contemplation of where you fit into the universe and what you believe about what life means. Remember the wonderful scene in the movie *A Beautiful Mind,* where actor Russell Crowe as mathematician John Nash points up at the stars and asks the woman he loves to "name anything" so that he can trace its essence there on the divine map: umbrella, octopus. In the same scene, he tells her he does not believe in luck, but that he does believe in "assigning value to things." The pursuit of spiritual joy—whether you are a mathematician, a priest, a poet, a painter, a pair of young lovers—is gained in the effort to find your place in the rich fabric of the universe.

Spiritual joy also means letting yourself live in the world, allowing yourself to love and to be loved and even to lose love. It means recognizing and appreciating the beauty and wonder of the natural world. And it always means coming back to yourself again to internalize what you've discovered and to let it become a part of you.

Your Spiritual Side

Whether or not you attend services or consider yourself a member of an organized religion, you do indeed have a spiritual side. Several studies in the mid-1990s, including one by the Gallup Organization, revealed that up to 90 percent of Americans believe in the power of prayer and/or meditation, and 95 percent of these people believed they have had a prayer answered. (Interestingly, some people claim to believe in the power of prayer but not in a "God.")

Although many people belong to religious organizations, many who don't still consider themselves spiritual. In his book *Spiritual but Not Religious* by religion professor Robert C. Fuller (Oxford University Press, 2001), Fuller reports that 20 percent of Americans describe themselves as "spiritual but not religious," choosing to avoid organized religion in favor of an independent spiritual search.

Others choose to engage in their spiritual search in fellowship with others of their faith through organized religion, and still others believe that spirituality is nothing more than the pursuit of an enriching life, whether or not they believe in any so-called higher power. Does that mean even atheists can be spiritual? We say yes, but that requires a qualification: What on Earth does spiritual mean?

We like Fuller's definition of spirituality, from his book:

Spirituality exists wherever we struggle with the issue of how our lives fit into the greater cosmic scheme of things. This is true even when our questions never give way to specific answers or give rise to specific practices such as prayer or meditation. We encounter spiritual issues every time we wonder where the universe comes from, why we are here, or what happens when we die. We also become spiritual when we become moved by values such as beauty, love, or creativity that seem to reveal a meaning or power beyond our visible world. An idea or practice is "spiritual" when it reveals our personal desire to establish a felt-relationship with the deepest meanings or powers governing life.

This broad-based definition of spirituality can apply to anyone, no matter his religious beliefs, traditions, or affiliations (or lack thereof). Nurturing our spiritual side adds a depth and dimension to our sense of self. To return once more to mathematician John Nash and the movie *A Beautiful Mind,* we were moved at the end of the movie when Nash declares, as he receives his Nobel Prize, that the highest answers he has found in his life quest are the ones inherent in the indefinable calculus of love; Nash then goes on to thank his wife, declaring "you are all my answers." Cast in the light of Nash's brilliance and his struggle to overcome mental illness, his realization of the power of love to reach and reveal his own spiritual nature and find expression in joy makes his accomplishments more poignant and hard-earned. Like Nash, we achieve spiritual joy, spiritual love, by working to understand who we are. Although pondering the meaning of life and our place in the universe might not be the first item on our to-do list, and although it might be easier to do just about everything else first, spiritual nurturing is just as important as any basic human activity. It is as important as eating healthy foods, exercising, and meditating.

We can find spiritual joy by becoming familiar with our internal compass, remaining open to the intuitive messages the universe has to offer us, proactively seeking self-knowledge through internal exploration, finding and defining a life purpose to give our life a deeper and more satisfying meaning, and by serving and giving to others. That might sound like a lot to do! Indeed, each individual spiritual quest is different but may include many different aspects and stages. Our first venture into our own spirituality may well be to craft our own roadmap to spirit.

Joy-Full Exercise: Charting Your Spiritual Roadmap

How do you nurture spirit? Drawing an actual map that visually represents your spiritual journey can help you to find your way. All you need is a large sheet of paper, a pen, a pair of scissors, a glue stick, and some pictures cut from magazines or printed from your computer that represent the things you believe are important in your life.

In one corner of your map, put a photo of yourself, or write your name and put a circle around it. Draw a winding line to the opposite corner of the map. On this end, put something that represents spiritual enlightenment or your spiritual idea: a sun, a star, the sky, a religious figure, an angel, or anything else that has meaning to you.

Now for the fun part! Look through magazines and other sources of pictures: mementos, postcards, photos of loved ones. Find pictures that represent the things you believe are important in life. What fulfills you? What fills you with joy? What do you consider the priorities in your life?

Attach these pictures along your road map. Don't worry about the order, just decorate the map with your priorities in visual form. You can continue to add to your map over time or finish it in one sitting. Roll it up or tuck it away in your journal and refer to it whenever you need a reminder about what is really meaningful in your life.

You may have heard of "out-of-body experiences," full of lights and visions. A true spiritual path demands something more challenging, what could be called an "in-the-body experience." We must connect to our body, to our feelings, to our life just now, if we are to awaken.

—Jack Kornfield (twentieth century), Buddhist meditation teacher and psychologist

Contemplative You

Your spiritual roadmap is just a beginning step in the quest to know yourself better. Many cultures consider the inner search for the self an integral part of the transition into adult life. Self-study is part of the yogic path to enlightenment. Buddhism and Islam are based on spiritual exploration, and the Judeo-Christian tradition also encourages the examination of the spiritual self, through prayer, contemplation, and the trust in a higher power to lead one through the inevitable "dark night of the soul" that precedes a higher level of spiritual understanding.

If you've never really thought about your spiritual side before, getting to know your spiritual self may initially feel like a challenge. Many of Gary's clients are at midlife, which many cultures note as a time of spiritual awakening. Indeed Dante, epic poet of the Italian Renaissance, 700 years ago began his famous poem, *The Inferno*, with just such a moment: *Midway upon the journey of life, I found myself within a forest dark, For the straightforward pathway had been lost* (translated by Henry Wadsworth Longfellow in the nineteenth century).

Some of us who, before midlife, have never before nurtured our spiritual side or even acknowledged that we have one, may wonder what is going on. What is that "still small voice" speaking to us, telling us to change our life direction or realign our priorities?

People facing their spiritual selves for the first time (or reacquainting themselves with their spiritual side after ignoring it for many years) might find themselves asking some serious questions:

- Does my current career mean anything to me?
- Do my relationships give me what I need? Am I giving enough in my relationships?
- Am I a spectator in the world or a participant? Am I involved enough in my community?
- Has my life become too narrow? Am I missing something?
- Am I creating a legacy? Will I be remembered?

Rather than dreading or avoiding questions like these, spiritual seeking helps us to take a serious look at these big questions. These kinds of questions are universal to all human beings, but it's easy to push them aside. Yet the price of neglecting them—of neglecting the great inner search into our spirit—is imbalance, and that imbalance can drain the joy from our lives.

Instead, spending time to consider these questions and to better acquaint yourself with your inner self can fill you with a confidence and an inner serenity, even if you don't ever quite come to all the answers. Spirit grows through the search for meaning, not in the finding of it, which makes the joy of spirit easy to apprehend: It begins the moment you begin your journey.

Self-study and the contemplation of the big questions in life can take many forms. You can write in your journal on a regular schedule to help yourself think through these questions. You can take up an art form, exploring your spirituality through drawing, painting, music, or movement. To fully nurture your spirit, these activities should be regular, not sporadic. Spend some time each day quietly focused on who you are, where your life is going, or what is meaningful to you. Five or ten minutes each morning and each evening in quiet meditation will put a meaningful frame around your day and help you to feel more grounded.

Journaling

In this book, we've already given you lots of cues to help direct the writing you do in your journal, but we hope you won't feel limited by our limited suggestions. Your journal can be much more than a place to visit occasionally. It can be a daily reflection of your spirit, and it can serve as a form of meditation.

While some people find writing difficult, others find it the most effective way to discover what they think and feel. Even if your journal consists of a regimented account of each day's activities, you can add a few paragraphs about what was meaningful to you, what you learned, what you discovered about the world. Or maybe your journal will be purely a source of spiritual contemplation.

Many a journal has spawned a great invention or given birth to a revolutionary idea. Let your journal be the fertile ground in which you plant the seeds of your spirit. Someday you may cherish the garden of volumes you have authored, and your children and grandchildren may pass these volumes down as treasured family history.

For those of you who can't seem to get in the habit of journal writing, perhaps another medium—reading, drawing, talking with others, meditation—will better serve your contemplative spirit.

Social Spirits

Spirituality-based social groups aren't just a fixture of organized religion. Some people simply think better in a group, when they can bounce their ideas off each other and share their feelings. If this sounds like you, you might find that your most valuable inner contemplation happens when your friends are around you.

If your friends feel the same way, consider starting a group that meets regularly to discuss issues and matters of spirituality, from the spiritual relevance of political events and decisions to philosophical discussions about the nature of reality. You might have a group to read and discuss parts of a spiritual text, or you might choose to meet in a natural setting, for inspiration. Your group might choose to meditate together for a period of time at the beginning of a meeting, or you might want to launch right into a discussion.

Whether you meet once a week or once a month, take turns leading the discussion and choosing topics; then be open to where the conversation turns. Or follow a study course to give a structure to meetings and discussion. However you organize your group, spiritual openness with friends can become a great source of joy in your life.

Inner Reflection

Sometimes, all it takes to know yourself better is to spend a little time every day on inner reflection. Morning is a good time for inner reflection, even if you think you don't have time in the morning for one more little thing. If you are used to despairing at the sound of the alarm, hitting the snooze button a couple times, finally rolling out of bed and hitting the shower, downing that coffee, and rushing off to work or rushing kids out the door for school (or both!), morning might not be your favorite time of day.

But what if you took those 10 minutes of snooze button time (are 10 more minutes of sleep really going to make any difference?) to sit all the way *up* in bed or even move to a chair or the floor, and just *think?* Focus on your day and how you plan for it to go. Then focus on your inner self. Think about how you are feeling and how you would like to feel throughout the day. Do you need to be energized? Are you hoping to feel relaxed? Set your mind in the direction of your day while breathing in a slow and relaxed manner. Then finish with an affirmation that will help to establish the tone for the day. You can use anything you like, but you might consider any of these:

I will live this day full of energy and life!

I will live this day with an inner tranquility.

I will live this day mindfully, relishing every moment.

I will live this day calmly and with self-control.

I will live this day aware of the needs of others.

I will live this day aware of my inner needs, so I can fulfill my potential.

If your morning inner reflection goes well, you may want to gradually shift this peaceful time so that it becomes a morning meditation. Meditation is a lot like inner reflection, and indeed, your inner reflection is a form of meditation, but a more traditional meditation session might be even more beneficial to your functioning if you choose to introduce this amazing discipline into your life.

Meditation 101

Meditation is a vast and complex subject, but integrating meditation into your daily life can actually be quite simple. Meditation does more than improve concentration through training the mind to focus. It can also provide you the ideal mental forum for getting to know yourself, considering your goals and values, and even contemplating how you might reorient your life in a more positive way.

Regular meditation will bring you more joy because it overhauls your mind/body/spirit balance in such a positive way that you can't help but feel more centered and more in-tune to your own being. Meditation encompasses the physical, the intellectual, and the spiritual as it balances the self.

People who have made meditation a part of their daily routine tend to get sick less often and have much lower levels of stress than control groups, according to extensive studies conducted on people practicing Transcendental Meditation, or TM. (This organized group presented themselves for scientific study, but anyone who meditates can enjoy these benefits.) Better health makes life more enjoyable, of course. Meditation tones and disciplines the mind as it trains you to focus better and think more clearly. And meditation makes a space for spirit to grow and flourish, touching every part of your life.

Meditation can take many forms, but perhaps the most basic is seated meditation. In Zen Buddhism, this form of meditation is called *zazen,* but many other traditions practice seated meditation, too. Seated meditation is a good way to begin meditating because it is simple in practice: You sit, you breathe, you focus. Sounds easy, right?

Actually, meditation is a challenge for most people because our minds are so filled with the details of our busy lives that we find it hard to focus. Just as exercise is hard when we aren't used to it, so is meditation! Of course, when we get in the habit of exercising every day, we gain strength and fitness, and exercise becomes easier and more enjoyable. The same thing goes for meditation.

How to Meditate

Find a quiet space where you won't be disturbed. Sit comfortably on a firm surface like the floor or a chair. You can sit on your knees with a pillow between your feet, or you can sit cross-legged. The ultra-flexible might like to sit in the traditional lotus position common in yoga meditation, with legs crossed and each foot placed on the opposite thigh. This position is highly stable but for most of us, it takes some practice, so don't rush it. A regular cross-legged position is fine. If sitting on the floor is uncomfortable, choose a chair with a high back and a firm seat in which you can sit up straight. Slouching isn't conducive to meditation because it crunches up your torso and doesn't allow energy to flow through your body efficiently.

Place your hands on your knees, palms facing up. You can make a circle with your thumb and index finger, a gesture, called a *mudra* in Sanskrit, thought to make a circuit of flowing energy so that it moves down the arm, out the fingers, back through the thumb, and back into the body. Or simply relax your palms in a gesture of openness toward the universe.

Anchor your posture by shifting on your sitz bones until you feel stable. Imagine your head lifting from the crown, back straight to open up your torso. Place your tongue on the roof of your mouth, which can actually help to anchor your posture and help you to feel centered. Relax your eyes and allow them to blur. Don't force them closed but don't direct any attention to them, as visual focus is not the point during this exercise.

Now, turn your attention to your breathing. Don't worry about making your breathing deep or long or slow, just breathe regularly and pay attention to it. Listen to the sound of it. Feel it moving in and out of your body. Let your entire focus center around the sound and feel and shape of your breathing.

Don't be surprised if your mind begins to wander, but when it does, gently guide it back to your breathing. Some meditation teachers advise counting the number of breaths, to help give your mind a more concrete focus. If you have a lot of trouble paying attention to your breathing, try counting: one inhale, one exhale, two inhale, two exhale. When you reach 10, start back at 1.

We won't kid you: Meditation is challenging. Who would have thought your brain was so full of chatter? Long ago, the Chinese dubbed this inner chatter "monkey mind," and we think that's a pretty apt description. You may not realize how loud and raucous those inner monkeys really are until you sit down to meditate. But these monkeys are worth taming, so keep at it. Start small: Five minutes is plenty for beginners. Once you are comfortable and focused with five minutes of meditation, increase your meditation time by one minute every week. When you are up to 10 or 15 minutes (some people meditate for 30 or even 60 minutes each morning), you will be a truly accomplished meditator!

When you have learned to focus your mind, you needn't continue to count your breaths. This is just a technique to help train you. The true meditative state is a state of pure awareness: Your solitary focus on the breath will eventually dissolve into a solitary focus on being. To meditate is to *be*, totally aware to the nature of reality, unattached to thoughts, feelings, or things. The meditator lives in the world, interacts with the world, even serves the world, but the meditator does not grasp the world and hold it tightly. The most amazing benefit of meditation is the eventual recognition that living *in* the world free from attachments and desires is a more vivid and ultimately *alive* way to exist than the way we existed before, chasing after all those little things we think we want at the expense of *seeing* who we *are*. What a joyful way to be!

But the only way to get there is with practice. Practice, practice, practice! Even before you think you are very good at it, meditation will begin to improve your physical and mental health—but, like exercise, regular practice is essential for real change. The more you meditate, the more it will balance you and the more amazing each moment of your life will become. Fifteen minutes of focused, relaxed meditation each day will change your life. We promise!

For more information on meditation, including how to meditate via many different methods, see the Resources section of this book, where we list many of our favorite meditation books, including our *The Complete Idiot's Guide to Zen Living*.

When you first begin to meditate—in any tradition—you suddenly become awestruck by all the things going on in your mind. With practice, an incredible empowerment takes place as you begin to recognize and even to stop the constant chatter of thought.

—Jean Smith (twentieth century), American writer

Joy-Full Exercise: And the Answer Is ...

Classic Zen sitting meditation is pure mindful awareness, but you can adapt meditation in many ways. Because meditation helps to relax your mind and body into a state of hyper-awareness, it puts you in a unique position to solve the problems you face in your life. During meditation, the simple presentation of an important question as a focus for meditation may yield surprising results. No question is too big or too small to consider during meditation:

Do I want to change careers?

Do I feel it's right to commit to this relationship?

Would I feel better if I apologized to my friend?

Am I prepared to adopt a dog?

Whether you think the universe or your own subconscious mind is helping you work out your dilemmas, the fact is that this technique really works. Begin meditating by relaxing and paying attention to your breathing. As soon as you feel relaxed and centered, present your question to the universe or to yourself: Who am I? How is my spirit? How am I doing? Where is my life going? Or whatever question you choose. This is your time, and you can consider any point of focus you like. The point is to focus solely on the question but without mentally striving to answer it. Just put the question out there. Consider it, as a question. Repeat the question, as a mantra. See where it takes you.

Spend 10 or 15 minutes in quiet contemplation, leaving your mind open for answers. Step back, mentally, and see what comes to you. Breathe, remain open, and you may be surprised at what suddenly seems obvious or right. This technique can almost seem like magic: You ask the question for which you thought there was no good answer or you contemplate a dilemma that you really didn't know how to resolve, then quite suddenly, without any mental effort at "solving," the answer is there in front of you, flooding your mind with truth: *a-ha!* So that's what you thought, what you knew all along. So that's what you should do.

Your answer might not be what you thought it would be. You might recognize the truth about something, and it might not be what you would have hoped was true. Yet this meditative technique can help you feel good about your conclusions and even fortify you with the resolve to carry them out. It's all a matter of finally getting comfortable inside your own consciousness. The answers were inside you all along.

The Meaning of Life

Carl Jung, the famous psychologist, believed humans have what he called a "natural religious function" that leads each of us toward metaphysical, or spiritual, contemplation. Jung believed that the disregard for this basic spiritual need could lead to psychological problems. If Jung is right (and we believe he is), that means that spirituality is not only enriching but also necessary for proper functioning.

In other words, the quest for meaning is a natural, human instinct. Denying this instinct is unhealthy. To fulfill this instinct is to fulfill a basic human need.

Not that you need an excuse to consider the meaning of your own life, not to mention life itself. Maybe you believe life has no ultimate higher meaning but that each life has its own individual purpose. Maybe you believe life is designed to teach us or help us evolve, spiritually. Or maybe you just don't know. The point is to ask the question, and to consider the answer.

Even if you think you know why you are on this planet in this body at this time, you can enrich your spirit further by pushing yourself to consider other possibilities. How do you do it? The world is filled with interesting opportunities for spiritual growth. Here are some ideas to get you started on your quest:

- Take a yoga class. Hatha yoga is a physical practice designed to facilitate spiritual awakening.
- Join a meditation group. Sometimes meditating with a group of people can help to refine your focus and help you stick with your practice.
- Take up tai chi. This Chinese movement program is designed to free the flow of energy to balance body, mind, and spirit.
- Read the spiritual masterpieces of other religions: the Bible, the Koran, the *Tao Te Ching,* the *Bhagavad Gita,* the Kaballah, the *Tibetan Book of Living and Dying,* the Confessions of

St. Augustine, or more contemporary classics like the writings of Gandhi, Eleanor Roosevelt, Martin Luther King Jr., Nelson Mandela, Pema Chödrön, Thich Nhat Hahn, the Dalai Lama, and countless other inspiring voices today.

- Considering more structured guidance? Investigate different religions and consider joining a religious organization.

- Surf the Internet. A great place to start: www.beliefnet.com. This clearinghouse for all religions contains fascinating articles, commentary from all sides on current issues, message boards, and great interactive resources including a "What's your spiritual type?" quiz to help you determine which belief system most closely matches your personal opinions and views.

- Talk to friends, informally or in a more formal discussion-group setting, about spiritual issues.

- Focus your attention on helping others. Sometimes this is the best way to find yourself! Volunteer for a local organization that serves a group you feel strongly about: children, the elderly, or animals, for example. Or get involved with an environmental or community action cause, or spend time with a needy family member, neighbor, or friend.

- Spend some time alone in nature, reflecting on the natural world around you. Long walks, camping, or simply sitting to observe for a while can enlighten and inspire you. Why does a beautiful natural setting fill us with joy? Now that's something to meditate on!

What Do You Mean?

As we grow and change, our priorities and our sense of what life means for us changes, too. Your Joy Journal is a good place to keep track of these changes. What does life mean to you today? Where are your priorities today? What brings meaning to your life? Give these questions some thought, then spend time writing in your journal about the meaning of life according to you, right here, right now. Next year at this same time, do it again, and the year after that, and the year after that. You might even devote a special journal section to your yearly "state of mind" address.

Joy and the Natural World

You don't have to be the outdoorsy type to find joy in the natural world. Something about natural beauty fills the spirit up with joy in a way that manmade masterpieces, though great and inspiring, can never quite accomplish. Maybe you see the natural world as the creator's ultimate masterpiece, or maybe you see it as ongoing evidence of the incredible process of evolution. Maybe you see it as both! But however you see it, spending time in the middle of it will change your spirit.

Studies show that even when looking at photographs of beautiful natural scenes, people experience a lowering of blood pressure, heart rate, and respiratory rate. Just the suggestion of nature relaxes us! Although we aren't going to tell you to take a full-blown camping trip (although it is something to consider!), spending a little time in nature every day can be as powerful a spirit-booster as meditation or exercise. When you combine the three into a meditative nature walk, then you've uncovered a serious life-enhancer!

The Japanese call walking meditation *kinhin*, a technique practiced within a *zendo* (a Zen meditation center) by walking slowly, deliberately, and mindfully around the room. While you can practice walking meditation indoors, we feel the practice is even more powerful—if different—when practiced in nature.

Vietnamese Buddhist monk Thich Nhat Hanh often expounds upon the benefits of walking meditation in the natural world for spiritual renewal. In his book *Peace Is Every Step: The Path of Mindfulness in Everyday Life* (see the resources section for more information), Thich Nhat Hanh advises:

Walk as if you are kissing the Earth with your feet. We have caused a lot of damage to the Earth. Now it is time for us to take good care of her. We bring our peace and calm to the surface of the Earth and share the lesson of love. We walk in that spirit. From time to time, when we see something beautiful, we may want to stop and look at it—a tree, a flower, some children playing. As we look, we continue to follow our breathing, lest we lose the beautiful flower and get caught up in our thoughts. When we want to resume walking, we just start again. Each step we take will create a cool breeze, refreshing our body and mind. Every step makes a flower bloom under our feet. We can do it only if we do not think of the future or the past, if we know that life can only be found in the present moment.

You might not think you have time to go outside and walk every single day. You might not think you have a place to walk that is close enough to the natural world, especially if you live in a city. However, nature is everywhere: a tree on the corner, a tuft of crab grass growing through the cement, a squirrel leaping from one gutter to another, a dog gleefully urging its human down the sidewalk.

If you are lucky enough to live near a natural area, consider it a refuge. Walk through the park, the forest, the botanical garden—even the outdoor greenhouse of a garden store!—with mindfulness and reverence for the natural world. Let nature fill up your soul and recall your primal relationship with our first mother, the earth. We are not so distant from nature after all.

Joy-Full Exercise: Seek Your Totem Animal

Many Native American cultures sent their young men out into the wilderness as a coming-of-age ritual. These young men would travel alone into the forest or into the mountains. They would immerse themselves in the natural world and find a totem—an animal with which they could identify on a spiritual level, with which they would be forever linked.

The practice of finding a totem may not be part of our contemporary culture, but you can do it anyway! Let this outing be a deliberate spiritual exercise. Find your totem animal and let its spirit become a part of yours.

First, locate a natural area where you can spend some time alone: a park, a wood, a pond or lake, a desert area, a hillside, a riverbank, a field—even your own large, woody yard if you tend to get a lot of wildlife. Set aside about an hour. Dress for the outdoors (wear sunscreen!) and bring a bottle of water and something to sit on, like an old blanket.

When you first arrive, take a moment to center yourself. Close your eyes, breathe, and think or say:

I seek my totem animal, my spirit partner in the natural world. Let us find each other.

Open your eyes, then set out into nature. Walk slowly and mindfully until you find a spot for sitting. Sit quietly and with respect for the nature and the many habitats around you. Once you are seated, turn your focus to your breathing, but keep your senses sharply tuned to the world around you. When your mind wanders, bring it back to your present moment. Look at the colors, the textures. See the trees, the plants, the stones. Feel the air, hear the sounds of bird song and wind. Wait, in openness.

You might see many different living creatures during your totem meditation: bugs, birds, squirrels, perhaps a deer, a raccoon, an otter. Or you might not see any animals at all. Continue to wait, breathe, and be.

When an animal comes into your realm of attention, focus on it. Let your spirit speak to it. Stay open to it. Does it look at you? Does it notice you? Do you feel any response from the animal? Or is that hawk circling overhead totally unaware of you?

Continue to wait, and let your intuition tell you when your totem animal appears. Even if that crow doesn't look at you, you may feel a connection to it. You might wonder if it senses you as it hops over the grass. Maybe that deer wanders by unaware of you, but your spirit latches on to it and makes it your own. Maybe that grasshopper lands on your knee and surveys you or that butterfly flutters in front of your field of vision as if sent there by some higher power.

The point of this exercise is to identify with the creatures in the natural world by reaching out to them with your spirit. Some people feel quite obviously chosen by an animal when they try this exercise, while others feel out of place in nature and find it difficult to relate to any natural creatures. If you have trouble with this exercise, don't make yourself unhappy. Recognize that you have just begun your introduction to the natural world, and try the exercise again on another day. The more you return to a natural setting for walking and sitting meditation, the more you will begin to feel a comfortable part of the natural world. If you don't find a totem animal on your first try, you will find one eventually. This isn't an exercise to rush. It is an exercise to savor, and the longer it takes, the more benefit you can gain.

Once you've decided that your totem animal is the crow or the squirrel or the deer or the beetle or the minnow or the moth or whatever you decide, write about that animal in your Joy Journal. Why did you choose it? How did you feel when you meditated in a natural setting? Describe the experience and how it felt to immerse your spirit in nature. Let the joy of the natural world infuse you, and remember to return to it often.

Coming Back to the Self

Finally, without caring for yourself, your spiritual power will wane. While focusing your energy and love on others, on the natural world, and on the study of spiritual thought can all build and grow your spirit, without basic self-care, you won't ever be able to reap the benefits of spiritual enrichment. You must protect and nurture your own spirit before it can reach out to anyone else, in the same way a child needs protection, nurture, and love in order to go out into the world and become a happy and useful member of society.

According to the book *Authentic Happiness* by Martin Seligman, Ph.D. (see the resources section), studies on personal happiness vs. longevity are difficult because so many different factors can contribute to longevity, but in a landmark study of 178 nuns whose lifestyles were virtually identical, the one factor that most closely correlated with long life was an inner sense of joy. Ninety percent of the nuns described as "cheerful" and "positive" by people rating their personal autobiographical sketches for positive language were still alive at the age of 85. Of the nuns whose sketches portrayed fewer positive emotions, only 34 percent were still alive at 85.

Nuns, as well as many other people who devote their lives to the service of others, don't have an easy time of it. They spend much of their time giving to others. Why do some of these nuns suffer from burnout, while others feel perpetually fulfilled? Seligman's theory is that those who act out of their own character and their own virtues are more likely to experience joy than those who believe they are entitled to joy without the exercise of personal strengths. He writes:

> The belief that we can rely on shortcuts to happiness, joy, rapture, comfort, and ecstasy, rather than be entitled to these feelings by the exercise of personal strengths and virtues, leads to legions of people who, in the middle of great wealth, are starving spiritually. Positive emotion alienated from the exercise of character leads to emptiness,

to inauthenticity, to depression, and, as we age, to the gnawing realization that we are fidgeting until we die. The positive feeling that arises from the exercises of strengths and virtues, rather than from the shortcuts, is authentic.

If Seligman's thesis holds, then the achievement of spiritual joy is not a right. It is an earned victory that takes some effort. It is being true to one's self. It is not only *having* beliefs and values, but acting them out as well. It is the exercise of character.

But why are some people able to exercise character, while others can't seem to summon the energy, not to mention the courage? To have character and conviction is to value one's own beliefs, to consider himself worthy of holding those beliefs sacred. People with character aren't filled with self-loathing. They are filled with self-love—not the conceited self-love that isolates humans from the world, but the kind of love that radiates outward and encourages each of us to be our best selves, to help each other in the service of humankind. It is to believe we are, as humans, worth preserving, worthy of a good life, worthy of love—worthy of the *effort* it takes to do the right thing.

If we don't care for ourselves, why bother to do the right thing? If we don't care for ourselves, how can we care for others? And so, at the heart of the argument for character is the argument for care.

How well do you care for yourself? How high up on your to-do list is *you*? Ask yourself these questions to help you determine how well you are taking care of number one:

- Do you take some time to yourself every day, for reading, writing, meditating, or just relaxing?
- How many people depend on you for their basic needs?
- How much time did you spend doing something fun yesterday?
- Do you feel fulfilled by your work?
- Does somebody love you unconditionally?
- Do you know how to love someone else unconditionally?

Although some of us are pretty good at taking care of ourselves, others of us are stretched so thin that we barely feel we have time to get the bills paid and food on the table, let alone relax in a bubble bath or write in a journal. Yet the magic of self-care is that the more time you take for yourself, the more energy you have to get it all accomplished. If you don't fill the car with gas, you aren't going to get very far!

If you are among the self-care-challenged, we suspect you feel your life lacks joy. Guess what? You can reach out and grab joy. You can take it all for yourself, revel in it, bask in it, because when you take joy, it just gets bigger, and soon you'll find you've got enough for everyone.

Spiritual love is a position of standing with one hand extended into the universe and one hand extended into the world, letting ourselves be a conduit for passing energy.
—Christina Baldwin (1946–), American writer

Joy-Full Exercise: Self-Care Strategies

We have an assignment for you. This week, we're going to make your to-do list just a *tiny* bit longer. Every day this week ... yes, *every* day ... we would like you to do one thing on the following list. You can choose the same item for each day or pick a different one every time. It's your choice. Your only requirement is to make one self-care strategy happen in your life once a day for seven days in a row. You can do this. It will bring you joy.

- Bring candles and a radio or CD player into your bathroom. Light the candles. Turn on the music. Take a bubble bath, or pour $1/2$ cup powdered milk and 1 teaspoon olive oil in the bath water. Unplug the phone and hang a "Do Not Disturb" sign on the door. Soak for 20 minutes. No less!

- Spend 15 minutes alone, relaxing and trying to picture your own spirit. What does your essence look like? Imagine a conversation between you and your spirit. What would you ask yourself? What would you answer?

- Go on a 30-minute walk outside in the fresh air. Pay attention to the world around you. Focus on your breathing, not on your thoughts.

- Call a friend to go have a cup of coffee or tea. Declare all stressful subjects off limits for 30 minutes. Instead, take turns telling each other what you like about each other. What are each of your best qualities?

- The simple act of petting a dog or a cat has an immediate beneficial effect on blood pressure and overall stress level. Spend 15 minutes with a cat or a dog, petting and talking to it. If you don't have a cat or a dog, ask a friend who has one if you can have a "play date," or visit the local animal shelter and ask if you can spend some time with some of the animals.

- If you are in a relationship, spend one hour of one-on-one time with your partner. Be extra affectionate. Kiss. Hug. Express your love. Should that lead to something more amorous, then more power to you!

- If you have children (or if you can borrow some—hey, your best mom friend probably needs a break!), put aside one hour to play. Forget about what isn't clean or accomplished. Just play. Run in the park, make believe, eat an ice cream cone. Let your children remind you how it feels to be a child. If you find yourself crawling around on all fours making animal noises or doing a barrel roll down a grassy hill, we are very proud of you.

We hope you feel better acquainted with your spiritual side than you did before you began this chapter, but don't stop here! Bringing mind, body, and spirit into balance is a lifelong, joyful endeavor, so keep taking care of yourself in all your many beautiful aspects as we wind down this second movement of our joyful symphony. Constant mindfulness about body, mind, and spirit will help you to maintain a joyful, lively sense of wonder in your world, and joy will become your constant companion, even when things don't always go as you planned.

The Third Movement
Reclaiming Joy

Adagio molto e cantabile
(Very slow, in singing style)

The third movement of Beethoven's *Ninth Symphony* is the *adagio*. *Adagio* means very slow, in a singing style, and in this slower, somewhat more solemn section, we will talk about some of the things you might find a little less easy to overcome in your life—those things that seem to block your view of the sun, let alone your vision of a joyful daily existence.

As we talk about the ways in which joy can veer off track and how to get it back, we would like you to envision the calm, centering sound of singing. As every symphony must eventually slow down and move through certain sections with a more careful, deliberate pace, so will we carefully and deliberately address those things that must indeed be handled with care, love, and a gentler brand of joy.

Chapter 7

Joy Misplaced: "Why Am I Afraid?"

As we strive to bring more joy into our lives, each of us will eventually become aware that some things are easier to overcome than others. Sure, we might worry a lot or stress out about work or family. We might not spend enough time on self-care, or we might wish our jobs were more fulfilling. But we also probably recognize that with a little effort and reorganization, we can do something about most of these daily annoyances of modern life. It might not be easy, but it at least seems do-able with a little effort.

But what about the big things? What about the bigger obstacles to finding simple joy in daily existence: the walls, as opposed to the curbs and stumbling blocks we addressed in the first movement of our book? Most of these obstacles consist of the psychological consequences of past events: the way we were raised, the things we lost, the tragedies we experienced. When something happens to us that seems too big to get our minds around, or when something happened to us in childhood that has become a part of who we perceive ourselves to be, we can feel helpless in its grasp: How do we feel joy if we can't climb out of despair? If we can't forgive? If we can't run fast enough to outpace our fear?

But we *can* win the battle against psychological barriers to joy, no matter how large they seem. Joy is the very essence of being alive, and if we've drifted away from that essence, be assured we are still connected to it by the very *fact* of our existence. We can find our way back to that place in our heart where we used to dwell. Did you ever see that early Tom Hanks movie, *Joe Versus the Volcano?* Rent it one night and look for the scene where Tom floats on a steamer trunk raft with Meg Ryan and watches in wonder as the moon rises huge in the night sky over the ocean horizon (an eerie foreshadowing of his later movie *Castaway*). Mesmerized by the clear light of this vision, Tom's character Joe whispers, "I forgot how big it is. Thank you God, for my life. Thank you for my life." Most simply put, joy is the fact of being alive and seeing it. It is simply being alive.

What makes us so afraid is the thing we half see, or half hear, as in a wood at dusk, when a tree stump becomes an animal and a sound becomes a siren. And most of that fear is the fear of not knowing, of not actually seeing correctly.
—Edna O'Brien (1932–), Irish writer

What Are You So Afraid Of?

We would like to begin this *adagio* section of the book by facing our fears. Fears? But aren't we grown-ups? What do we have to fear? We are too old to be afraid of the dark. We are too old to believe there are monsters under our beds. We are far too old to fear the adult world because we are a part of it, right?

Actually, many of us face fears as adults, and we don't just mean fear of heights or closed spaces or public speaking (although these in themselves can be debilitating). Just because we are grown-ups doesn't mean we are no longer afraid, even as we assure our children they have nothing to fear from the ominous closet, the cavernous space under the bed, the creaky tree outside the window. We all have our closets, our creaky trees, our dark spaces that wait just below us as we sleep.

As adults, our fears are likely to take a somewhat different form. We may not fear the bogeyman, but we might very well fear success, or failure ... or both! We might fear rejection, or change, or stagnation. We might fear aging or death, or we might be afraid we will turn out just like our parents ... or that we *won't!* We might simply feel afraid and not be sure why ... and we might fear looking too deeply into the question because we are afraid of what we might discover about ourselves!

Sometimes, fear can actually help us. Author Erica Jong once said, "Fear is a sign—usually a sign that I'm doing something *right.*" Fear can alert us to danger and can signal us that something important is about to happen. Fear only becomes a joy drain when we let it rule us or keep us from acting in a positive way. Author Marilyn Ferguson once wrote, "Fear is a question: What are you afraid of, and why? Just as the seed of health is in illness, because illness contains information, our fears are a treasure house of self-knowledge if we explore them." Fear can be an important indicator of what we need to think about and how we need to proceed. If we use fear, it can help us grow. If we become paralyzed by it, we will stagnate.

When we carry fear too far—and indeed, contemporary society encourages us to do so—we may fear constantly! We love that scene from the Steven Soderburgh film *Sex, Lies, and Videotape* where Andie MacDowell's character is talking to her psychiatrist about worrying obsessively about all the garbage the world is generating and where we are going to put it.

Hype about negative events often gets so blown out of proportion by media exposure that we grow to believe we have more to fear from certain events than we really do. We aren't downplaying the importance of child abductions or pesticide on vegetables or the greenhouse effect or aggressive dogs or road rage or even garbage for that matter, but latching on to every story we hear and letting it fuel our fears about our own everyday experience of life in the world has no beneficial effect. Instead, it keeps us from participating fully in our lives.

The Nebulous Reality of Fear

What is fear, exactly? We can't touch it, but we can feel it. We can't see it, but we can sense it. We can't quantify it, exactly, but we can measure its effects on the body.

Fear is certainly real ... isn't it? Actually, fear is no more, and no less, real than the body in which it dwells. But let's consider that body.

Health and contemporary Ayurvedic guru Deepak Chopra, M.D., author of many books on the ancient Indian science of holistic health, likes to use an example to demonstrate the delusional nature of presence of the physical body. Look at your hand. See the fingers, the knuckles, the veins, the skin. Turn your hand over and examine your palm. Notice the creases, and then, the finger lines. Now imagine looking even closer, so that you could see the individual cells of your hand. Go further in, and see the molecules that make up these cells, and further to the atoms that comprise the molecules. At this atomic level, we can see that matter is really just tiny spinning particles surrounded by space. That hand isn't really solid at all.

The same technique works for fear. Rather than looking at the source of our fear, let's look at the fear itself for a moment. The following visualization can help us see that our fear may be a far less solid thing than we think.

Fear is born in uncertainty, and nourished by pessimism.
—Lois Wyse (1926–), American advertising executive

Joy-Full Exercise: Clearing Your Room of Fear

Sit quietly and imagine that your fear is a room inside the house that is your body. Visualize this room inside you, then imagine you stand outside the door. The door is closed. What do you feel when you look at the door?

Don't worry about the source of the fear—that thing, or things, you think you are afraid of. Just look at the feeling of fear, represented by this room. What is it? A feeling of nervous anxiety? A feeling of dread? Of withdrawal? Look closer at the feeling. Does it manifest as failure to act? Or too-rash action? Does it manifest as heart palpitations or sweat? Fatigue? Insomnia?

Move closer to the door. Remember, the source of fear is outside your body, not inside—it is far away in space and time. Only the fear itself sits inside, waiting, a remnant from your past experience or a shadow of your current attachments. Go to the door. Put your hand on the knob. How do you feel? More nervous? More anxious? Calmer?

Open the door and imagine stepping inside the room that represents your fear. Imagine a light switch next to the door. Turn it on. Imagine the room flooding with light. Walk in. Look around. Where are you? In a thought? In an emotion? Imagine the thoughts and feelings associated with your fear are pieces of furniture in the room. Step inside those. Look around. What do you see?

Look at each piece of furniture: the couch that is your self-doubt, the wingback chair that protects you from rejection, the ottoman that keeps your feet up so you don't act, the pictures on the wall of worry, anxiety, sleeplessness. Sit on the couch. Sit in the chair. Put your feet on the ottoman. Survey the décor, the color scheme of the room, the lighting fixtures, the window treatments.

Imagine that you decide this room needs redecorating. Why, it's furnished with hand-me-downs and other people's things! You want new furniture. Pick up that couch. Wow, it's lighter than you thought—almost as if it is made of foam. Take it to the door, and toss it out. Do the same with the chair, the ottoman, the pictures, the lamps. Take it all down. Pile it up outside the door until the room is empty.

Now, stand in the middle of the room and look around. This place that you feared ... it contains only space. There is nothing left. The space is clear. You turn to look at the door, and you see that all the furniture has already been whisked away. You walk back out of the room and shut the door, and suddenly, the door dissolves into nothingness. The room has disappeared, and you realize it was only there because it was furnished with those thoughts and feelings—so easily cleared away—that kept your fear in place. Once you let these go, the fear goes with it. It wasn't real after all.

There would be nothing to frighten you, if you refused to be afraid.
—Mahatma Gandhi (1869–1948), Hindu religious leader and social reformer

From Whence We Came

So where did all that furniture of fear come from? Childhood is short but incredibly influential in terms of what kind of psychological strengths and barriers we carry as adults. Even when the things we fear exist in our present life, we may fear them solely because of patterns we have built up from childhood or because we are inadvertently imitating the actions of fearful parents.

Dream analysts often compare the self to a house, and claim that dreams about houses are about the self, so to continue the metaphor from the previous visualization, all that hand-me-down furniture within the house of you is probably furniture your parents (and other adult influences from your childhood) might have chosen. But is it what you would choose? Maybe some pieces are valuable antiques, others junk that should be thrown away. Sorting through these influences can help you to determine why you fear the things you fear and what exactly is holding you back from experiencing the natural joy of living in this world.

The Bible tells us to "put away childish things" and many of us have taken this message to heart, most likely in a way in which it was never intended. Do you live with a sense of obligation to act like a grown-up, or are you comfortable with your childish side? Joyful behavior is never wrong, and even if some might call it immature ... who cares? Joy is right, and even self-evolved, which exceeds maturity.

Is Peter Pan at Home Today?

Today in your Joy Journal, spend some time writing about your attitudes regarding grown-ups and children. In what ways do you feel like an adult? In what ways do you still feel like a child? Do you automatically assume it is better to be mature or much preferable to remain relatively immature? How do these assumptions manifest in your life? Try to be specific and use examples and stories from your own life to help you best understand your attitudes and preconceptions about growing up ... and not growing up!

If you grew up in a highly controlled or regimented household, you may feel guilt about having too much fun. If you never witnessed your parents acting joyful and having fun, you may have a hard time actually embracing joy as acceptable, and no wonder! We learn what we live, and our parents are our first role models.

Much of how we act and what we believe comes from the adults who taught us how to behave in society when we were children. If your parents lived during the Great Depression or were heavily influenced by parents who did, you may even view joy as frivolous … or slightly scandalous! Even if you know, logically, that joy is good, your inner voice may keep pulling the rug out from under your convictions by whispering into your inner ear: *What's wrong with you? Your life isn't serious enough! Be quiet and behave yourself.*

The effect of our parents reaches even deeper. Some of us may even feel guilty about having a more enjoyable life than our parents did, not to mention being more successful, more educated, or wealthier. Parents have a hard time with this, too. It's not easy to see that "child" they always took care of picking up the tab at dinner or offering to help out with expenses. Some parents are so ingrained in their roles as caretakers that they find it virtually impossible to concede that their children are no longer financially, not to mention emotionally, dependent on them.

So now it's definition time. Think about your parents. Visualize them. If only one of them is/was an influence, just visualize that parent (although absent parents also have their influence). If you were raised by adults other than your parents, visualize them instead.

First, think of all the things they have taught you that have enriched your life. What did you learn from your parents? How have they shaped you in positive ways? In what ways did, or does, your relationship with your parents bring you joy? Write down some specifics:

_____

_____

_____

_____

_____

_____

_____

_____

Now, from a place of confidence, hold up your fears and doubts in front of this visualization of your parents. What are they? Are you afraid to be more successful than your parents? Are you afraid to be happier than your parents? Are you afraid your parents don't or wouldn't approve of your life? Are you seeking and not receiving their approval? Are you afraid you have, or will, disappoint them? Give voice to your specific fears regarding your parents, and write them here:

_____

_____

_____

_____

_____

_____

_____

_____

Now, read over what you just wrote. Think about it. Imagine your parents reading it and thinking about it. You might even choose to share it with them.

Maybe your parents never meant to instill those fears in you. Maybe they would never begrudge your success or tell you not to feel joy. Maybe they admire you even more than you could ever know. And even if they don't, you know what? All you need is within you. The fears and feelings having to do with your parents are not the core of you. Those fears are only furniture, and you can use the pieces you like and discard the pieces that don't work for you. That isn't the same as discarding your parents. It is only discarding the useless remnants inside you that they may or may not have meant to leave behind.

Letting go of the psychological remnants of our past isn't easy, and we don't mean to make it sound easy. However, recognizing that the thoughts and feelings within us are only those—thoughts and feelings, not defining characteristics—can help us feel more comfortable in letting them go. Meditation can make this easier, too. As we meditate, and stand back mindfully from our seemingly complex mental drama, we can see how it all plays itself out on a stage. That can make it easier to shut the curtain or flip the channel to a different show.

In some cases, we might find ourselves unable to get a handle on our fears. If you feel unable to control your fear, or if your fear is interfering with your life functioning, consider talking to a professional therapist. He or she can help you sort out your feelings and put things into perspective so that you can regain mastery over your own life, re-seeing what things are important, what things constitute legitimate objects of thought, and what things you can finally release.

To be truly joyful, we must learn to let go because attachment to the transitory will lead us in the wrong direction. Loss of control can be frightening, and so can much of what it entails: relinquishing power we *thought* we had, facing exactly what we can and can't change, and looking inward at who we really are.

To be able to release our fears, we must first do some housecleaning, resetting the mind toward mindfulness and the practice of seeing rather than holding on, understanding what we tend to hold on to, and recognizing that the only thing we can control is what is inside us. We can't control what our parents say or said, do or did, but we can reshape our inner environment in any way we choose. That's a lot of power! But to accomplish this housecleaning, we must commit to self-care and personal reflection so that we feel safe and confident.

To fear is one thing. To let fear grab you by the tail and swing you around is another.

—Katherine Paterson (1923–), American children's writer

Gary's father always told him to take life seriously, work hard, and always be ready for the worst-case scenario. That's just what Gary did, and in college, having superseded his parents' education level, he felt obligated to prove he could do it. He was out there, sailing through life without role models, having gone in a different direction than either of his parents. How very serious. How very sobering.

And yet, just before Gary's father died, he took Gary aside and told him to be sure to have more fun in his life than he, Gary's father, had had. Gary's father told him to take more vacations; balance making and saving money with spending it; build a nest egg of money, but don't forget to build a nest egg of fond memories as well. Suddenly, Gary recognized that the patterns and lessons he had inherited weren't fixed in stone. Having fun was just fine. It was okay. Suddenly he had permission!

But even if your parents never give you permission to fill your life up with joy, you are an adult. You can do it anyway! It isn't wrong, it isn't naughty, it isn't irresponsible. It is the fulfillment of your potential, and you have a responsibility, not to anyone else, but to your own spirit, to provide the joy necessary for becoming the person you are meant to be. You know the one we mean ... the joyful one!

Joy-Full Exercise: Are Those Your Parents?

Imagine yourself sitting with your parents under happy circumstances. This visualization can be based on a memory or a could-have-happened scenario. Step back from the scene and watch you and your parents all enjoying life together (even if that never happened or one or both parents were absent). What are you doing together? Watching a movie? Throwing a Frisbee on the beach? Sitting around the kitchen table drinking coffee?

Examine the way your parents express their joy in your visualization. Do they do so in the same way you do or in their own unique ways? What have you learned from them about joy? What have they learned, or could they learn, from you? Visualize yourself thanking your parents for the lessons they have taught you. Imagine, very specifically, your parents acknowledging what you have taught them about embracing life. Let this scene sink into your consciousness and live there.

When I Fight Authority ...

"Oh yeah? You're not the boss of me!" How often we may wish to say those words, even to someone who *is* the boss of us, at least in the work-place! Too often, out of fear of reproach or punishment from some "higher" source (a parent, a god, our conscience, or any authority figure), we find ourselves suspicious of feeling joy openly. Gary realized that he has an automatic habit of putting on a serious expression in the presence of an authority figure, and Eve recently realized that no living member of her family has an employee boss or supervisor of any kind because they are all self-employed, perhaps largely due to authority issues!

The concept of authority is a tricky one for Americans. We don't like it much, and yet we recognize that in many instances, authority figures are necessary. We need law enforcement. We need government. Children need parents. Companies need people to run them in various capacities. It's how America—and human society in general—works.

But working with authority is a lot different than fearing authority (or raging against it, for that matter). As rational adults, why would we fear someone who tells us what to do? Because someone else who told us what to do a long time ago made the experience fearful, that's why. We might have learned to "behave" by doing whatever was expected, or we might have learned to "misbehave" and suffered consequences, but whatever our individual situation, if we have difficulty with authority figures, it's worth considering why.

We would never tell you that you should blindly obey authority, and we believe that recognizing the real power authority has, rather than the power you may perceive its having, is the key to balancing your attitudes about it. We also would never tell you to defy authority for no good reason (although defiance has its place for a good cause, as does cooperation with authority, for a good cause). The trick is to see an authority figure for what it really is: someone with a position different than yours. If he abuses his power, that is his problem. You needn't let it touch your inner core. Stay focused. Keep meditating. Be who you need to be. Let yourself feel joy, and you'll regain your perspective.

I believe in a lively disrespect for most forms of authority.
—Rita Mae Brown (1944–), American writer

Joy-Full Exercise: You're Not the Boss of Me!

Who do you consider an authority figure over you? Your parents? Your employer? Your older siblings? God? Try this exercise, to help sort out your reactions to authority figures.

First, list all the people you feel have authority over you. These can be people you know, as well as groups in general such as law enforcement officers, doctors, or politicians:

_____

_____

_____

_____

_____

_____

_____

_____

Now, find a timer and set it for two minutes. Look at the first person on your list. Meditate on the name. Look at the letters. Focus totally on that name and only that name. Whenever a negative feeling associated with the name drifts into your mind, imagine mentally circling it, then drawing an X through the circle. Consider that thought null and void, then return your focus to the name itself. When the timer goes off, set it for two minutes again, then move onto the next name.

Continue until you have reached the end of your list, then consider the specific thoughts that came into your mind as you did this exercise. What were they? Did you realize anything about your reaction to these people that you hadn't thought of before? Write a few lines about your experience with this meditation:

_____

_____

_____

_____

_____

_____

_____

_____

The point of this exercise is to help you see that all your feelings about authority figures are only that: feelings. They drift in and out, they seem to attach themselves to the name or the person, but they can also detach themselves. In each person's essence, they are just a person. Their authority is a societal construct. At the core, they have no authority over you, although it may work to play those roles to keep society running along smoothly.

Look at the list one more time, as a whole, and see if now, having meditated on each individual name, you can begin to see the list of names for what it really is: a list of names. Nothing more, nothing less.

My Bootstrap Broke!

Pull yourself up by your own bootstraps! It's the American way. American culture idealizes people who work long and hard, who make a lot of money, who "succeed." Those who embrace their work with a passion and consider it their life's calling may work long hours and succeed in many ways. Others, however, are so fearful of failure that they let their work consume their lives, rather than improve it.

At the same time, others are paralyzed from moving forward or ahead ... or moving at all! ... by the fear of success. Fear of success is as insidious as fear of failure, and once again, the fears we attach to our working lives can keep us from experiencing careers that bring us joy, whether those fears keep us in jobs we dislike or income brackets that simply don't meet our needs. Work fueled by passion brings us joy, but work fueled by fear steals our joy away.

Fear of failure can push one into overdrive. While some people work exuberantly out of a love for the work they do, others work obsessively, out of fear that they might get left behind. You might fear failure if you:

- Are a workaholic, spending most of your time at work, working on work, thinking about work, and talking about work.
- Are never satisfied with your position because you are always planning how to move up or make more money.
- Feel a lot of stress from your job but are afraid to cut back on workload or delegate tasks to others. What if someone does something wrong and you get blamed?

Fear of success can have the opposite effect, but it may be intimately tied to the fear of failure. You may stagnate, afraid to try to move ahead even if you think you deserve it. Could you handle more responsibility? What if you were so good that people began to see you in a whole new way? Could you handle that, or is it easier just to *feel* superior to everyone from your safe vantage point? And at the same time, what if you couldn't handle it and failed?

The funny thing about fearing success or failure is that while both fears seem real, they are both based on something that hasn't even happened yet. We'll talk more about the work you do and the implications of it in Chapter 9, but for now, consider whether fear is impacting your work. Are you afraid to pull yourself up by your own bootstraps? Or are you afraid you might just be able to do it? In either case, you are missing out on the opportunity for joy in your work because fear pushes joy out of the way.

Love, Loss, and Longing

Ah, love! We all seek it, we all pine for it, and when we find it, we spend a lot of time complaining about it! Sometimes it seems every movie we see, every song we hear, every book we read idealizes romantic love and sends us the message that if we don't have it, our lives won't be complete. So many of us spend our lives desperately seeking love and settling for something that isn't right for us because we are too afraid that we will never find anything better.

Fear colors our love lives in many ways. If you aren't afraid to be alone, you may be afraid to commit to someone. Humans are social animals, and we do indeed have a biological imperative to seek a partner and procreate, but we don't have any biological urge for marriage or long-term relationships, so where does that leave us? Doomed to a life of short-term relationships? Culturally stuck in a marriage that doesn't work? Or able to rise above biology and form a lasting partnership that improves everyone's life and fills both partners with mutual joy?

Re-Visionist

Think about an event from your past having to do with work or love or family. Rewrite the story in your Joy Journal, changing the facts to see how it might have gone a different way. Explore through writing this revisionist scenario. Rather than using this exercise as a source of regret, let it be a source of joy, teaching you how to consider many different options in your past, present, and future.

Love does more for us than create children (indeed, many people decide not to have children). Love provides us with companionship, emotional support, and someone to care for us. Some people are perfectly happy living alone and keeping social relationships on a less emotionally intimate basis, but most people buy into the idea that life is better with a partner.

Yet life may not always be better with a partner, and it is certainly can be *worse* with the *wrong* partner. Although men and women both may live with the fear of never finding anyone, we are all a lot less likely to settle for someone incompatible because both men and women are more capable than ever of supporting themselves. We are an independent lot, we Americans, and the old-fashioned "married with children" model doesn't suit nearly as many of us as it once did.

Meanwhile, the partnered among us live with our own fears. Does every fight signal the end? Do incompatible beliefs doom long-term potential? Can you really live with somebody who would *wear that sweater?* Relationships are difficult to maintain, no doubt about it, and we'll talk more about the relationships in your life in Chapter 10, but for now, consider your fears relative to the people you love.

Fear binds you, and without it, you can trust in your own ability to love someone who is right for you, even to leave someone who isn't. Releasing fear can also set you free to understand that you are whole, with or without a partner, and that no one else "completes you," as movie character Jerry Maguire so famously uttered, to the detriment of relationships everywhere. When you let the fear go, the self emerges, and that is where you will find the answers.

Joy-Full Exercise: Meditation to Dissolve Fear

You are greater than, and separate from, your fears. You can come back to this knowledge, even if you've tricked your mind into believing that fear rules you. Let meditation put you back into balance. First, check the following statements that apply to you:

- ❏ I'm afraid to be alone. I could never make it!
- ❏ I'm afraid to commit to someone long-term. What if I meet someone better?
- ❏ I'm afraid to give in to societal pressure to be in a relationship. I don't have to!
- ❏ I'm afraid to let myself love. The inevitable loss would be too painful.
- ❏ I'm afraid to trust. I know my partner could find someone better.
- ❏ I'm afraid of fighting. I might say something I would regret and screw up the relationship.

Maybe your fears lie elsewhere. If so, add to this list:

_____

_____

_____

Now, sit quietly with this list in front of you and look at it closely. Some of the impulses behind your fears may be legitimate. Maybe you have a reason not to trust your partner. Maybe you really don't want to be in a relationship right now, or ever. But the fear you attach to these impulses isn't helping you.

Take three deep breaths, then speak these words:

I release the fear and place my trust in myself.

Repeat the words slowly and rhythmically, using them as a mantra to focus your mind. When your mind wanders, bring it back to these words: *I release the fear and place my trust in myself.* Continue to relax and repeat these words for five to ten minutes, and sink your entire being into their meaning.

Your Joy Arsenal

When Eve's seven-year-old, Angus, gets a little nervous at bedtime, having just seen (or even thought about) a scary image, he likes to arm himself with plastic weaponry. He sleeps under a plastic medieval-style shield with a plastic Samurai sword and a loaded squirt gun under his pillow. This kind of arsenal makes him feel perfectly safe against the onslaught of imaginary dream demons.

Even though Angus knows his dreams and imaginings are just that and not real, he still fears them and still takes action. In the same way, we can take action to combat the fears that plague us, even when we know they aren't real. Fight off your demons with your arsenal of joy, and watch them dissolve like a bad dream hit with a squirt gun.

> Where there's a will, there's a way, and where there's a child, there's a will.
> —Marcelene Cox (1900–), American writer

Wielding the Sword of Joy

We like to think of affirmations as a joyful sword. Whenever you need to invoke a joyful moment, wield an affirmation. We like to collect them and memorize them for easy access (And you'll be full of pithy quotes at just the right moments!). This book is full of affirmations, but here are a few more to try on for size, coined by some famous people:

- Panic is not an effective long-term organizing strategy. (Starhawk, b. 1951, American writer)
- Sex is never an emergency. (Elaine Pierson, b. 1925, American doctor)
- To see what few have seen you need to go where few have gone. (Buddha)
- I never think of the future. It comes soon enough. (Albert Einstein, b. 1879, American physicist)
- I won't think about that now; I'll think about that tomorrow. After all, tomorrow is another day. (Scarlett O'Hara in Margaret Mitchell's novel, *Gone with the Wind*)

Bearing the Shield of Joy

The shield of joy is meditation. Meditation builds a shield around you that protects your joy by warding off the "slings and arrows of outrageous fortune" (to quote Shakespeare). Meditation helps you to step back from the fray and recognize what is important, what is real, what is worth pursuing, and what you may be prone to grasp and hold on to at the expense of self-awareness.

Bear your shield by meditating, even for just a few minutes, every day (see Chapter 6). Rather than hiding you from the world (Scarlett's affirmation is perhaps not the best long-term strategy), meditation helps you to live fully in the world, in the present moment, with mindfulness.

Dwelling in the Geodesic Dome of Joy

We recently encountered an Internet ad for a company that manufactures Geodesic Dome homes (www.domehomes.com). No, we aren't thinking of building one … at least not this year. However, we couldn't help but notice the metaphor. Okay, maybe we manufactured the metaphor, but it works!

Geodesic domes are built by connecting a network of triangles into a dome shape. The triangle is one of nature's most stable structures, and interestingly, the triad is also a spiritual metaphor in almost every culture: Maiden, Mother, and Wise Woman. The Father, Son, and Holy Ghost. Birth, Growth, Death. Body, Mind, Spirit.

The website about geodesic domes states:

Domes are stronger and safer homes, and have proven to withstand tornadoes, hurricanes, and earthquakes far better than ordinary, conventional box homes. All the space you pay for is usable, providing complete flexibility for placement of interior partitions, fixtures, and furniture ... 100% efficient.

Some people visualize the protection of a bubble around them, but we like the idea of visualizing a geodesic dome. Whenever you feel the need for protection from fear, worry, or anxiety, visualize a clear, glowing geodesic dome surrounding you, anchored to the earth to protect you and to allow your true self a space to expand and shine, safe from the sway of thoughts and feelings that buffet your consciousness like a storm.

Permission Granted!

Finally, just in case you never received permission to feel joyful and to leave fear behind you from your parents, your teachers, your siblings, your friends, even your religion, we would like to step in and act as a conduit for the universe: We give you permission to feel joy. We give you permission to release your fear and trust yourself. We give you permission to appreciate who you are and what you are becoming as you work on your personal evolution. We give you permission to feel safe. And we give you permission to love. Who are we to give you such permission? Fellow human beings, that's who. We are all part of one universe, and we are all connected; so when we give you permission, it's not that much different than anyone else giving you permission ... even yourself.

Now go forward fearlessly. You've got an exciting life yet to live. Let it be a life filled with joy!

Chapter 8

Joy in the Crucible of Tragedy

In the face of tragedy, joy can seem very far away indeed. When something happens to us, something in our immediate lives that we find it hard to climb out of, or even something in the world that strikes us to the core, how do we recapture our sense of joy? Should we? Is it wrong, or disrespectful? Can joy fit in the same body as sadness, grief, and despair?

Joy celebrates life, but when life turns to sorrow, when something horrible happens to us or to those we love, how can we celebrate? How can we even think of looking for joy in those challenging moments or situations?

Actually, part of dealing with personal tragedy is by recognizing that life is a complex and amazing process of ups and downs, gifts and losses, life and death, pain and good feeling. To celebrate life, we must embrace all of it, stepping back from events and from our feelings to see what is happening and to consider our place and our role. What can we learn? What can we *do*?

This doesn't mean pushing tragedy down and covering it up with a false layer of happiness. Of course not! Rose-colored glasses fail, as author Alice Walker so eloquently puts it, to help us "honor the difficult" experiences in life. We need to recognize what life really encompasses across its entire spectrum, across our entire life path. The way is not *always* strewn with roses. But committing to the experience of life, both the tragedies and good times, allows us to bring joy and purpose to all of our lifetime. The joyful soul understands how to live life—all of life—fully and mindfully.

Of course, this isn't so easy to do when we are in the midst of a personal or national tragedy. On the day we wrote this chapter, the space shuttle *Columbia* broke apart in the sky only 15 minutes or so from safe landing. The seven astronauts aboard perished. As this chapter is being edited, experts postulate that the disaster could have its roots in events from *Columbia*'s launch. Who knew what tragic potential was woven into that moment of lift-off when humankind once again reached for the sky and the stars? Is this a reason not to reach? To fail to strive? To fail to feel in our own hearts the astronaut's incredible joy at the sight of earth from the heavens?

On a grand scale, how do we look at an event like the loss of the space shuttle *Columbia* and reconcile it with joy? On the smaller, more intimate scale of our own circle of loved ones, how do we reconcile personal tragedy, illness, or the death of a loved one with joy? Perhaps we look for the answer to these questions by acknowledging and honoring the incredible rush of living life fully in the moment—of daring, on a grand scale and in the intimacy of our own circle, to reach for the stars, to explore, to discover, to understand, and to love while we live, to honor the spirits of the intrepid.

In this chapter, we'll help you work through different ways to deal with personal and public tragedy, because you *can* weave joy into your life in all its stages. Living mindfully through your life in all its incarnations teaches you to live alive and aware rather than deluded by attachments. You can fully experience and move through tragedy without holding on to it. Tragedy is part of life, but it needn't destroy your life. It really *can* make you stronger ... and even more joyful.

Moving Through Pain

Who doesn't want to feel good? Feeling strong, healthy, energetic, and awake makes joy easy to capture, but what about when you are in pain?

Chronic pain is a true challenge to joy. Millions of Americans have suffered from chronic pain, and some people struggle with it for many years.

Whether you have a chronically achy lower back or arthritis pain or pain associated with a disease, if you have to live with pain, or have had to do so in the past, you know the cycle: pain leads to anger and frustration, which contributes to a lack of sleep, which contributes to fatigue, which contributes to more anger, frustration, and pain.

To lessen the suffering of pain, we need to make a crucial distinction between the pain of pain and the pain we create by our thoughts about the pain. Fear, anger, guilt, loneliness, and helplessness are all mental and emotional responses that can intensify pain.
—Howard C. Cutler, M.D., from *The Art of Happiness*

But you don't have to get caught up in this cycle. While your healthcare professional can talk to you about treatments for your pain, we can tell you that if you live with pain, one revolutionary modality for dealing with pain is to *live with pain.*

Jon Kabat-Zinn, Ph.D., is the founder and director of the Stress Reduction Clinic at the University of Massachusetts Medical Center and the author of several books, including *Full Catastrophe Living: Using the Wisdom of Your Body and Mind to Face Stress, Pain, and Illness* (see the Resources section for more information). Kabat-Zinn instituted a pain management program at his clinic based in mindfulness. According to Kabat-Zinn, if pain is part of your life, you can try to mask it or forget it, but you may have more success taking the opposite approach: *Experience it.*

In Kabat-Zinn's book, he proposes a mindfulness experiment with pain. The next time you hurt yourself—bumping your shin on that darned coffee table again or stubbing your toe or catching your finger with a hammer—step back mentally and as quickly as you can, become mindful of the flow of pain sensations. Follow the flow of sensations as you do whatever you do to treat your pain (ice, rubbing the area, or whatever). Remain as mindful as possible, and you might notice something interesting. Kabat-Zinn writes:

In conducting this little experiment, you may notice, if your concentration is strong, a center of calmness within yourself from which you can observe the entire episode unfold. It can feel as if you are completely detached from the sensations you are experiencing, as if it were not "your" pain so much as just pain. Perhaps you felt a sense of being calm "within" the pain or "behind" the pain.

While a mishap such as Kabat-Zinn describes results in an example of acute pain (sudden severe pain, as one might experience in an accident or a heart attack), the technique works for chronic pain, too. Of course, pain can help us survive because it alerts us to danger—that stove is hot, that knife is sharp—and in this sense, pain is necessary and even "good." Pain in itself is just pain.

And this is the key to helping us live with chronic pain: the recognition that pain is pain, and not us. Pain is pain, and not the suffering we attach to it.

Pain *is*. Becoming mindful of pain as part of what is happening to us can help us put it into this perspective. Through regular mindfulness meditation, we can regain our sense of self. We can find that core of calm that sits and observes the fluctuations of pain. We can learn to see that pain moves and flows and changes just like our emotions and our thoughts. It isn't attached to us, even if it hangs around our being. This kind of mindfulness helps us to let go of our attachment to the pain and the negative emotions we drag behind us.

Mindfulness can help us to unhook those emotions from the pain and let them float away, so that even as pain may remain, we can see it. We can experience it as a thing, but a thing that is not us, just like any other thing about our physical bodies is part of our experience but is not a part of or inner core of being.

The same technique can help us to deal with serious illness or injury. Cancer, heart disease, diabetes, multiple sclerosis, spinal injuries, broken bones, brain injuries, and thousands of other health conditions are a part of the daily lives of millions of human beings. Many of these conditions come with pain as part of their manifestation. As we seek treatment from qualified medical professionals for our disease, it can be easy to feel helpless, as if doctors were manipulating our fate without any input from us.

Aversion to pain is really a misplaced aversion to suffering. Ordinarily we do not make a distinction between pain and suffering, but there are very important differences between them. Pain is a natural part of the experience of life. Suffering is one of many possible responses to pain.

—Jon Kabat-Zinn, Ph.D., from *Full Catastrophe Living: Using the Wisdom of Your Body and Mind to Face Stress, Pain, and Illness*

But as the medical profession seeks to treat our physical self as we contend with the experience of serious disease or injury, we can be an equal player. Our job is to attend to our spirit and to keep returning to our inner core of being so that our physical circumstances don't overwhelm us. Actor Michael J. Fox, who lives with Parkinson's disease, wrote in his best-selling memoir, *Lucky Man*, that he would not trade his experience after diagnosis, however difficult, for the life he could have had disease-free, because his struggle with Parkinson's gave him insights, gifts, and life lessons he values deeply and that have made him who he *is*.

Just as pain is a part of physical existence, so is illness, so is injury, and inevitably, for all of us, so is death. Those of us used to defaulting to negative attitudes may see this simple fact as reason for despair, or at least, a good argument why joy is a superfluous emotion. Nothing could be further from the truth! Instead, the tendency to attach despair to pain and illness with the little fishhooks of our minds is what makes these processes seem negative.

Yes, we all have a survival instinct. We fight to live. We fight pain because it is an instinct, designed to help us survive. But once we are doing everything we can medically to ensure our survival, this instinct is no longer relevant. Therefore, we can use our higher brain—the part that interprets our basic instincts—to override this vestigial tendency to attach anxiety and despair to pain and illness.

Many studies have examined the different attitudes of people who live with illness or injury. Some people become depressed, but many others (often after an initial adjustment period) claim that they are happier than they ever were before. How can someone be happy with a debilitating disease or an injury that impairs functioning? They can because the body is not the self, because the illness is not the self, and because a dramatic experience like a cancer diagnosis or an accident that causes paralysis can help to put life into perspective. All those little things that used to seem so important suddenly shrivel up to nothing in the face of an experience that challenges our entire perception about what it means to have a satisfying life.

But how do we get to that place? Like anything else, putting pain and illness into perspective takes practice and commitment. Yet if we face dramatic personal health challenges, we may have a better incentive than other people to get back to our self and to put our challenges into place. Mindfulness can become a mental survival technique for us—one that results in a heightened sense of joy in every aspect of our life.

A Conversation with Pain

Imagine that your pain or your illness is a being all its own, someone who lives with you right now and who hasn't been behaving in a manner you would expect from a roommate. In your Joy Journal, dramatize a conversation between you and your pain. What do you say? What does the pain say to you? Keep writing, developing the conversation until you come to an agreement or some sort of resolution.

Joy-Full Exercise: Body Scan

When you contend with pain and/or illness in your life, you can help to keep it in perspective and under your control with regular body scans. The body scan is a technique for becoming aware of physical sensations. Kabat-Zinn teaches this technique at his clinic, but you can do it on your own at home. Here's how.

Find a firm surface where you can lie comfortably on your back, such as a clean floor covered in carpet and/or an exercise mat. You can use pillows under your knees, lower back, neck, and head to make yourself more comfortable. (You can do this exercise on a bed but the firmness of a floor can help you to tune into your body, plus help you to stay awake.)

Settle into your body as you lie on your back. Consciously try to relax your hips, your shoulders, your neck. Imagine your body sinking softly into the floor.

Now, mentally scan your body for areas of tightness. The first step in the body scan is to relax. Begin at your feet and release tension from your arches and ankles. Move slowly up your body, consciously releasing tension from your calves ... knees ... thighs ... hips ... buttocks ... abdomen ... chest. Relax your shoulders, your biceps, your elbows, your forearms, your wrists, your palms and fingers. Then, move your consciousness to your neck, releasing tension. Release tension from your scalp, your face, and then back down your body via your spine, imagining your entire core melting and relaxing into the floor.

As you relax, be aware of your breathing, letting it slow down and deepen to infuse your body with oxygen and energy. Take some time in this place of deep relaxation to get comfortable.

Now, begin your body scan. Mindfully turn your attention to your toes, then slowly and deliberately let your attention scan upward over your body. Notice physical sensations, but try not to attach feelings or judgments to those sensations. Just be aware of them.

Let your attention scan slowly up and down, up and down your body. Where do you notice tightness? Where do you notice particular pain sensations? Try to describe those sensations in a distanced way: do you perceive stabbing sensations, throbbing, a low-grade ache, a soreness? Try to visualize the shape of the pain and its movement.

Keep scanning up and down. Let your scan be an opportunity to step out of your body and watch its sensations objectively, as a thing you live with, like a house. Continue your scan for 10 to 15 minutes, then after you've scanned your entire body several times, let your mindfulness slowly expand to encompass your entire body all at once. Move away from your body and watch it, labeling the feelings and thoughts you have about your body, mentally circling them, then moving on.

Practicing the body scan at least once a week and whenever you begin to feel overwhelmed by some aspect of your physical body can balance you in a way that lets joy flower inside your body.

.:. Mental afflictions do not disappear of their own accord; they don't simply vanish over time. They come to an end only as the result of conscious effort to undermine them, diminish their force, and ultimately eliminate them altogether.

—The fourteenth Dalai Lama of Tibet (1935–), from *An Open Heart: Practicing Compassion in Everyday Life*

Loving Past Loss

Losing someone we love may be the most difficult barrier of all to a life full of joy. Nothing can compare to the loss of a loved one—a parent, a partner, a child, a friend—these losses leave holes in our lives and sadness in our hearts. And yet, even loss can become a source of joy.

We are human, and we develop important and deep connections with other humans. When we lose them, it hurts because we miss them, whether we lose them through death or because of a separation like a divorce or an estrangement. We may feel guilty or responsible for the circumstances surrounding the loss, even if we know, logically, that we aren't. Or we may simply feel stricken with grief.

How do we get past a feeling like that? It isn't easy, and it can be a harrowing journey, but it is indeed a journey. Grief and loss are akin to suffering and pain; loss is a part of life, but grief is the attitude we attach to it. It is a feeling, and while it belongs to us, we can experience it, face it full-on with an awareness that it doesn't define us. It happened to us. It is not who we are. Only in facing it and feeling it and then letting it go according to its time can we incorporate difficult experiences like this into our life experience.

In her beautiful book *Loving-Kindness: The Revolutionary Art of Happiness* (Shambhala, 1997), Buddhist writer Sharon Salzberg talks about how opening the heart against the separation of all beings from each other can help us to release fear and move into partnership with all sentient beings. She writes:

> As we open, we uncover the mind's inherent ability to heal, to grow, to change. Being still, we see the power of the mind, which is the strength of our own capacity to love and connect. Actual love is the true seeing of our oneness, our nonseparateness. As we discover this capacity to love, we develop intimacy with ourselves and others. We develop the strength and compassion to live with integrity and, one day, to die with peace.

This notion of openness means moving outside the realm of self in the wake of tragedy to reach out to others.

How often have we seen the outpouring of love, hope, and help from communities around the world when a tragedy happens? But when our tragedy is personal, we can also reach out to others and let them reach out to us. Not the least of this bonding with the river of life is in the connection to those we have lost. Remembering the gifts that people we have lost have given to us, re-experiencing that remembered joy, and continuing to move rather than getting stuck in one traumatic place can help us to see tragedy as meaningful, even if it is also painful.

Once we've let ourselves feel the grief of loss, we can better feel the joy of having been blessed with people and experiences, being joyful for the gifts they have left us, the lessons they have taught us, and the way they have added to the magnificent picture of life can help to lift tragedy back into perspective. Once we commit to staying in that river of life and letting it take us where it will, we can let the spirits of those we have lost stay with us on their own. We won't need to hold on to them because they will always be there, integral to the nature of that flowing river.

Our life has certainly changed. Whether we have lost someone we love or even a part of our self, we can learn to let those truths stand, be, and become a part of who we are. This is the key to finding joy after a great loss or personal setback.

Letting the Universe Speak

About 10 years ago, back when AIDS was a definite death sentence, Gary was a caregiver for someone with the disease. He will never forget leaving the elevator on the fourth floor of the hospital one day and recognizing that just in front of the elevator door the hall forked: the medical surgical ward was in one direction and the neonatal ward was in the other. Gary remembers thinking how ironic, and yet how balanced, it all seemed at that moment. One late night, after his friend had had an especially bad evening, Gary left the hospital tired and worn with care. He entered that same elevator with a nurse carrying a baby in a glass incubator. He remembers holding his hand up to the cube and watching the baby reach out to try to touch him. Somehow, amidst his grief, Gary suddenly saw this baby as a symbol for all the life ahead: the bigger picture, the view beyond personal tragedy, the infinite potential of life.

The universe speaks to us, particularly when we are filled with sorrow and when we are filled with joy, because during these moments when our hearts are overflowing with feeling, we may be particularly open. On the day Gary's father died, a friend had a baby. On the day a friend of Eve's died, she gave birth to her first son.

159

When we first experience tragedy, we may despair that the universe doesn't make sense, but the more we let ourselves feel and observe those feelings without holding them tightly, the more we can step back to see how it all fits together.

> Birds came, and left again, and came, and perched, and flew, and fluttered around the branches, just outside my mother's window, just after she died.
>
> There were no birds there the day before. I know because I was sitting in exactly the same place, by my mother's bed, at exactly the same time. I would have seen them. But on Wednesday morning, the moment of her death, the birds came and sat on the branches outside her window, while we were sitting inside in her room.
>
> I'm glad the birds came. In fact, I think I was expecting them.
>
> —Reeve Lindbergh, on the death of her mother, Anne Morrow Lindbergh, wife of aviator Charles Lindbergh

The trick, in separating feelings from attachments, is not to confuse letting go with denial. When something dramatic happens to us, this is part of the human experience. Feeling it, no matter how painful it is, grows us as humans. It teaches us to experience a full range of emotions, to love better, to appreciate what we had, what we have, what we will have. It takes courage to face emotions that hurt, but only in moving into them can we let go of them.

Experiencing these feelings, however, is much different than holding on to them. If we can make a clear distinction between the feeling of grief and the attachment of regret or doubt or resentment or guilt to that feeling of grief, we can see how what we feel needn't come labeled with a value judgment. We can feel grief; we can feel pain, and that's okay. We should feel it, learn from it, then open up those fists and let the experience become a part of us, free of those labels. We need to let the resentment go; let the regret and doubt go; let the guilt go, and we will know what true grief is, but then we will also learn what true joy is when we come out on the other side of grief, stronger and wiser, more grateful and more able to see the human experience, having lived through its most difficult hour.

When we can see these patterns, when we can step back and see how it all fits together, we will become even more open to signs and signals of that union. It will all make more sense to us, once we've integrated our experiences and allowed ourselves to see them and let go of the negativity we attach to them. The universe is whispering to us: We are all in this together.

Joy-Full Exercise: A Breath of Fresh Air

Sometimes, in the thick of grief, it can be hard to figure out what to feel, and even though meditation is an excellent way to help us step back from the situation and identify the ebb and flow of our emotions, there may be one thing we are lacking right now: exercise.

When we feel sad, depressed, angry, or any number of emotions associated with a traumatic event, it's natural to close down and stop normal activities, but in times like these, it is more important than ever to get ourselves out into the fresh air. No matter how we feel, no matter what has happened, we need to step outside for 15 minutes and breathe, walk, be mindful.

Mindful walking is important at this time because you will be especially prone to sinking back down into your spiral of negative thoughts. Actively propelling yourself through the fresh air with your thoughts fixed on what you see in the natural world around you can be an incredible relief, for one thing. For another, it can help you to look beyond that barrier your mind has erected at this time. Mindful walking helps you scale that fence and at least take a glance at the world around you— the world to which you will soon return.

A mindful walk during a traumatic period isn't a way to escape your grief. Not at all. But it is a way to lift you out of attachments to that grief, and studies have proven that exercise is an effective mood lifter. No, you don't "deserve" to stay sad, and a walk won't fix your grief, but it can reorient your perspective while getting your body moving in the way it is designed to move. It will help to put you back into balance.

We are nature. We are nature seeing nature. We are nature with a concept of nature. Nature weeping. Nature speaking of nature to nature.

—Susan Griffin (1943–), American poet

Finding Joy in an Unstable World

The first few years of the twenty-first century have been full of vast, dramatic changes and traumatic events on an international scale. How can a world in crisis be a joyful world? How can anyone even sleep at night, knowing how easily our lives could end, how quickly it could all fall apart?

Stop right there! Read one newspaper, and you may quickly begin to believe that destruction of society as we know it is imminent, that nobody is safe anywhere, and that you can't trust anyone. Certainly, life has proven unsafe for many people, and there will always be tragedies. Certainly, it pays to be cautious, within reason. But it doesn't pay to be afraid, to live in a state of constant pessimism, or to lose trust in humanity.

When the world begins to seem like a threatening place, the reason is usually separation. We begin to think the "other people" are dangerous or evil or … well, *other*. That's where fear stems, not to mention hate and violence. *He* did it. *She* did it. *They just might do it to us, so we better do it to them first!*

In unity, there is no fear because if the other is the same as the "I," we know what to expect. We know there is no enemy, only a mirror.

In her book *Loving-Kindness: The Revolutionary Art of Happiness*, Sharon Salzberg tells a lovely story of building up fear regarding a large aggressive dog in her neighborhood until she finally encounters the dog and makes a connection:

> Fear is the primary mechanism sustaining the concept of "other," and reinforcing the subsequent loneliness and distance in our lives. Ranging from numbness to terror, fear constricts our hearts and binds us to false and misleading ways of viewing life. The fallacy of separate existence cloaks itself in the beguiling forms of our identifications: "This is who I am," or "This is all I can ever be." We identify with a fragment of reality rather than with the whole.

When we lose the "us vs. them" framework binding up or thinking in *otherness*, we might find that we still need to protect ourselves on occasion, that we still need to view honestly the actions and motivations of others. But in viewing our interactions with others from a set point of unity rather than opposition, we can act with greater confidence in the rightness of our actions.

As we do so, if we continue to reach out to others with openness and compassion, we will be helping to shape a society based on those values, rather than contributing to one based on fear and suspicion. This can make the world seem like a much more joyful place to spend our lives.

Joy-Full Exercise: Shaping a More Compassionate World

The world might feel unstable, but you can help to make your world, or at least your community, a little more stable by promoting unity rather than division. Consider how you might make a difference in unifying your community by brainstorming, perhaps with a few like-minded friends. Make a list of all the projects you might consider, from small scale to large scale. Here are some ideas to get you started:

- Invite several neighbors over for a get-better-acquainted dinner.
- Write a letter to the editor of the local newspaper about how we are all more alike than different.
- Start a meditation group, so you can all benefit from meditation as a unified force.
- Organize the planting of a community garden.
- Volunteer at a soup kitchen.
- Spearhead an organization that promotes unity in a more formal and public way.

The more you imagine ways to unify the world, the more you may get inspired, even to make small steps, shift your thinking, modify your knee-jerk reactions to certain situations (we all have them), and eventually, inspire others to move more toward unity along with you. Acting out of compassion for your fellow humans, who are indeed all just fellow humans, can change your life. You'll see joy everywhere, and when the people you reach out to look at you, they'll see it, too.

Joy comes in the moment of reaching, striving, or doing. The outcome is not sure, but to be fully alive, the action must be taken! Will astronauts take the same chance and board the space shuttle again for a trip to the heavens? You bet! No doubts! Get in the act, right now, this moment.

If it is sunny out, go outside and reach toward the sun, feel the warmth on your face and breathe. Discover. You are alive. If it is cloudy and rainy out, go outside and reach toward the rain, feel the wet drops on your face and breathe. Discover. You are alive. If it is dark out, go outside and reach for the moon and the stars, see your infinite potential in those infinite points of light, and breathe. Discover. You are alive!

Now, go get someone you love and experience it together. Together, at this moment, you are alive. Discover. How incredible, how beautiful, how full of joy!

Chapter 9

Embrace Your Life Purpose

What do you do? The question hangs in the air over all of us. We ask it of each other. We consider the opportunities open for ourselves. When we hear the phrase "What do you do?" we automatically know as a culture that we aren't asking, literally, what you *do,* in general. We mean, *what is your job?*

Americans work longer hours and take fewer vacations than most other countries in the developed world, but what we *do* can be more than the job we have. It can actually be what we *do,* with purpose and mindfulness. What do *you* do? What you do can be just this: Embrace a life purpose.

Some people seem to be born knowing their life purpose, while others struggle through their lives trying to find one. Some people are mired in the past, always obsessing about some mistake that won't be fixed or some stroke of luck that won't be duplicated. Stuck in that rut, those people filter every new moment and opportunity through the prism of the past and risk missing out on benefiting from the new gifts (or challenges) the future might bring. Some of us look ahead ever-forward to some ideal life goal we hope to reach *some-day,* dreaming about the future, planning for the future. It's great to have goals, but when we live our lives always looking toward the future, we once again miss recognizing something precious: the present moment.

It doesn't make much sense to *struggle* to find a life purpose. Your life is happening right now, and the way to begin working toward a purpose is to begin living your life right now. Living for the present moment is the best way to understand what your life purpose is.

Life isn't a dress rehearsal for what might magically happen someday, so why do so many of us live it that way? Life is magical right now. We are amazing right now. So what is your life purpose, or what would you like it to be? Just be, and your life's purpose will float to the surface of your consciousness like a lotus flower on a lake. There is no better time than the present to start living it.

What Humans Want

What do we want? Do we care about a life purpose? Does the idea in itself stress you out? Or does it excite you and fill you with ideas? Most of us have some vision of our future, but do we have a vision for our present? Or is the thought of a present plan overwhelming—why, you can barely get to the grocery store!

Fear not! A life purpose is anything but intimidating and far from being one more excruciating item on a life to-do list. A life purpose is the motivator that brings out your passion. It is the thing you *love to do*, the thing you are *good at*. A life purpose is the reason you put up with to-do lists in the first place, and for many, it is the reason they put up with jobs that may be less than ideal in other ways. If your life's purpose is to save the rainforests, you may hold down a regular job to help fund your environmental excursions or your independent environmentalist newsletter. If your passion is jazz piano, you may work all day in a job that supports your family so you can spend your nights doing what you really want to do: playing jazz. If you are all about leadership, perhaps you will run for office, holding down a job that can be beneficial in a peripheral way to your political career.

Take a moment to think about your life as it exists right now. Is this the life you want? Or are you waiting for something to happen, someone to change, or some authority figure to swoop down and fix everything?

Embracing a life purpose means deciding what you want and then reaching out to achieve it, starting right now with no waiting, no fruitless dreaming. Every day, today, there is one new thing you can do to get closer to the joy of living a life authentically *you*.

The idea came to me that I *was,* *am,* and *will be,* but perhaps will not *become.* This did not scare me. There was for me in *being* an intensity I did not feel in *becoming.*
—Nina Berberova (1901–1993), Russian-born poet

Living right now is the best, the easiest, and the most pleasurable way to take personal responsibility for your life. Mindfulness helps you nurture yourself to keep yourself strong and relaxed and healthy as it releases your attachment to the future. The future will come, one way or the other, but for now, it is *now,* and that is where you live. Let your life purpose happen today.

But what if you still have doubts and aren't sure what your life purpose is? Look at your strengths and the things you love to do. They don't have to be a part of your job, but maybe they are. Or maybe your strengths are in your relationship to others or in your creative power. Are you a humanitarian at heart who feels called to serve humankind, either on a small personal scale or in a big way? Are you an artist whose passion is to create beauty and truth? Are you at your strongest as a leader or a behind-the-scenes make-it-happen person? Are you destined for a life of spirituality or a life vividly in and of the world? Were you meant to help preserve the earth and its creatures or to build great monuments to humankind?

Some people know exactly what they are meant to do, but for others—including those who don't exactly believe anybody was "meant" to do anything—it can be tough to pinpoint a life purpose. Your life purpose doesn't have to be ingrained, however. You can choose it … and you can change it. It needn't be limited to a single purpose, either. Some people follow an ever-evolving purpose or purposes, and that's great! There are no rules in this game. You get to design your life in whatever way suits you. It's your life! It's your *joy!*

Joy-Full Exercise: My Life List

To help clarify your life purpose, your goals for now and those goals you see for yourself that you can start working toward right now, spend a little time writing up a plan. Plans can help focus your efforts and hone your vision, as long as you don't get so attached to them that you are unable to change with circumstances and adapt your plan as you evolve.

Consider this exercise a chance to stretch your creativity, not a way to pigeonhole yourself. Let your mind run wild and let limits dissolve beneath your pen.

First, begin by answering some questions about yourself. This can help you to understand where your strengths lie. Some psychologists believe that the most effective strategy for understanding a life purpose is to understand where your strengths lie, rather than concentrating on your weaknesses. Maybe you never volunteer, but look how you inspire people through your art! Maybe you don't have a creative bone in your body, but you really know how to reach out and make other people feel like worthwhile human beings. Maybe you aren't a natural-born leader, but present you with a plan and you can make it happen. Think about what you can do well, what you enjoy, what everybody knows you for. That is your first clue to your life's purpose.

1. The best thing I ever made was:

   _____

2. I'm best at lifting other people's spirits by:

   _____

3. Am I a better planner or a better do-er? In what ways?

   _____

   _____

   _____

4. A time when I acted bravely was:

   _____

   _____

   _____

5. I'm really glad that I have these qualities:

_____

_____

_____

6. People compliment me on my:

_____

_____

_____

7. I once stood up for myself when I:

_____

_____

_____

8. I'll never forget the time I won …! Here's how it happened:

_____

_____

_____

9. I get really passionate whenever I talk about:

_____

10. I bet I would make a really good:

_____

Feeling good? Feeling strong? Feeling confident? You should! These questions can help you not only reflect on your positive qualities and strengths but see your past as a sort of gearing-up for this present moment. Seeing what makes you joyful and what you are good at might help clarify your life's purpose for you. And if not, just keep living right now. That may be your purpose in and of itself: to learn how to really *live*.

In the movie *Castaway*, Tom Hanks's character, Chuck Noland, is a FedEx executive who thought he had it all figured out and lived his life by his passion for the clock. Through a twist of fate, Noland finds himself stranded for four years on a remote island. Daily, Noland struggles to find his courage to keep moving from day to day, moment to moment, to find meaning in his life when all the familiar surroundings of life are stripped away. Off the island and back in the midst of everyday life, Noland realizes he is faced with the same challenge he had on the island—the courage to get up every day and just *breathe*. Whether we live on a desert island, an Iowa farm, or in a Manhattan high-rise, it seems we *all* face the same challenge and need the same courage to keep breathing and to find our way in life, our purpose. And as Noland learns, this task takes our whole focus, our whole concentration, and our whole self to be patient and alert to life's possibilities for each of us.

The Working World

Once you've got a better idea of your strengths, let's consider how you can fit those strengths into your life and use them for your direct bene-fit and daily joy. Some of us have jobs that directly tap our greatest strengths, but some of us have jobs that help to earn money to support our hobbies, the place where our life purpose really reigns supreme. And some of us may be best at simply living. That's a life purpose all in itself. Does your job support that purpose?

One of the basic Buddhist precepts is to practice *right vocation*. Buddhists believe that one's chosen occupation can have a direct effect on one's inner self, and therefore, this belief system discourages work in fields that result in harm of others (like the manufacture of weapons) or that promote intemperance (selling intoxicants like drugs and alcohol).

While this precept was written long ago and might not always be rele-vant in contemporary society, at its core, it is indeed an important aspect to consider about the work you do and the way you spend at least eight hours of your 24 hours, day after day. The way you spend your time impacts your consciousness in many ways, so that you can't help but be affected by your job. If you feel good about your job and what you do, if you feel you are somehow making a positive contribution to the world (and you can do this in many, many ways via all sorts of jobs), that time spent will be time spent well.

The mind, of course, is just what the brain does for a living.
—Sharon Begley (twentieth century), American scientist

170

However, if you don't feel good about the work you do, if you have a gnawing sense that your work is somehow harmful or degrading or otherwise mismatched to your strengths, if you don't enjoy it and it saps your energy and your joy, then it is crucial to consider how to change this situation. Do you really want to spend a third of your life steeped in dissatisfaction? What a waste of your time that would be!

When you feel neutral about the work you do, but it supports your passion outside the working world, your job may indeed be worth holding on to. And if you examine your negative attitudes about your job, you might find you can adjust them. Maybe the work you do is worthwhile and you are too focused on society's attitude about your job, not on how well you do it and how much you enjoy it. Think long and hard about whether or not you feel good about the work you do, and why. Does it contribute to the world, based on values you support? Is it just a means to earn money in whatever way will earn it most efficiently? Or is it stealing away your life energy in an insidiously slow way, keeping you around with one hand through offers of security and sapping your soul with the other?

The corporate culture that glorifies workaholics has more than its fair share of competitive spirit, and competition can be a good thing when it energizes us. It can inspire our creativity and help us to achieve in ways that grow our spirits. But when competition turns to distrust, stress, and greed, a good job can go sour. The blue-collar workforce often faces just as much stress and pressure for less prestige and less compensation. Killing yourself over a job that doesn't feed your soul may seem like your only option ... but maybe it isn't.

The work world is changing, slowly but steadily. Gone are the 1980s when work was all about materialism. The new century is remarkably more enlightened about the needs of human beings in the work place. The new wave of 20-somethings in the workforce work hard and play hard, too. They spend long hours, but lots of that time is spent having fun. Employee lounges may boast pool tables and pinball machines in addition to the requisite coffeemakers, and creativity is what it's all about. Sure, some of these high-flying businesses crash and burn (consider the youthfully driven dot.coms of the late 1990s), but America is indeed enjoying a movement toward work that is fun, that allows people to be both adult and child at the same time.

But we aren't all able to have jobs with pool tables in the break room, and many people don't make enough money to meet their basic expenses. So what happens when you think you are supposed to pull yourself up by your own bootstraps? Do you settle for a job you dislike because you need the money? Do you take the leap to try a job you love but can't afford to keep? Do you risk building a whole new career because you think you might be able to have it all? What if others depend on you for financial support? Is it selfish to risk it all, just for a little more joy?

You might be surprised to hear us tell you that we think whatever you do for a living can bring you joy. You don't have to have a glamorous career or be famous or fabulously wealthy to find joy in your work. Those kinds of career qualities are all about the external world, but when it comes to living a joyful life, it doesn't matter if you are a CEO or a store clerk or a stay-at-home mom/dad or a waitress or a movie star. Who you are inside is what makes for joy. Is your soul employed, or just your body?

If you are good at what you do and it brings you satisfaction, that's great! However, if you despise what you do and drag a slew of negative emotions with you to work every day, your job won't bring you joy. Even so, in the later case, it isn't the job that kills your joy. It is those negative feelings you attach to your job!

Resumé of the Soul

In your Joy Journal, write your resumé—not the one you would give to a potential employer but the one your soul would write. Put your name at the top of the page, then write your Statement of Life Purpose in 25 or fewer words. What kind of life purpose do you seek? Then, list your qualifications for the job: your strengths, your accomplishments, your relevant qualities, your experience. Spend some time with this resumé, crafting it so that you feel it truly expresses your inner self. As you work, you may find that you want to adjust your statement of life purpose, and that's fine. Do a few drafts until you are satisfied.

After you finish, put your soul resumé away for a few hours, then go back and read it over as if you were the employer looking for someone to fill the job.

Hire yourself.

Now, we aren't saying that what you do doesn't matter. The work you choose does matter, and if you engage in work that you think matters, you will derive more pleasure from your job. However, deciding what job matters to you is different than determining a societal attitude about your job. You might find great satisfaction in painting houses or doing medical transcription or working in a factory. Someone else with a career you might glamorize in your own mind—a lawyer, a doctor, a senator, a supermodel—may not get satisfaction from his work because of an inability to truly embrace and accomplish that work well on an inner level.

So where does that leave you? We suggest considering mindfulness before turning in that resignation letter. First, learn to do your job mindfully, with full and total attention and absorption. Do your job well. Take pride in it. If you can reach a place where you see your job exactly as it is, without attaching feelings and attitudes onto it; if you can learn to simply do your job with full awareness, then you can be in the best position to judge if it is the right job for you. Dissatisfaction, resentment, ego, and competitiveness will follow you into any job. Only when you see the job as the job and the job alone can you judge whether this is the job for you.

If it is, great! Consider your job a source of spiritual practice, and if you have other needs—creative or intellectual or physical—find ways to develop other aspects of your life to fulfill them. But if you feel that your job doesn't reflect who you are and what you believe, begin today to move in a direction that will allow you to fulfill your life's purpose.

Joy-Full Exercise: *Right Now* Life-Shaping Strategies

You don't have to quit your job or take off on a spiritual pilgrimage to Nepal or even change much of anything about your life to begin to re-shape it in a way that satisfies and fulfills you. Try these small-scale high-powered strategies, and start your journey toward a more gratifying life today:

- Take up a hobby. What have you always wanted to do? Research what you need to do to get started. (Check out a book on life drawing at the library? Register for a cooking class? Research fine wines on the Internet? Price antique dollhouses?)

- Brainstorm ideas for turning your already-established hobby into a small business "on the side." Everybody loves those dried herb wreaths you make and give as gifts. Could you sell them at a craft show? You are so good at teaching animals how to behave. Could you train pets professionally? You love to play sports or feel passionate about your yoga practice. Does the local community center or health club need a part-time fitness instructor or yoga teacher? You have a knack for writing. Could you freelance in your spare time?

- Call the local school and ask about volunteer opportunities. Could you tutor or mentor a child? Help kids learn to read? Assist with special events?

- Take up an art form. Paint, begin learning how to play an instrument (yes, adults can take piano lessons, too!), sign up for a dance class, or sculpt with clay. Let your creativity shine!

- Finally, if all this thinking about how you could change your life begins to seem like too much, consider that maybe … just maybe … your life is pretty good the way it is. Maybe you don't need to change anything!

Let him who would enjoy a good future waste none of his present.
—Roger Babson (1875–1967), American statistician and author

Spending Your Time

Do you really spend your time, or does it slip away almost unnoticed? Sure, we spend a lot of time at work and another good chunk of our time sleeping, and none of that is time wasted if we work mindfully and sleep enough to keep our bodies healthy and efficiently functioning. But what about the rest of the time? How do you spend it?

Me, Me, All About Me!

Sometimes, you may feel stretched so thin that all you want to do in your spare time is relax. Guess what? That's a *good thing!* Relaxation is an important part of self-care, and when you need it, you should do it. To be fulfilled, you need to take time to yourself to refuel and refresh your mind and spirit. Let yourself be lazy. Let yourself bask in a hot bath or "waste" two whole hours talking to a friend on the phone or hang out at a coffee shop reading a magazine just for fun.

Spending time for yourself isn't selfish. It is *essential.*

What's that? You say you don't *have* any spare time to relax? We know the feeling! Some of us take on too many things, either because we want to or because we have to, and suddenly find ourselves without any available time to ourselves. Maybe you're in the midst of a frantic and impossible work schedule or deadline. Maybe you're a single parent who must work and do all the caretaking duties for young children, or maybe you have an aging parent who requires constant care.

When we put too much emphasis on one aspect of our lives—work, caretaking, keeping a spotless house, and so on—we throw our lives out of balance. As a self-employed writer and single mom of two very energetic little boys, Eve often feels so overextended that she can't think straight, and sits at her computer staring catatonically at the screen. Talk about a waste of time! When things get to be too much, it's time to do some serious scaling back. Believe it or not, you *can* find "me time." It just takes a little creativity and a big commitment to paring down that insidious "to-do list" in ways you might not have thought of before.

This life de-cluttering is actually kind of fun, in the same way it can be fun to clean out a closet and donate 300 pounds of junk to charity. Here are some tips for de-cluttering your days so that you can be more efficient, more calm, and more energized in accomplishing the non-negotiables in your life:

- Review your periodic "obligations." How many of those clubs, meetings, and societies do you really need to attend? Would you feel more relaxed if you quit some of them? Or if you don't want to quit, maybe you could take some time away from them until your life slows down again.

- Can you do more work at home? More and more people telecommute, working from home a few days each week. It might help to calm you and make you more efficient if you can get things accomplished in the privacy of your own home, without the distractions of co-workers.

- Overwhelmed with kids? Set up a baby-sitting co-op with a few friends. Take turns watching each other's kids during times when you would have your own kids anyway. Use those times when you don't have kids to recharge.

- Overburdened as a caretaker? Establish mental boundaries so you know exactly what you will and will not do, and so you have a clear sense of where the person you are caring for ends and where you begin. In some cases, hiring temporary care to give yourself a break is well worth the money. It isn't selfish because you are doing what you need to do to be a better and more effective caretaker.

- Overburdened by financial constraints? Consider scaling back. Could you move to a smaller space and still be comfortable? Do you really need two vehicles? Could you streamline your eating habits to waste less food? Do you really need all those cable channels? What could you do on the weekends for fun that doesn't cost a lot of money? The possibilities are endless for simplifying your financial life. Think of creative ways to cut back, re-assess, and scale down, but don't cut back on the things that mean a lot to you, or you will feel resentful and deprived.

- How many of your bills could you pay automatically or online to streamline your financial duties? Could you balance your checkbook online or through special software designed to organize your finances? These resources can save you hours each month.

- Make simplicity your hobby. Get inspired by *The Simplicity Reader* by Elaine St. James (Smithmark, 1999) and go from there. Simplicity is addictive, and you may find that simple living punches a hole in your routine through which all your stress leaks away.

- Remember who you are. In all the rush and bustle and anxiety of life, it's easy to forget how unique and interesting and amazing you are. Look at all you do! Stop for a moment each day to appreciate yourself, not for what you do or who you do it for or what you accomplish or what you make, but simply for who you *are*.

Once your life is beginning to de-clutter, look for opportunities to spend time with yourself, taking care of yourself. If you are one of those people who is so accustomed to giving your time to other people that you don't even know how to spend some time on yourself, here are some helpful hints. Just watch how a few minutes of self time every day increases your energy and improves your attitude, inspiring you to forge ahead and improve your life in other ways!

- Turn off the television. Remember all that time you didn't think you had? Do you really need to keep following that one-hour drama or that string of "must-see" sitcoms? The TV has its merits, and now and then it can be a nice way to escape, but it also saps your energy and atrophies your brain. Spend half an hour reading a book or soaking in the tub instead.

- Read a poem out loud. This takes maybe two minutes, and no matter how overextended you are, you can take two minutes out of something to try this exercise. According to *Redbook* magazine, new research reveals that reading poetry out loud can be just as relaxing as meditation.

- Eat an apple while concentrating fully on eating it. The vitamins and fiber will nourish your body, and the mindfulness exercise will focus your mind and relax you. You have to eat anyway, right?

- Get a massage. Just do it. It's worth the extra few bucks, no question, and the relaxation benefits will make you more productive, adding more efficiency to your day.

- Decide not to do one annoying thing you thought you had to do today. Delegate the chore to a family member ... or just let it go undone. (Is the world going to end if you don't make the bed today?) Spend those precious few minutes relaxing, deep breathing, or meditating.

- Add a few drops of lavender oil and a couple of lemon slices to your bath. Instant aromatherapy session! Lavender is relaxing and lemon is inspiring.

- Remember what it is like to socialize in person. Have a friend over for a visit. Face-to-face human communication is energizing and can drain the stress from your day. (And you thought instant messaging was just as good ...!)

- Go off your diet. Who needs it? Just eat healthy and forget about the scale. You'll feel a lot better, and think of all the time you'll save when you stop worrying about following those little meal plans!

- Soak your feet in warm water, then rub them with petroleum jelly and put on some socks. The joy of soft feet in the morning will energize you, especially when you don't have to contend with dry skin sticking to your socks or hosiery.

- Play tag, statue, red rover, keep-away, kick-the-can, or any other fun kid's game you remember from childhood. Your kids (or the neighbor kids) don't remember how to play? Be recreation director (participation required!). Or enlist a few playful adult friends. You could all use the temporary physical regression time.

- Eat a handful of walnuts for a snack today. Filled with phyto-chemicals and healthful fats, walnuts are a nutrient-dense snack. Plus, you'll be energized and you'll get more accomplished.

- Suck on a peppermint to energize you. Keep a bowl of them on your desk.

- Or better yet, have a lollipop. Why the heck not? There's no fat, just a few calories, and lots of fun. (Brush your teeth afterward!)

- Whenever you feel overwhelmed, take just two minutes to breathe slowly, deeply, and rhythmically, and you have instant regeneration!

Your Hobby, Your Joy

Most of us have some kind of hobby, whether it's photography or ori-gami, reading mystery novels or building model airplanes, juggling or practicing yoga. A hobby is anything we do just for the fun of it, the love of it, the fulfillment of it.

If you don't have a hobby, now is the time to get one. Hobbies can help us to discover what we truly love to do and can fill up parts of our soul that don't get filled elsewhere. Sometimes, hobbies can become such a passion that they morph into careers, but even if yours never does, that doesn't matter. Some people claim they would never want their favorite hobby to become a career because that would take the fun and relaxation out of it!

Finding a hobby can be as easy as flipping through the pages of a cat-alogue listing community education classes like photography, writing, language classes, or ballroom dancing. It can be as easy as surfing the

Internet for inspiration. It can be as easy as becoming engaged by the hobby of a friend.

Making time for a hobby is a lot like making time for yourself because what you choose as a hobby should fill you with joy and satisfaction. If it doesn't, then why bother?

Here are some hobby ideas to get you thinking:

- Tai chi or yoga
- Kite building and flying
- Contra dancing
- Making (and eating!) sushi
- Studying ancient cultures
- Crafting
- Politics
- Organic cooking
- Cake decorating
- Ecology
- Bird watching
- Rock collecting/fossil hunting
- Computer programming
- Writing poetry
- Collecting and tasting teas or coffees
- Wine appreciation
- Calligraphy
- Stamp collecting
- Financial planning/investing
- Movie making
- HAM radio

Something catch your eye? Stir your soul? This list could go on and on, of course ... the point is that anything you love can be a hobby and anything you love is worth your time. So get excited and let a non-job-related activity fill you with joy.

Sharing Your Gifts

When you have gifts—and everyone does—you can magnify them and increase their power to bring you joy by sharing them with others. This could take many forms: community involvement, volunteerism, mentoring, writing, sharing your art, even sharing your financial resources.

When you share your strengths with others, you empower both yourself and someone else by reaching out with a gesture of unity. This isn't always easy, but learning to give can be addictive ... in a good way!

Many of us have a self-protective mechanism that keeps us from feeling comfortable about volunteering. Maybe we think we will feel too vulnerable or have to look at our own lives in a new way if we get too close to someone who is different than we are—less advantaged, in greater pain, older, sicker. But once we see this barrier for what it is (a fear reaction), we can let it go. Open yourself up to the joy of immersion in humanity, and you may just discover a powerful hidden gift within yourself: the strength and courage to see yourself in others.

The love of our neighbor in all its fullness simply means being able to say to him, "What are you going through?"
—Simone Weil (1909–1943), French philosopher and mystic

Being with Your Family

Most of us say we want to spend more time with our families ... so why aren't we doing it? Are we under the impression that once we succeed at work, our children will revert to infancy and we can enjoy their lives to the fullest? Do we think our parents will wait around forever for us to spend time with them and tell them how we feel? Do we think our siblings don't need to interact with us until we make something of ourselves?

Many of us have to work during the day and can't be with our families all the time. That's just part of life. But when you come home at the end of the day, when you finally do get to be with your family, do you know how to *be with your family?*

It's a simple thing to stop what you are doing and look a child in the eye when he talks to you, to really listen to what he says and respond to it with respect. But how often do we do something else at the same time, listen with one eye on the television, answer with vague assents or a wave of the hand? How often do you say, "Not now, I'm busy?" Every day?

It's a simple thing to make time to visit your parents or your siblings, especially when they live near you, but how often do you feel that stab of resentment when you get that call: "When are you coming for a visit?" "When I have a little *time, mother!* I'm really *swamped right now!*"

The people we love won't be around forever and neither will we. Of course, we all know this, but we forget it day-to-day when our routines overwhelm us. But just like with any other way we spend our time, mindfulness with our family will deeply enrich and grow our family bond.

Learning to be with your family, fully and totally in mind and body, when it is time to be with them, is an amazing experience. Your child's behavior will change, becoming calmer and more loving. Your partner's stress will begin to melt away, and he or she will become more open to what you have to say because of how well you are listening. Your parents will feel loved. Being present for your family is among the most important gifts you can ever give them, so practice mindfulness with your loved ones every day.

Joy-Full Exercise: Turn a "No" into a "Yes"

Sometimes, the best way to mitigate the stress in your life is to learn how to say "no" more often to commitments and requests made of your time. But then again, think of all the things we say "no" to in our lives just because we don't want to get engaged in something we think we don't have time for, even though it might be an experience that could shake up our day a little and bring us some serious joy.

Maybe you always say no to that magnificent dessert tray at the lunch buffet (you can't spare the calories!). Maybe you always say no when a friend asks you to ditch the household chores on a Saturday and go for a hike (you have too much work, you have to keep up!). Maybe you always say no when your parents want to take you out for dinner (you don't have time for socializing tonight!).

While some parents probably give in to their children too often, many of us spend a whole lot of time saying "no."

Often, the "no" is for a good reason: to keep a child safe, to teach limits, to guard against overindulgence. But sometimes (admit it!) those no's are because you don't have the time or the inclination to engage in some silly kid thing you don't want to do.

Today, instead of saying no, choose one opportunity to do something joyful: have that triple chocolate torte, forget the paperwork for now and go on that hike, tell your child that yes, you will take her to the park today and yes, you will even swing on the swings! Let yourself say yes, just once, when you would have automatically said no, and feel how joy filters into the rest of your day.

> If only we would stop trying to be happy, we could have a pretty good time.
> —Edith Wharton (1862–1937), American novelist

Making Each Moment Count

Finally, remember that each moment is your entire reality. The past is gone and you can't change it, so why live there? The future is uncertain and you never know what will happen, so why live there? The present is right now. It is the only place to live and the only reality. Sink in and stay a while because every moment of your existence can matter.

Even when you practice household chores or other menial tasks that seem like necessary evils or a waste of time, remember that as you do them, it is still *now*. Vacuuming a carpet, stirring a soup, filing … you can achieve total focus and a deep appreciation for every moment, no matter what you are doing, if you live in mindfulness.

When you live mindfully, you begin to see how no one activity is any better than any other activity … not really. Being is all there is, no matter what you are doing, so whether you are taking out the garbage or listening to a symphony, *be there in joy*. Whether you are filled with anxiety or serenity, *be there in joy*. No matter who you are or what you do, what your strengths are, how you look, or who thinks what of you, *be there* to capture the joy, perceive the sorrow, and embrace your life exactly as it is, because that's exactly how it should be.

The Fourth Movement
Spiritual Renewal: Spreading Joy

Presto
(Very quick)

The more we fill up our own lives with joy, the more it spills back out and flows out into the universe to touch others. And so begins this final section of our book about joy: the fourth movement, played *presto,* or "very quick."

Letting joy flow outward to others is as important as letting it flow into ourselves, and the more we open our lives to joy, the quicker and more exuberantly it can spread to others. As you consider how to recapture the joy of childhood and the ways to magnify your joy by spreading it over your community, your country, and your world, imagine the quick, lively presto tempo of Beethoven's fourth movement, which includes what we know as the famous hymn, the "Ode to Joy." Your joy is contagious, just as joy should be, so let it proliferate ... presto! Lift yourself to the joy divine.

Chapter 10

Joy to You and Me

Throughout this book, we've talked a lot about the importance of community and of recognizing what we all have in common, rather than worrying about or feeling threatened by our differences. We need each other, and for that reason, relationships with other human beings can be one of the most profound sources of joy in our lives.

Yes, we need to love ourselves so that we know how to deeply love others, but at the same time, loving others openly and honestly can increase our own confidence, self-esteem, and personal sense of life satisfaction. Relationships generate joy by increasing the flow of joy from heart to heart, as a river flows into and out of lakes and ponds, oceans and tributaries, to finally fall into that great ocean of the human spirit.

The verb "to love" in Persian is "to have a friend." "I love you" translated literally is "I have you as a friend."
—Shusha Guppy (1938–), Iranian-born writer

Love, American Style

Americans are fascinated with the concept of romantic love. We make movies about it, we write books about it, we sing songs about it. When we see what we think is romantic love between two people we know or even two people we don't know, we envy it … and often, at the same time, poke fun at it. ("Get a room, you two!")

But deep down, how can we help but buy into the notion that somewhere out there is a soul mate just for us, that perfect match, that ideal someone who will bring out our best, support us when we need support, back us up in all our causes and opinions, make us feel incredibly sexy … someone who wants us more than anyone else, someone who, when we finally find them, will catalyze that "happily-ever-after" ending we've all been waiting for.

The problem is, it just ain't so.

The Myth of Romantic Love

We're not saying you can't find someone to play "romance" with. If you both love to be romantic, that can be a great source of joy for two! We're also not saying you can't find someone who makes you feel giddy and weak-kneed, or someone that you can develop a lifelong relationship with, someone you can deeply love and cherish.

However, to believe someone else can be responsible for your happy ending is to take the power of your own happiness away from you. No relationship is effortless, and nobody will agree with you all the time, support you all the time, or even like you all the time! People in loving, committed relationships get in arguments and must sometimes compromise what they want for the sake of the relationship. Only in recognizing the true nature of a relationship with another human being—someone as lovable but as fallible as you are—can a relationship succeed, on equal terms and in a way that makes life better, not worse, for both people in the relationship.

But then we see another Meg Ryan/Tom Hanks movie and all our good intentions may crumble: Why can't he be like *that?* Why can't she treat me like *that?*

Anthony deMello, a Jesuit priest who studied meditation and Eastern thought before his death in 1987, once said that romantic love only exists because we develop a pre-conceived notion about someone. The relationship works if the person decides to play the role of what we want, and if we are willing to play the role of what that person wants. If, instead, our preconceived notion is foiled by reality, the relationship falls apart. In either case, the relationship is, or was, based on illusion.

Love is the image of ourself until ourself destroys us.
—Jean Garrigue (1913–1972), American poet

And yet, we take a slightly more optimistic approach to relationships. Even if the notion of romantic love is largely elusive, that doesn't mean we can't engage in it just for the joy of it! We think romance is great fun, and satisfying, in the same way a really good piece of chocolate or a massage or an aged cognac is great fun and satisfying. So why not go for it? If your partner enjoys romance, too, then let it become a part of your relationship.

But notice that we said *a part of your relationship*. Romance cannot be the core of your relationship, just like chocolate and cognac can't be the core of your diet, and a massage can't be the core of your exercise routine. The core of a successful human relationship is to trust in the bond between two humans, to be open and honest, to communicate, and (this part is important) to expect to put some work into maintenance.

Does a car run without maintenance? Does a house? A furnace? To keep your relationship stoked and running smoothly, you have to work on it, and you have to expect that sometimes things will break down and need fixing. Sometimes the person we love won't do the thing we would have done or say the thing we would have said. Sometimes, the person we love will embarrass us or anger us or hurt our feelings. To build a relationship means to encounter these issues without throwing in the towel—to say, "Uh oh, we need to fix this!" instead of "Uh oh, time to trade up!"

Once we let go of the expectations for perfection, once we admit that no living human being could possibly fit the profile of our perfect soul mate, we can get down to the much more satisfying business of building a human connection with a real live person who is headed in the same life direction. That's the stuff on which strong, long-term partnerships are built.

Love Without Attachment

Oh how we want to hold on to the things we love! Oh how we want things to work out! Sometimes they do. Sometimes they don't. In either case, holding on won't help. It is more likely to cause problems.

Loving without attachment means accepting responsibility for our part of the relationship. We can decide to encounter issues without giving up and from the positive point of view of benefiting, not diminishing, the relationship. We can decide to stick with someone even when he or she proves to be imperfect, and we can recognize that relationships take work. But what if our partner doesn't decide or recognize the same things?

We can't force anyone else to make a relationship work, just like we can't force anyone else to love us. Loving without attachment means loving in the best way we can, and *letting* our partner love the best way he or she can. We can't control what anyone else thinks or feels. We can only remain open to listening and accepting the thoughts and feelings of someone we love.

The fruit of life is experience, not happiness.
—Amelia E. Barr (1831–1919), English-born writer

That's not to say you can't do or say things to help your partner trust you or feel more comfortable with your relationship. You don't have to sit back and be a victim of someone else's whims or insecurities or baggage. You can proactively fight for a relationship, but somewhere in that fight is a boundary you can't cross, even if you try. Loving without holding on is empowering. Loving while grasping tightly results in co-dependence at best, and at worst, loss.

How do you love without attachment? It takes self-confidence, that's for sure. Open communication and trust make it a lot easier, too. If you trust someone, you won't feel compelled to hold on to him or her. If you stay open about what each of you is feeling, you will have an easier time staying confident about your relationship. But to truly unattach yourself from someone you love is, in a sense, to go against human nature. If we want it, we grab it and we hold on so nobody else gets it from us! It's the cave person in us, the wild animal (or maybe the toddler): Get away from my friend! Mine, mine, mine! Stay back, or I'll bite!

Just imagine for a moment loving someone while defying that primal instinct to hold on. What would happen? By attachment, of course, we don't mean a literal holding on but a mental holding on. Visualize the person you love for a moment. Breathe deeply and focus on your mental image of that person. What thoughts and feelings rise up into your subconscious?

Probably you will envision many different kinds of thoughts and feelings, affection, attraction, maybe jealousy, maybe some guilt. Maybe you envision physical interaction or a conversation you had. Maybe you envision the future: commitment or moving on.

Now, consider what would happen if you let that person go in your mind—still loving him, but unhooking all those thoughts and feelings from your conception of that person. Would he drift away? Would you forget him? Would he sense it and physically leave you? Are your judgments and expectations about the person you love what holds him or her to you, or is it something else? Is it hooks and traps, balls and chains, anxiety and striving? Or is it simply love?

Part of the problem with attaching to love is that we begin to mistake the other person for a part of us. Sure, in a romantic moment you might utter sweet nothings such as, "You are a part of me," but to take that literally can be detrimental to any relationship. Your life with and relationship to another human being can certainly contribute to your life experience, which helps to shape your thinking and your feelings, but each of us is a unique and complete person.

To love is to appreciate the unique wholeness of another person so much that you develop a special bond and an understanding, but that bond doesn't diminish each whole, even when it binds two wholes together. To detach from a loved one is to let go of the notion that you need someone else to be whole. Within a relationship, give yourself space to evolve into completeness alongside someone you love, and you will form a bond stronger than any two humans struggling to fill up each other's emotional voids.

Ten Things I Love About You

Amidst the challenge of growing a relationship, you need to balance letting go and releasing expectations with acknowledging love and appreciation for the fellow human being you are getting to know and love so well. In your Joy Journal, make a Top Ten Love List. What are the 10 things you love the most about your partner, your parent, your child? Open your heart and let your appreciation flow through your pen. (If you think of more than 10 things, all the better, but we just *know* you can think of 10.)

Love Without Expectation

Part of learning to love without attachment is learning to love without expectation. Even when the people we love meet our expectations, relating to people via what we expect them to do or say or be destroys or foils mindfulness. If you expect someone else to make you happy or meet all your needs or complete your life, you are bound to be disappointed. If you expect someone to read your mind or behave in a certain way that embodies romantic perfection, you will be living in a dream relationship that doesn't really exist. You won't know the person you are with; you will simply hold up expectations in front of that person and hope he or she lines up. This isn't a true relationship, this is simply an illusion.

So how can you live in the present moment, truly be there with someone, if your mind is living somewhere in the future of what you expect? That's a tricky one, because letting go of expectation isn't easy. It may be one of the most difficult things you ever do in your relationship ... and one of the very best.

How much simpler and more rewarding it is to stop expecting and just be? Act according to your needs; communicate about your plans; fulfill your promises; and be who you are. If your partner does the same, expectation will become irrelevant.

But shouldn't you "expect" to be treated well? Respected? Listened to? Loved? Shouldn't you "expect" to be nurtured, made an equal partner, emotionally supported? Actually, no! Of course, relationships are best when they contain these qualities; when both partners nurture each other, treat each other well, respect and listen to each other, love each other, emotionally support each other, and act as equal partners. It's just that expectation clouds the reality of the situation.

A relationship is what it is. That certainly doesn't mean you can't improve it! But expecting doesn't enact improvement. If you feel emotionally unsupported, expecting to be supported won't help. *Asking* to be supported might help, however. Being supportive to the other person *yourself* might help. And if it doesn't, then all the expectation in the world won't fix the relationship.

You can accept the things you can't change in a relationship, or you can leave the relationship. Should you accept abuse, disrespect, being ignored, bad treatment? Certainly not! If you can't change these things, you need to free yourself from a relationship that harms you physically, emotionally, or spiritually. But again, to expect the relationship to be good won't *make* the relationship good. Communication, action, and behaving as a loving and respectful partner yourself can make all the difference in the world. Once you let the expectation go, you can get down to the business of actually *having* a relationship!

When we expect, we can't experience the joy of surprise, and we set ourselves up for potential disappointment. Even when we get what we want, we may raise our expectations until no one can meet them anymore. Or we will take the relationship for granted. Your wonderful, loving partner supports, nurtures, and loves you? What a beautiful thing that is! Appreciate and cherish a loving relationship for what it is. Let it be new and fresh and miraculous each day, rather than dwelling on those inevitable things you don't like in another human being.

How often have you been disappointed in an expectation and then used that disappointment against the person who disappointed you? We expect, someone fails us, and then we get attached to that disappointment. We hold it and stroke it and use it to feed our dissatisfaction. Soon, expectation turns toxic and undermines our relationship from the inside out.

But to love without expectation is to love free of all that psychological flotsam. As humans, this is a tough job. We expect out of habit and because it is an ingrained part of our culture. But we can learn to recognize our expectations, and in recognizing them, we can release them, one at a time, little by little, until all that is left standing before us is the person, unadorned—a person to love, or not to love, as the case may be, but unclouded by expectations so that each relationship can stand on its own and move toward its potential. How much easier it suddenly becomes to let love flow unimpeded. It's like taking all the rocks out of a river.

Love Without Barriers

We would venture to say that it is impossible to love too much. Excess love can only help to correct the imbalance caused by lack of enough love in the world. To love fully and with an open heart is an admirable quality, not easy to accomplish. It makes us feel vulnerable, even a little silly.

But love without barriers is different than love without boundaries. "Love" that manifests as a constant need to be with someone, to know that person's every move, to watch constantly and to devote one's life to another isn't really love at all. It is dependent attachment. Children and dogs are allowed to engage in dependent attachment, but unless you qualify as one or the other, dependent attachment won't take you very far in a committed relationship (unless the other person is the same way, in which case you've got co-dependent attachment, which isn't conducive for spiritual growth).

But these aren't really love boundaries; they are behavioral boundaries. Certainly all human relationships require behavioral boundaries because each of us is an individual and needs a certain amount of room to grow and maintain that individuality. Love, on the other hand, needs no boundaries. Let your love wash over your life and the lives of the people around you, and it will brighten all your colors, adding depth and gloss like a glaze over a Renaissance painting.

Joy-Full Exercise: Detachment Affirmation

To practice nonattachment, nonexpectation, and the dissolution of barriers in the love of the people in your life, visualize a loved-one in your mind and then speak these words:

I release my attachment (deep breath).
I release my expectation (deep breath).
I am complete (deep breath).
My love is complete (deep breath).

Chapter 10: Joy to You and Me
The person I love is complete (deep breath).
I commit to love, just as it is (three deep breaths).
(Repeat)

Navigating the Dating Scene

Whether you are a dating pro or have been recently tossed back into the dating scene, you already know that dating can be thrilling, baffling, and frustrating, stroking your ego or plunging you into embarrassment ... and sometimes all in one date!

Dating is more than courtship; these days, it has even become fodder for entertainment! So-called "reality television" has jumped on the dating bandwagon with shows that try to match up singles with millionaires (or fake millionaires), follow people on blind dates, set up couples on dates with other people, or throw them onto deserted islands with "sexy singles" to see if their relationships can take the pressure. Good television? Some might think so, but shows like this can also infiltrate our consciousness, setting up unrealistic expectations. Why shouldn't we be able to have our choice of 50 gorgeous suitors? Why shouldn't we get to marry a millionaire—or become instant millionaires just by agreeing to put our romantic escapades on public view?

Dating is practically tailor-made to drag expectations right into the game. The point, of course, is to find someone—for a casual or not-so-casual relationship, but whether we expect something short-term or long-term or even just a little physical attention in the very short term, we still tend to expect.

A date sets up an expectation. It says, "I like you, you like me, let's see what happens," and once we put a "let's see" into our heads, our minds tend to take it and run. Whether you find yourself envisioning how she'll look in that wedding gown or how you'll eventually have to let the poor sap off the hook when he becomes obsessed with you, if your mind runs away with you before you've even met a person very well, you can be sure that expectations are to blame.

The problem with expectations during dating is that ...

- They are based on scant evidence, as you have little actual experience with this new person.

- They are heavily colored by your personal desires, which have nothing to do with a well-established relationship (as a long-term relationship doesn't yet exist).

- They cloud your ability to really get to know this person, who might actually be a good potential partner or, at least, a friend.

- They are influenced by that early thrill of infatuation and physical attraction, which evolves (or doesn't evolve) into something more solid and lasting.

But how do you go on a joyful date without expectations? Use mindfulness, of course! Throw in a dash of kindness, compassion, and honesty, and you've got a great date ... or at least, a date that won't lead you in a false direction.

New love is difficult, but dating is really no different than meeting anyone else new or getting to know a friend better. It doesn't matter if you've been set up by a friend, if you are meeting someone you've been chatting with on the Internet (the twenty-first-century version of the bar scene), or if you've been dating someone for a while now and your relationship is progressing. If you decide to *be* on your date, really pay attention rather than dwelling in the future, then you have a much better chance of making a human connection.

The Dating Game

In your Joy Journal, write a paragraph "review" of each date just after it's over. As you sort through your very human relationships or as a relationship progresses, you can look back and read all about your first impression of each encounter. Sometimes memory tricks us, and while dwelling on past impressions can be detrimental to the future, a brief reminder of what happened and how it made you feel can help to reorient your perspective in a helpful way when you aren't sure how you feel about someone. And if you do end up "together forever"? You'll have a delightful (or embarrassing or hilarious) opportunity for reminiscing.

Mindfulness will also help you recognize past behaviors cropping up that aren't relevant to the date itself. Are you making assumptions based on what someone else said or did once? Are you taking something personally because of a past situation? Mindfulness can also help you to observe your own reactions to this other human being: Are you attracted sexually but not in other ways, or do you feel a connection in beliefs, attitudes, and personality?

Kindness and compassion can be a huge help on a date, too. The other person may be feeling just as awkward or embarrassed or insecure as you feel ... or maybe much more than you feel. Taking that into account when processing what the other person says and does can help to keep you from *assuming* that you know the motivations and inner thoughts of someone you barely know.

Finally, honesty is crucial at all stages of a relationship, and no less so than in the beginning. If you know you won't be interested in dating someone again, be honest—not in a hurtful way, but don't lead him on. Be kind, but be honest, and if you do have a connection with someone that you both want to explore, you'll be starting out in a way that will build a solid foundation for any future communication and interaction.

As you think about all these aspects of dating, though, don't lose your sense of humor. Dating is actually kind of funny ... two people who don't know each other very well trying to figure out if they could ever fall in love. A sense of humor will help keep the mood light, and if you are taking things lightly, you won't be obsessing over "where it's all going." Plus, you'll both have a lot more fun.

I've got a heart like a college prom. Each one I dance with seems the best of all.

—Ilka Chase (1905–1978), American writer

Life Partnership

We date, and date, and date ... and one day, we meet "the one," or we simply decide that a partnership is working well and why not just stick with a good thing? Whether we've been with the same partner for a long time or are just now deciding to take the plunge into commitment, deciding to be with someone for life is a sound and very human way to feel more secure and supported, not to mention having a friend who doubles as a sexual partner in the same household.

We would never try to characterize an ideal life partnership or say which "types" are most likely to work because we've seen them all, from opposites who attract to couples who almost seem like twins. People of drastically different ages, income brackets, cultures, religions, people of any gender and every possible personality can fall in love and make it work with joy.

But we can make some generalizations based on what we've seen. Life partnerships tend to work best when ...

- Both partners are committed to making the partnership work.
- Both partners make an effort to spend some time communicating or being together every day, even if only for a few minutes.
- Both partners are forgiving.
- Both partners are willing to be vulnerable, open, and honest with each other, even about things they might not want to admit like insecurities or fears. Likewise, when one partner admits insecurities or fears, the other is open to hearing and working through the problem.
- Both partners have fun and laugh together a lot.
- Both partners look for, and find, the joy in each other. Then they strive to nurture that joy and increase it, in ways large and small, every day.

A life partnership can be a most fulfilling and long-term human relationship, so it is worth our time, our attention, our presence. Be there together, and you'll continue to be there together. Life is long, and it's nice to travel through it with someone.

On the other hand ... if you are still looking, still waiting, still hoping, still despairing, remember that a life partner isn't necessary for any kind of completion. If you spend all your time looking ahead to when you'll finally "find someone," you are missing out on your life. It's always going to be *your* life, and you will always be an autonomous human being, so start acting like one!

Many people claim that when they finally stopped looking for someone else to make them whole and concentrated on the business of simply *being* a whole individual, they ran smack into the love of their lives. It's no coincidence: People who are happy with their lives and content within themselves are more attractive to others. In other cases, simply recognizing that you are finally at a point in your personal evolution where you are ready to enter into a relationship is enough to bring a relationship to you. Speak your intention to the universe, and love may be drawn to you. That's just how it happened for Eve, two years after her divorce. She told a friend, out loud, "You know, I think I'm finally ready to have a relationship again." Two weeks later, she met someone she is still seeing today.

The point is that forcing love is antithetical to a productive relationship. You can only influence *you:* who you are, and how full and rich and aware your life is. Your life is as beautiful and has as much potential for joy as anyone else's, whether they happen to be partnered at the moment or not. Plenty of partnered people are unhappy and have little joy in their lives. It's all a matter of what you have inside, not a matter of who is lying next to you in the bed. Yet recognizing the beautiful and full nature of your own being and living your life in awareness may actually draw someone else to you: someone who is headed on a similar path and with whom you can build a relationship that can enrich both your lives. Just let go of the striving and let your life unfold, and you'll find a new freedom, to love and to let yourself be loved without expectation or the need to control others.

The Joy of Sex

And speaking of that bed ... good sex is good. It can deepen your relationship and fill your day with joy. Good sex is also good for you! Studies show that regular (safe) sex in a monogamous relationship can help to alleviate depression, decrease the chance of reproductive cancers, lessen stress, improve sleep, and even help to alleviate certain kinds of pain like menstrual cramps and (ironically) headaches (so much for that excuse!). People who have sex once or twice a week have more immunoglobulin A, a chemical secreted by the body that directly fights the common cold (although people who have sex more often actually had levels equal to those who never have sex, so once again, moderation wins!).

For women, sex can also help to regulate the menstrual cycle, can help prevent endometriosis, and may even alleviate depression; while in men, regular sex is beneficial to the prostate as well as the mood. Regular sex keeps both men and women feeling more bonded to their partner, and in better communication, and it also stimulates more loving feelings. What's not to love about love?

But somehow, sex gets all muddled up with attachments and expectations, just like all the other aspects of relationships (and indeed, of human life!). Because it feels so good, it can also be addictive, and we can seek it out without considering the person we are getting it from. These days, that's more than spiritually degrading; it's downright life-threatening.

The Indian sage Patanjali, whom many consider the father of modern yoga practice and whose *Yoga Sutras* mark the first organized written record of yoga philosophy, penned a set of do's and don'ts for "right living," in an effort to help the practitioner of yoga most easily reach enlightenment, and in his list of do's, called *niyamas,* Patanjali wrote about chastity.

This *niyama* is challenging for Westerners for whom sex is a part of life, but the original intention of this moral principle probably was not abstinence because many yoga practitioners in ancient India were married with families. Instead, chastity means cultivating reverence and respect for the person with whom one is intimate. It means honoring the sexual process and valuing it as a sincere and deeply meaningful communion between two people. It means avoiding casual sex, degrading sex, sex that hurts someone, or sex just for the sake of pleasure and pleasure alone, outside the boundaries of a relationship.

You might argue that if you want to have sex, you should be able to have sex, and we won't disagree with you! Sex, as we said, can be a joyful experience and a great life enhancer. The trick is to use it in that way, however, and not as a means to get what you want, to manipulate people, to use them, or to stroke your own, um … ego. Sex is, we would venture to say, practically essential for a close, intimate, bonded love relationship. But as a recreational drug, well … that's not joyful. When using any drug that results in a temporary high which leads us astray by way of desire, we follow the desire. When it vanishes, we run off looking for more, losing track of ourselves again … and losing track of the joy that stays with us because it comes from within us.

It *is* something big and cosmic. What else do we have? There's only birth and death and the union of two people—and sex is the only one that happens to us more than once.

—Kathleen Winsor (1920–), American writer

Loving Your Friends and Family

Of course, our romantic relationships aren't our only human relationships. We love our friends and we love our families, but these relationships can challenge us, too. To make the most of the people we love in our lives, sometimes it's easiest to stick to a few basic principles. We like to call them our Ten Commandments for loving our friends and family:

1. **Forgive the past so it doesn't haunt the present.** Your parents made you feel inadequate as a child? Forgive them. Your teenager said he hates you? Forgive him. Your friend began dating your ex? Forgive him or her. We don't have long on this earth to spend with the people we love, and wasting time resenting the past lets the precious present escape unnoticed.

2. **Be patient.** Parents require it, children require it, in-laws certainly require it, even friends require it when they seem needy without giving anything in return or borrow your favorite sweater without asking. Patience can help you release your irritation at the foibles of others. You have them, too, you know. Consider it payback for all the times people have been patient with you. (Yes, there have been several!)

3. **Be tolerant.** Everyone is different, comes from different experience, processes thoughts and feelings differently. The more tolerant you are of the differences of your loved ones, the more you will feel unified.

4. **Be kind.** Do you have to make that jab, hurl that sarcastic remark, comment on that ... interesting fashion statement? No, you don't. Be kind to the people you love, and kindness will flow back to you. (You know the old axiom about doing unto others, right?)

5. **Embrace empathy.** If you can move into someone else's heart and experience how he is feeling, you have a great gift, but we can all be more empathetic. The next time you find yourself reacting against something your sister or father or best friend said or did, stop your negative thought flow and put yourself in your loved one's position for a few minutes. Maybe you'll see what's going on with a clearer vision, and even if you don't, let the negative thought flow continue on its way without your brain in tow.

6. **Acknowledge your bond.** If you have a history with someone, that matters. Sure, it may be living in the past to rehash it all, but a relationship that has lasted for years, that is the source of fond memories and connection, is worth a little effort to preserve.

7. **Learn how to apologize.** Sometimes (admit it), you are in the wrong. More often, a miscommunication or a misspoken word sets off a chain reaction. We all say and do things we later regret. If you learn not to fear being the one who says "I'm sorry" first, you can reinstate the joy of friendship a lot more quickly. Try not to *expect* an "I'm sorry" back, at least not right away ... it's like expecting a gift in return for a gift, which negates the whole point of a gift! In other words, don't use "I'm sorry" as a way to coerce an admission of guilt out of someone else. Say it and mean it, and you'll get a lot more mileage out of it.

8. **Don't waste time.** When you are with the people you love, be there with your full attention. Don't wait too long to tell people you love them. Be free with your hugs and kisses. Appreciate people and tell them what you appreciate. You'll fill up the lives of your loved ones with joy.

9. **Share yourself.** Are you the relative or the friend everyone comes to with a problem but who never goes to anyone else? Let yourself open up to your loved ones and let them help you. It might help them more than anything else you do, to know they make a difference in *your* life.

10. **Love yourself.** You are a beautiful, unique soul worth exploration, nurture, and love. No one knows you like *you* do, but even you can know yourself better. Commit to the relationship with *you,* and all your other relationships will begin to fall in place.

You've identified your joyful calling, or at least, you are thinking about it. You've earmarked your most treasured relationships as ideal opportunities for joyful mindfulness. And now, before we get any more serious, let's jump into the sandbox or the wading pool. Let's eat a Popsicle. Let's short-sheet the camp counselor. Just for fun! In other words, let's remember the joy of *play!*

Chapter 11

Remember How to Play

Think back … way back … to your early childhood. What do you remember? Think about the way you envisioned life, as an impossibly lengthy, winding road ahead of you, full of adventures and at the end, that mysterious state called "adulthood."

Remember how much time it took to get from one birthday to the next? The time between the seventh birthday and the eighth, or the eleventh and the twelfth, or the twelfth and that excruciatingly long wait to become an age with the prestigious word *teen* attached to it … how long it all seemed to take, and how fun and painful and yet … *fun* it was to pass that time. Childhood seems to last forever, and once we grow up, the time flies by, with birthdays bumping up against each other with seemingly no time at all between them.

Time is a funny thing. We know that a minute is a minute and it is always 60 seconds long. We know how long a year is or a decade, but somehow, time used to be a languid river we meandered along in an inner tube. When did it turn into running the rapids?

Part of the reason life speeds up when we are adults is because we lose track of life. We stop paying attention. We stop wondering and waiting and reveling in the small moments, the games, the smell of the air, the toys, the deep and abiding sense of play that used to master our days. When we had grown-ups to worry for us and all we had to do was be children, we had the time to let time expand. We didn't have to hurry, and neither did the day.

But now that we're all grown up, with responsibilities and jobs and all those other trappings of the adult world, can we ever recapture that sense of wonder we used to have? Can we remember how to play? Can we find a space where we can be both a respectable adult and playful child? Joyfully, yes! We know lots of people who have done it, and you can, too. Let's begin by letting our minds wander back, back, back in time …

The World as You Once Knew It

Think about how you related to the world as a child. Remember summer, those long afternoons, the shadows that stretched down the sidewalk making you look like a skinny giant? Remember sidewalk chalk and hopscotch, jump-rope rhymes and skateboards, jacks and hula hoops? Remember riding your bike, hearing the rumble of thunder, and heading for home with anticipation about the coming storm? Remember those long, starry summer nights, the sound of cicadas in the trees and crickets under the house, sleeping with the window open and watching for shooting stars?

Now remember how it felt when summer wound down into fall. Remember the feel of the chill in the air, the color of the turning leaves, the thrill of shopping for school supplies and a new backpack. Remember the dark sky and the whipping wind blowing your Halloween costume around your legs as you ran down the street with your bag of candy, gleefully shining your flashlight into the shadowy tree branches and trying to recognize your friends behind masks and makeup?

And even if you were in some prison the walls of which let none of the sounds of the world come to your senses—would you not then still have your childhood, that precious, kingly possession, that treasure-house of memories? Turn your attention thither.

—Rainer Maria Rilke (1875–1926), German poet, from *Letters to a Young Poet*

Remember the dusty smell the first time the furnace kicked on, winter mornings with steaming cups of hot chocolate, pushing the marshmallows under the sweet, steamy brown liquid and watching them bob back up again, eating them when they were just soft enough to melt in your mouth but still hold a shape? Remember how it felt when somebody built a fire in the fireplace and you sat and watched the flames in your bathrobe and slippers? Remember building a snowman on that day when the snow stuck together like magic, making it effortless to roll a giant snowball around the yard until it was big enough, finding sticks and rocks for the eyes and arms, and searching the refrigerator for a carrot?

Remember looking for the first shoots of bulbs on the side of your house in the spring, breaking through those thin sheets of ice over the puddles with a satisfying crunch under your snow boots, feeling the first warm breezes, and rejoicing on that glorious day when your mother or father told you that yes, you could go out *without* your coat today?

Remember when the most important thing in the world was meeting your friends at twilight for a game of kick-the-can in the cul-de-sac or getting a chance to ride that pony at the fair or finally achieving 1,000 jumps on the pogo stick? Remember what you dreamed, what you believed, how deeply you *felt* the beauty of the world?

Childhood can be sometimes hard, sometimes scary, even painful. But it is also magical, by its very nature. Because you were new to the earth (or new to the earth *this* time around, depending on what you believe), you weren't yet heavily colored by its cultures and attitudes. You really *were* seeing life for the first time, experiencing each new thing for the first time. It felt magical. Think back. You can remember.

Joy-Full Exercise: Recapturing Your Childhood Memories

We know you have your own fond memories of childhood, things you may not have thought about for a while. Think of them now! Let yourself spend time meditating on how you thought, how you felt, how you saw the world as a child. See how many details you can capture in your mind. Think of the things you loved to do, to play, to feel. Let your mind wander back into the past, to the magical parts of your childhood where the world was a wonder and everything was new.

Reclaiming the Kid Inside

Childhood joy doesn't have to end! For some of us, childhood was a time when we were shorter and didn't know as much about the world, but as for the aspect of play, it is still a part of our grown-up adult lives. Then, too, we all know the kinds of adults who are "serious types." Maybe you are one of them! Being a "serious adult" can result in lots of money and success (although it doesn't always), but is it fun? And does fun matter? Are grown-ups supposed to have fun?

Of course they are! What's the point of making money, having a job, having a family and kids, a dog, or a cat, if you can't enjoy what and whom you love? Adults can play, even though we may play differently and our toys may be slightly more sophisticated. Do we really need Palm Pilots, Blackberries, or laptops? (Don't you love those playful names?) Maybe we do, or at least, maybe now that we have them they have become integral to our work lives, but even if we need them, we also like to play with them! (Admit it ... you're not scheduling a meeting on that PDA, you're e-mailing your best friend in Paris!)

When play is at the heart of daily life, joy will hang over our years like a tent-house blanket over the kitchen chairs, and we won't ever forget how to play peek-a-boo with a baby or hide-and-seek with a grandchild. And we'll always have a deck of cards ready for a round of Hearts or Spoons or Euchre when friends come to visit.

But you don't have to have kids or even know any kids to reclaim your inner child. You *were* a kid once, remember? You don't need kids around you to inspire you to play again, you have all the experience you need inside you. A sense of play, imagination, and fun is absolutely essential to a joyful life. Why should kids get to have all the fun? Grown-ups need to play for balance, for stress relief, and simply to feel more joyful.

What one loves in childhood stays in the heart forever.
—Mary Jo Putney (twentieth century), American writer

Some adults take to play easily, delighting in toys or games or flights of the imagination. For others, remembering how to play is more difficult, especially for people who grew up being criticized for childlike behavior. However, now that you're all grown up, you can play if you want to, thank you very much! Who is going to complain? Certainly not your kids. Certainly not your dog. Certainly not your partner, if he or she gets to play, too. (Besides, some games are *just* for grown-ups, *wink-wink!*)

You might want to limit the really obvious play on company time. Your supervisor might not approve of the game of marbles on the floor of your cubicle. But that doesn't mean you can't read the latest best-seller on your lunch hour or ride your bike to the office instead of driving. It doesn't mean you can't enlist the help of co-workers over break room coffee to try to remember how to make a cat's cradle or a witch's broom or a Jacob's ladder with a loop of string, or to remember the lyrics of old camp songs or funny sitcom themes.

No, you can't and shouldn't be silly all the time. Even kids aren't silly all the time. Sometimes they settle down and have a serious conversation, do their homework, or just relax for a while. In the same way, we have work to do, houses to clean, errands to run. Sometimes we have to buckle down and get things done, have a serious conversation, or "deal with" stuff.

But when it's appropriate, like on a break, in your free time, or at a social gathering, why not leap into the spirit of play and have a really good time? Eve remembers spending an entire evening at a so-called grown-ups party singing snippets from the Bugs Bunny opera cartoon with Elmer Fudd and his magic helmet, with everyone supplying the parts they remembered. (But that's not surprising, as Eve doesn't know any "serious adults.")

We can learn a lot from the way kids lead their lives. They have a fresher, newer, less cynical, but in many ways wiser approach to living life than we do. They know how to live in the moment. They know how to let loose and really enjoy life, and when they get hurt, they know how to let loose and cry until they feel better. Then, it's on to the next game!

Joy-Full Exercise: Playtime!

It's funny how easily we forget how to play. Begin retraining yourself today! Go to the store and buy a toy, maybe something you would have loved but never had as a child (a dollhouse, a remote control car). Or buy something you used to have but lost long ago. (A Lite-Brite? A Magic 8 Ball? A set of Tinker-Toys or Lincoln Logs? Legos? Yep, they still make them all!) You don't need to spend a lot of money. Just buy something you think looks fun to play with. Take it home. Delegate 30 minutes—minimum!—and play with your toy!

Your Play History

One of Gary's fondest memories of his father was his love of toys. Gary's father didn't have many toys as a child, so he loved to buy his own children toys, and he wanted to play with them, too. His favorite pastime was model airplanes, and eventually, radio-controlled airplanes. For Gary's father this hobby became a true source of joy. Play for grown-ups, this meant a lot to him, even as he preached about taking responsibility in life, earning a living, and following all those other "serious" adult dictums.

Gary, on the other hand, wasn't too interested in toys. He found his joy in reading books. Eve remembers dolls who were like best friends and elaborate games in which bedrooms were transformed into wonderlands of clouds and candy (all it takes is a little construction paper, a pair of scissors, some cotton balls, and a big imagination). Eve will never forget making a giant paper airplane out of a newspaper, carrying it to the top of the bunk bed, sitting in it, and scooting off the side, totally convinced she would go sailing across the room. (Don't try this at home!) And don't even get her started about the Skipper dolls that got to live free of their Barbie sisters by faking their own deaths and taking over an abandoned mansion (the bi-level coffee table in the family room).

When we talk of leaving our childhood behind us, we might as well say that the river flowing onward to the sea had left the fountain behind.

—Anna Jameson (1794–1860), English/Canadian/Irish art critic and historian

Eve's kids have their own modes of play, too. Angus is seven, a serious collector of trading cards, fossils, and crystals, and a whiz at video games. Emmett is almost five and loves to engage grown-ups in elaborate games of pretend, especially the one in which he is the puppy in the pet store and Grandma is the nice lady who comes in and buys him, only to discover that he can morph into a cat, a mouse, a bird, and (surprisingly), Spiderman (who then becomes Peter Parker, who then turns back into the puppy).

How about your own history of play? What did you love to do as a child? Were you a book hound, a rock hound, a bug collector? Did you love to explore outside or build tents inside? Did you play with Barbies or action figures? Or were you more interested in playing with real people? Think back. What were your favorite toys? A stuffed animal? A realistic newborn baby doll? A battery-powered robot? A baseball glove? Crossword puzzle books? Paper dolls? Blocks? Legos?

Did you collect spoons or postcards from family vacations? Were you interested in animals or attached to your family pet? Did you have an imaginary friend? Eve's son Angus had an imaginary friend named Loop, who was a flying loop of string with a face and Angus's very best friend in the world at the tender age of two. (Who said play has to be realistic?)

Remembering your own play history can help you to get back in touch with what you find to be fun and a source of joy. Remember that dollhouse you loved? Why not build one now and begin collecting miniature furniture (an expensive hobby, but it sure is fun!). Or maybe you adored that model train. Hey, who needs a guest room? Change that room into a model train room and build a track around the room complete with realistic landscape. If it brings you joy, it is not a frivolous endeavor but a sacred one.

Remembering your history of play can also help you get back in touch with the part of you that dominated your personality when you were young. If you haven't seen that intrepid child adventurer part of yourself for a while, never fear. If the child you were so many years ago did not have permission to blossom and play, then give permission to yourself to do it now. Your joyful, inquisitive, precocious inner child is still in there somewhere. You just have to dive in and look into the dusty corners of your heart.

Your Play Memoir

In your Joy Journal, write your memoir ... your *play* memoir! Write the story of how you loved to play as a child. Describe your favorite toys and the games you used to play with them. Were your stuffed animals residents of a magical forest? Were your dolls an oddball group of travelers visiting different countries around the world (different rooms in your house) in a plastic truck?

Did you go through periods of playing with nothing but pick-up sticks or barrel-of-monkeys or tinker toys? Think back and include as much detail as you can. Save this memoir in your Joy Journal and refer to it whenever you are feeling a little too grown up. If you didn't have the opportunity to play much as a child, then use this exercise to explore the kind of play you desire as a part of your life now.

The Intersection of Fun Street and Silly Avenue

If play seems like a leap for you, we're here to help. You can fit more play into your life in little ways, and the more you play, the more comfortable it will become.

Imagine that play is already a big part of your life. Don't fear being silly or goofy. People will find you easier to relate to if you are a little bit silly, and kids will think you are the greatest grown-up they ever met. Parents who know how to play can be more intimately involved in the lives of their kids and may even be better at understanding their children's point of view.

Play is fun and right and good. You can live in a world that is fun and right and good and full of joy. You really can! If we can do it, you can do it. You can live a life graced with a sense of play and a fresh wonder in the world around you, no matter how much you have lived and experienced. Every day is a new opportunity to feel and experience the joy of childhood again—or for the first time!

See if you can squeeze at least one playful activity into your life every day. Here are some ideas to set you on the right course:

- Remember how fun it was to draw pictures, before you were self-conscious about whether or not they were "good"? Draw just for fun, whatever you want to draw: a horse, a race car, a flower gar-den, a beach scene complete with a sun wearing sunglasses, or your favorite cartoon character. Or do silly portraits of your family.

- Windy today? Fly a kite. Find a wide-open space like a park or a field and get a sturdy, quality kite that won't smash apart at the first crash landing. Kite flying takes some practice, and as an adult, you may have the added benefit of patience, so keep at it. (That kid over there might be able to give you some helpful hints, too. Her kite is really soaring!)

- Look for locally organized nature walks. A guide will point out flora and fauna, which can help you look at your natural surround-ings in a whole new light while you get to enjoy the fresh air and meet new friends.

- Go bird watching. A pair of binoculars, a field guide, and a note-book are all you need to start this fun hobby. The more you learn, the more you'll see. If you get the bug, consider joining a bird watching group and going on trips to try to spot rarer and rarer examples of our flight-blessed friends.

- Paint by number. These kits are inexpensive in the art store and make a great meditative tool in addition to being fun. When you're done, you'll think, *Hey, I painted that!* Yes you did!

- Take an art class and learn how to throw pots or paint with water color or take really good photographs.

- Take up square dancing or belly dancing or Irish contra dancing or tap dancing or ballroom dancing. Or just go dancing at a local disco. Or slow-dance with one you love in your living room. Something about moving the body to music automatically induces a free-spirited sense of joy.

- Play a game! Get the family together for a rousing game of Taboo or Trivial Pursuit or Scattergories or Pictionary or Encore or any other fun "talky" game that gets everybody laughing together.

- Play improv. Get together with friends or family and present differ-ent situations. Have pairs of people get up and act out the scene, just for fun. Or join a local community theater group or take an acting class. (No, you're not too old!)

- Hold a talent show. Let friends or family members take turns performing for each other. Who sings? Who plays an instrument? Who can juggle or do back handsprings or twirl a flaming baton? Who wants to read a poem? You might have so much fun that your talent show becomes a regular event.

- Get a group of friends together to visit a comedy club. Research shows that laughter has a healing affect. No comedy club around? Rent a funny movie and watch it with friends, or even by yourself. Pop popcorn or enjoy your favorite childhood movie candy (Raisinets, anyone? Jujyfruits? Goobers? Hot Tamales? Snowcaps? Dots?)

- Watch cartoons on Saturday morning in your pajamas. Laugh. Eat some pancakes. Drink milk. Feel good.

- Make a collage out of magazine pictures representing the things you love or that interest you. A large piece of paper or poster board, a glue stick, a pair of scissors, a stack of magazines, and a little imagination are all it takes. (Kids love to do this, too.)

- Bake your favorite cookie. Chocolate chip? Oatmeal raisin? Snickerdoodles? Monster cookies? If you don't have a recipe, check out a cookbook at the library or search the Internet (you can find just about any recipe on the Internet). Eat some cookies, and then, if you are afraid you will eat them all, give the rest to someone who would appreciate the gift, like a neighbor or co-worker with children.

- Hang out at the park for a few hours. Walk around, check out the playground equipment, read on a park bench, feed the birds or the squirrels, breathe the fresh air, notice the colors.

- Read a book, not because "everyone" is reading it or because you think it will be good for you, but just because it would be fun. That means choosing a book you actually *want* to read. A mystery? A romance novel? A medical thriller? A courtroom drama? A sci-fi adventure? Fantasy? Whatever sounds like fun. (Are you caught up on the *Harry Potter* books yet? Well, what are you waiting for?)

- Become a weather watcher. Start a weather journal and record the daily temperature and conditions. While you're at it, what do you think that cloud looks like? A bear carrying a pitcher of lemonade?

A clown standing on his head? A mother elephant with a baby elephant holding her tail?

The clouds hung above the mountains like puffs of white smoke left in the wake of a giant old-fashioned choo-choo train.
—Sue Grafton (1940–), American writer, from *B Is for Burglar*

- Think back to a moment in your childhood when you laughed really hard. Remember how that felt.
- Play dress up. Put on a costume and pretend to be someone else. Wear your grandmother's hat or your partner's bathrobe, or amuse your kids by putting on something of theirs and pretending to *be* them. Give them something of yours and let them pretend to be *you*.
- Whatever you are doing right now, see it anew, as if you were seeing it for the first time. At least once a day, try to look at something with the fresh perspective of a child. You might find you get creatively inspired in ways you never imagined.

Joy-Full Exercise: Collection Craze!

Kids love to collect things, and you probably collected things when you were a child. Lots of grown-ups collect things, too, and find great delight in their collections of model airplanes, antique dolls, folk art, pottery, China figurines, novelty lighters, or any other passion.

If you don't collect anything, this is a great time to start. Think back to what you collected as a child. Marbles? Dolls? Colored rubber bands? Cool rocks you found while exploring? Then consider what kind of collection you would enjoy today. It doesn't have to be expensive. Start up that rock collection again, or collect interesting leaves, or press wildflowers and put them in a scrapbook. Search flea markets for antique bottle openers or matchbox cars or baseball cards or cigar boxes or hat pins. Or collect pithy quotes you hear or find out in the world.

Of course, like anything else that brings pleasure, collecting can become an obsession, which defeats the purpose of finding more playful delight in your life. Let your collection exist lightly in your life. Add to it in ways that bring you joy, and keep it in sight where you can appreciate it.

When Exercise Was Called Play, Not Work(out)

Why do we call it a *work*out? Exercise should be fun. No wonder so many of us don't keep it up for very long. Who wants to run like a hamster on a wheel? Wouldn't you rather run through the park or play tag? We will even go so far as to say that we aren't making exercise fun, we are having *fun* in ways that just happen to double as exercise. Now that doesn't sound so bad, does it?

Here are ways to have fun and get fit all at the same time, kid-style:

- Forget the aerobics class. Jump rope and enjoy great cardio benefits.

- *Don't* forget aerobics class, but go to one that's fun! Aerobic classes these days are more creative than ever with versions centered around dance moves, belly-dancing moves, kick-boxing (pretend you're Jet Li!), and using fun props like rubber balls and resistance bands. Aerobics classes come tailored to many different fitness levels, from beginner to advanced; look for a class that matches your level and won't be too hard or too easy.

- Skip, gallop, run on all fours, do a cartwheel, do a somersault, run sideways, and do it all again. What a workout! (Warm up first, though. That first cartwheel in 20 years can be a doozy, and you don't want to pull anything.)

- Try taking a class in African dance or joining a drum circle. Let that beat bring out your inner wild child!

- Don't just walk the dog. Teach the dog how to retrieve. Play fetch. Play Frisbee, or teach him the competitive sport of flyball, a fun relay race for speedy dogs. Or get into dog agility, an obstacle-course competition that is so fun, it's hard to believe grown-ups are allowed! (Plus, you get great exercise running around that agility ring directing your dog.)

- Play tag with a group of kids. You're it!

- Break out that old hula hoop or buy a new one. They only cost a couple dollars, and you'll get way more than that out of them in the way of fun, not to mention exercise. (*Warning:* It's hard to keep that hoop going, so you'll have to practice. Stretch out your lower back before and after.)

- Swing. Swing to your heart's content. Ride that fantastic arc of flight and let it fill up your heart as you work those arm and leg muscles.

- When the snow falls, go sledding! If sledding is a little too much for you, what about cross-country skiing?

- Go bowling or play miniature golf. Bring the kids and don't keep score, to help lessen the stress of competition.

- Play a sport. Hit baseballs at a batting cage, play beach volleyball, get together with friends for a weekend game of flag football or basketball at the park or in the local recreation center, play racquetball or squash or tennis on a free afternoon, or join a league for more organized play.

- Remember statue? Twirl each other around, let go, and freeze the way you land. Hold the freeze like you would hold any yoga pose while you hone concentration and build muscle tone!

- Play Twister with your family. This certainly encourages flexibility (in body and mind!).

- Dance around wildly to your favorite music—rock 'n' roll, soul music, even Vivaldi! Use whatever gets your heart pumping. Enlist others, or do a solo performance ... just for fun!

- Ride bikes. Get in better shape, and travel farther. Visit roads untravelled. (Wear a helmet and reflective gear, just like any responsible kid would!)

- Take a walk and practice looking at the world the way you did as a child. (Hey, did we just see you skipping again? And why not? It tones the calf muscles and lifts the spirit.)

- Have a running race, from here to that streetlight and back. If you win, jump up and down 100 times with glee. If you lose, jump up and down 100 times with glee for the winner.

- Take a yoga-for-kids class with your child and have fun doing poses that imitate animals, trees, and mountains.

- Have a sack race or a three-legged race. Or both. Can't get any kids to play? Find some fun grown-ups, and provide refreshments. (Popsicles, anyone? Rice Crispy treats? Peanut butter and jelly?) Make it a party. (Where is that Twister mat ...? You just had it ...!)

Kids move when they play, and so can you. Movement plunges you into a more immediate, physical awareness of yourself and your surroundings, and it keeps you healthy, too. So get moving in the spirit of play, and feel lithe and energetic as a kid again!

There's no such thing as excess eating, only inadequate activity.
—Dorothy Harris (twentieth century), American sports physician

Joy in the Little Things

One of the wondrous things about kids is the way they see the world. The little things give kids great pleasure. They may dream of big things like vacations in the tropics or sports cars, but give a kid a fudgsicle or a ride in a wagon and you've filled them with joy.

The more we live, the more we acquire, and the more we know, the more we tend to lose interest in the little things as we keep on striving for bigger and better things. We want a nicer car, a bigger house, more expensive clothes. But we don't have to lose our joy in the little things. It just takes a little mental reorientation and a dose of mindfulness to appreciate the wonder and magic of a warm beam of sunlight casting a toasty square of light on a wood floor (move over, cat!) or a the smell of a chocolate-chip cookie baking or the genuine smile of a friend.

As adults, we tend to get so busy with our responsibilities and the management of our lives that we forget to notice the day-to-day beauty of the world around us and the mundane unfolding of daily life. Yet little joy gifts lie in wait all over our days. Hunt for them, and you'll enjoy bursts of joy all over the place.

Moving through your day mindfully is the way to begin. When you live mindfully, you are particularly tuned in to what goes on around you, but at the same time, you stand back and don't let those things mentally engage you. You can see the beautiful slate color of a spring sky without engaging in anxiety that it might rain just when you are running from office building to the car. Did you leave the windows open? Why did you have to park so far away from the building today? And where is that umbrella ... hold it right there! Remember, we are being mindful, and those thoughts are flying all over the place! Come back to that slate sky with its cloud textures and shadows. See the beauty stretched out over-head. Really see it!

Here's another example: dusting. Dust collects on our things and we have to clean it off, right? End of story? It doesn't have to be! Notice the powdery surface, the way the surface gleams when you buff it clean, the way the dust forms gray patterns on the rag, the way the whole room comes alive when you are done with an extra brightness and shine.

Or consider cooking: How incredible, the way pale green broccoli gets brilliant and glossy in the wok or the way a bar of chocolate mixed with butter and melted turns into a velvety sauce. Really taste the buttery, sat-isfying crunch of popcorn or the full green garden of flavors in a salad sprinkled with fresh herbs.

Life is really just a string of little miracles punctuated by a few big ones. Why miss any of it?

Play Is Contagious (and We're Glad!)

The more you bring a sense of play and wonder into your life, the more others will be compelled to figure out why you are having such a good time. We love the short film *The Grumpy Bug* by Robert Scull (featured on the Nickelodeon channel during their Nick Jr. morning children's shows) about the bug that was so grumpy nobody would play with him. He finally, despite himself, started to have a really good time jumping in puddles all by himself, at which point all the other bugs gathered around to see what was so fun and at last, shyly asked, "Can we play?" This, of course, dissolved the grumpy bug's grumpiness and everyone had a rol-licking good time. (Check it out online at www.nickjr.com/grownups/home/misc_articles/justforme_stories_1.jhtml.)

Imagination is the highest kite that can fly.
—Lauren Bacall (1924–), American actor

When you learn how to play and how to have fun in your daily life, before you know it, other people will begin asking if they can play, too. Bring them into your circle of play and forge bonds of friendship based on joy. We're glad play is so contagious because it cements relationships with the people we love and creates memories we will treasure forever.

Plus, who needs any more excuse than the simple fact that play is fun, grows our spirits, exercises our bodies, challenges our minds, and makes us feel young? That's all the reason we need.

So anyway ... who's up for a game of hopscotch?

Chapter 12

Hold the World in Your Hands

Twelfth-century Zen master Kakuan illustrated the search for ultimate truth through a series of pictures called the Ox-Herding pictures, sometimes called the Ten Bulls (see the following figure). These 10 pictures show the progression of the mind on a quest for enlightenment.

In the first picture, we search for the bull we have lost. We know something is missing from our lives, and we seek truth, but where is it? In the second picture, we uncover footprints and think we will find the bull, but our search continues. Each of the drawings illustrates the search—glimpsing and chasing the bull, grabbing the bull, harnessing and taming it, riding it, putting it away and resting, and transcending the experience. These pictures represent the transcendence of illusions and the apprehension of truth, a re-seeing of the world, and then, finally … a return to the world, not necessarily to spread the word, but to live enlightened, free of delusion, immersed in joy.

When Zen Buddhists talk about achieving enlightenment, that final expansion of the spirit in which reality is at last apprehended and all attachment, expectation, and illusion falls away effortlessly, inherent in the conversation is that in the end, enlightenment doesn't mean holing up in a cave somewhere. It means going back out into the world, free of ego and filled with compassion, to serve and help others and to help alleviate the suffering of all sentient beings.

In that spirit, we will devote our final chapter to the ways you, too, can move out into the world with compassion, subtly making the world a better place in which to *be*, and leaving joy in your wake. How do we go out to serve and help and live with a joyful spirit in the world? Let's consider that question.

1. The search for what is missing in our lives.

2. Footprints! Embarking on the path of searching.

3. A glimpse of what we seek.

4. Seizing our consciousness.

5. Taming our consciousness.

6. Mastering our consciousness.

7. Resting in perception of truth.

8. Transcending our selves.

9. Perceiving the inter-being of all things.

10. Returning to the world to live in joy.

The mind on a quest for enlightenment, joy!

The Joy of Tolerance

Any group of people will usually result in a wide variety of personalities, experience, opinions, beliefs, and personal histories, not to mention genders, races, and abilities. While humans may tend to fear what they don't know, tolerance for difference builds a foundation in a community, so that everyone can feel accepted, safe, and free to pursue a life that works for them.

Without tolerance, people become isolated from each other. They grow suspicious of difference. If you grew up in a household free from prejudice, tolerance might come naturally to you, but many of us grew up in a household with attitudes that may have subtly influenced our interactions with people who are different than we are.

Different cultures have different kinds of practices and different belief systems, and noticing those differences isn't the same as being intolerant of them. The world contains an amazingly diverse population, and anyone living mindfully will easily observe these differences, even within a very small community. But the practitioner of mindfulness will also learn not to attach judgments to these observations.

Differences in accent or language, skin color, and features, as well as difference in habits, values, and priorities are facts of life. Believing that one language or color or feature or habit or value or priority is better than any other, or has less value, or worse, deserves some kind of punishment or exclusion ... that is prejudice, and that is what tears down a community from the inside out.

My illusion is more real to me than reality. And so do we often build our world on an error, and cry out that the universe is falling to pieces, if any one but lift a finger to replace the error by truth.
—Mary Antin (1881–1949), Russian-born writer

If you were raised with prejudice, if your parents were raised with it, if your grandparents were raised with it, you *can* break the cycle. The things we learn in childhood become deeply ingrained in us, but just as you can learn to value your contribution to the world even if you felt devalued in your youth, you can also decide to practice tolerance even if you have to fight a little harder at first to recognize when you are devaluing others based on assumptions about who they are.

Tolerance toward and empathy for the beliefs of others creates an openness between people in a community and increases good feelings and communication. Reaching out to others to offer physical, mental, emotional, or spiritual help increases your own joy on each of these levels and sets an example in your community.

If you recognize and value the life path of each individual you encounter (and even of those you never meet), no matter how different that path is from your own, you will begin to recognize that deep beneath those differences runs that river we keep talking about—that river of the human spirit that runs through the soul of each of us. We are all a part of that flow, and the more we feel it, the more we encourage others to dive into it, the more deeply we will feel the joy of universal being.

Joy-Full Exercise: Challenge Yourself Through Art

Many artists have captured their thoughts and emotions about prejudice in their work. Challenge your own assumptions by viewing some of these works, watching these films, or reading these books:

- Watch the video documentary *Strange Fruit,* about the life of Billie Holiday and her protest song, by the same title, adopted as the anthem for the anti-lynching movement. Take a look at the many modern film classics currently conceived by African American film director Spike Lee.

- Read Virginia Woolf's classic book *A Room of One's Own.* Published in October 1929, the month of the great crash that sent business men and stock brokers tumbling through plate glass windows, the book explores the creative fate and future of women writers. In a letter to a friend, Woolf wrote of *A Room of One's Own,* "I wanted to encourage the young women—they seem to get fearfully depressed."

- Go online and experience the thousands of testimonials of Holocaust survivors preserved by the Survivors of the Shoah Visual History Foundation, www.vhf.org. American film director Steven Spielberg established this foundation after completing work on the film *Schindler's List.*

- Research and read about American Indian heritage and the contribution this culture has made to our own. Look at the writings of Oren R. Lyons, traditional chief of the Onondaga Nation, Iroquois Confederacy, or Peter Matthiessen, or Louise Erdrich.

- Take another look at Tom Hanks's brave portrayal of Andrew Beckett in the movie *Philadelphia,* a story about a brilliant young homosexual lawyer battling against both AIDS and a wrongful discriminatory dismissal from his law firm, and notice the beautiful performance of Denzel Washington as the heterosexual African American lawyer who defends him.

- Check out the Artists Against Racism organization at www.vrx. net/aar/page2.html.

- For a truly global perspective, go online and access the complete list of winners of the Nobel Prize for Literature: www.nobel.se/ literature/laureates/. The site lists the name and year of each winner. Click on a name to find a brief biography, country, and information about that writer's particular genius and contribution to the world of ideas and letters. In the list of winners you will find a compelling and diverse group of writers, who create a portrait of our world in all its complex and dense cultural richness, full of challenges and potentials yet to be fulfilled. Look for people like China's Gao Xingjian, Poland's Wislawa Szymborska, our own Toni Morrison, Columbia's Gabriel Garcia Marquez, Egypt's Naguib Mahfouz, Japan's Yasunari Kawabata, and many, many more.

Letting Go of the World

Sometimes we humans are very self-important. We think we are responsible for the happiness of others. We blame ourselves for the misfortunes of others. And when big, terrible things happen in the world, somehow, we wonder if we could have prevented them.

One of the most important lessons of this book, one we reiterate often, is that we can only control what *we* do. We cannot control the behavior or actions or thoughts of other people. In the same way, we cannot control the complicated workings of the human race on a global scale, let alone the thoughts and feelings of those to whom we are closest. This is key for recognizing what we should and shouldn't try to control and what it is productive for us to worry about, even to think about, on every scale, from the personal to the public. Because suffering is in the mind—the perception of or reaction to certain conditions—we can only control our own degree of suffering and our own degree of joy.

In grief, part of the pain comes from our feeling that we should not suffer so that it is fundamentally alien to our being, this even though we all suffer, and frequently. Yet we reject suffering as a basic human truth, while greeting joy as integral to our very substance.
—Sister Wendy Beckett (twentieth century), British nun and art historian

We don't control world events and we can't prevent or cause them. *On the other hand* (and isn't there always another hand?), consider the serenity prayer: *God grant me the serenity to accept the things I cannot change, the courage to change the things I can, and the wisdom to know the difference.* Practicing mindfulness and letting go of attachments isn't the same as behaving passively or giving in to whatever happens to you. Mindfulness actually helps you to discover exactly what you are obsessing about pointlessly and which specific things might really make a difference.

For example, it doesn't do any good to worry about whether you are safe in your community, but it may well do a lot of good to organize a neighborhood watch, spearhead a local peace initiative, or volunteer to mentor teenagers who don't have reliable adults in their lives. Maybe getting involved in politics can help to influence policy that in turn influences government decisions about safety, whether locally or on a national level. Maybe organizing a local group to educate the community about cultural or lifestyle differences could help lessen hate crimes.

If we act when it matters without holding on to negativity, fear, and anxiety, we won't necessarily be any safer, not to mention any wealthier or more popular. But we will be sowing the seeds of joy in our community, acting in accordance with our own personal beliefs (whatever they may be), and building character by living with integrity. To let go of the world is not to leave it. It is to live in it without grasping ... leaving both hands free for reaching out to help.

Storm of Change

What could you do to change your world? Brainstorm ideas in your Joy Journal, even those things you *could* do but probably *wouldn't* ever do (because you never know!). From walking your neighbor's dog to handing out mittens in the winter to people on the street who don't have them, be as creative as you can. Add to your list whenever inspiration descends, and you'll find you're more often in the mental mode to improve your world.

Joy Infusion

Have you ever noticed how some places are just nicer to be in than others? Some cities, some towns, some communities have a warmth and a pervasive sense of cheerfulness about them, while others seem cold and uncomfortable. While each of us brings our own preconceptions and expectations to a place, people often agree generally on a place's qualities like a feeling of safety, of acceptance, of openness, of beauty.

Each of us can help to infuse our own communities with more joy by proactively spreading joy as a community member. Hillary Clinton said it takes a village to raise a child. We would agree, and we would also add that it takes a village to create joy. The effect of joy created by many is greater than the individual efforts of each because each act of joy spawns so many more.

How can you help to foster a joyful sense of community? Here are some ideas. Just watch how joy spreads outward like a wildfire.

- Smile at people in a friendly, nonthreatening way. You may surprise more than a few grumpy, hurried commuters, but we're betting you'll get a few smiles back, and maybe even a "Hello!" or a "Good morning!"

- If you see trash on the street, pick it up and toss it in a trashcan.

- If you see someone who looks like he needs a hand with a heavy grocery bag or a stack of packages, offer to help. (Ask first, though—don't just grab the packages, or you might scare someone! People tend to be distrustful of strangers, often for good reason.)

- Be friendly. Sounds simple, but it's so much easier to pretend you don't see any of the other people on the street or in that elevator or standing there on the bus or subway. Strike up a friendly, casual conversation, or offer a sincere compliment. Make someone's day.

- Be really nice to the frustrated cashier or waitress or postal clerk. Stop their frustration in its tracks. It's like handing them an emotional flower.

- Speaking of flowers, send someone flowers. A recent study showed that people who received flowers felt less depressed for days afterward.

- Talk to your neighbors. Get to know them. Be a helpful neighbor, too, offering to help when your neighbor needs a cup of sugar or a short-term baby-sitter or a snow shovel. (You'll be glad you did the next time you are short a cup of flour or you can't find your hammer.)

- Take an interest in the children in your community. Some day, they'll be running things. Even if you don't formally volunteer, you can get to know the kids in your neighborhood. Just because they are short doesn't mean they aren't human!

- If you have your own kids, get to know their friends, and be involved with their lives. Volunteer at the school. Know who is who and who may need help.

- Visit a local retirement center. Make a few friends. Think about how it would feel to go for days without a visitor. Stop the cycle and be a visitor.

- Diversify your friend portfolio. If all your friends are just like you, make an effort to make friends with different kinds of people, to broaden your own horizons and increase your own sense of tolerance. Everybody should have at least one friend who is a child, at least one friend who is past retirement age, and at least one friend from another culture or country. Really get to know people who are different from you, and you'll discover how much you have in common.

- Join a group that makes a difference. Whether you get involved with a church, a philanthropical institution, or start your own group for community improvement, you can enjoy the strength in numbers.

The imagination needs moodling—long, inefficient, happy idling, dawdling and puttering.
—Brenda Ueland (1891–1985), American writer

Laugh and the World Laughs with You

Laughter is infectious. The more you laugh, the more the people around you laugh, and the more joy bubbles into the air around you. Studies have demonstrated that laughter can help people heal more quickly after surgery, plus laughter lightens your mood and makes you feel great.

Just ask members of the Association for Applied and Therapeutic Humor, founded in 1988 by Alison Crane. This Phoenix, Arizona–based group promotes humor and laughter in healing and offers the annual Doug Fletcher Award for Excellence in Therapeutic Humor, the first recipient in 1999 being physician Patch Adams, whose life was made into a movie of the same name starring Robin Williams.

Laughter can also be a spiritual practice. Practitioners of laughing meditation sit in groups and laugh together, and the laughter rolls over the group in waves. The laughing Buddha, Ho Tei, is a fixture in Buddhist lore—a fat, jolly figure who never wore shoes and took life lightly, reveling in the prosperity of joy.

Have you ever noticed that your best friends are the ones you laugh with and that your most cherished intimate relationships thrive on laughter? Laughing is a simple thing to do, and the more you do it, the more its joyful energy will spread; so laugh often and sincerely.

Seek out humor in your community and encourage it. Add to it when you can. We aren't saying you should bombard your friends incessantly with jokes because they probably won't find that funny. But a little genuine humor goes a long way. Meet regularly with friends to watch funny movies or even practice your own informal version of stand-up comedy. Develop an appreciation for humor in art, humor in music, or humor in literature.

Some other ideas to make you laugh:

- Hang out on www.humor.com. We especially like the photo gallery. For even more web-based humor, check out the clearinghouse of humor sites at www.humorlinks.com.

- Envision Baubo, the Greek Goddess of Belly Laughter. Baubo inspired her fellow Goddesses, in times of despair, with her bawdy jokes and her tendency to lift up her skirt and flash people. No, we aren't telling you to do that! But you might get a snicker out of thinking about a Goddess doing it, and let's face it … bellies are pretty funny! They jiggle when you laugh, and they have that little button! Baubo was said to travel the countryside singing and laughing and telling jokes to keep the spirit of joy and revelry alive in the Greek deities. Keep her in your own heart and let her inspire you, too.

- Teach a kid a joke. You might just find the funniest part is in hearing the jokes kids try to make up before they really understand the concept of a joke. Laugh with them, not at them. Jokes that don't quite work as jokes can be pretty darned funny!

- Don't stifle your laugh in public. Smile and let it be known. If others look interested, share the joke.

- Use mindfulness to find humor. If you step back and look at a tense situation, you might suddenly find it funny!

- Humor starts at home. Encourage mirth in your family, whether that means playing more games, watching funny movies together, or reading jokes out loud.

- Get a group of people together and do MadLibs. Somehow, these are always funny. Can't find any in your local bookstore? Order them at www.amazon.com or www.barnesandnoble.com.

- Finally, the only kind of laughter we would encourage you to tone down is the kind that happens at the expense of someone else. Because really, when someone else gets hurt or embarrassed, that's not funny.

Seriousness is a sin, and it is a disease. Laughter has tremendous beauty, a lightness. It will bring lightness to you, and it will give you wings to fly.
—Osho (1931–1990), Indian spiritual writer, speaker, and philosopher

Joy-Full Exercise: Pay It Forward

The novel *Pay It Forward* by Catherine Ryan Hyde, is a story about a social studies teacher who gives his class an unusual assignment. Published in 2000, it sparked a movement, the Pay It Forward Foundation, and a Warner Brothers movie of the same name starring Haley Joel Osment, Helen Hunt, and Kevin Spacey.

In the story, a little boy named Trevor institutes a "pay it forward" project as fulfillment of his teacher's assignment to "Think of an idea for world change, and put it into action." The idea works like this: Do something nice for someone else, but don't expect anything in return.

Instead, ask that the person pay the favor forward, rather than paying it back, by doing something nice for someone else and, in turn, asking that person to pay the favor forward. The favor needn't necessarily be big, but it should be meaningful to the person.

As each person "pays it forward," help, compassion, and miracles spread quickly outward like ripples on a pond. The Pay It Forward Foundation has helped to institute Pay It Forward programs in schools and other organizations all over the world, and the Foundation has inspired the creation of many other similar organizations.

You can contact the Pay It Forward Foundation at www. payitforwardfoundation.org/educators/index.html. Or simply begin the process in your own life. Do someone a favor and ask him to pay it forward. Do it again. And again. And watch love spread and joy multiply.

We Dare You to Dream It

Finally, every community has different needs, different qualities, and a different character, just as every nation, every family, every individual is unique. To take a good hard look at the world around you and to present yourself with the challenge of trying to make it better is to take joy and make it proactive.

We hope you have come to the conclusion that you are not a victim of fate, but that by detaching yourself from your negativity, your desire, your attachments, and your expectations, you can begin to see the world, and yourself, for what they really are: vibrant, living, beautiful beings who are *being* right now. We are all part of the same thing, and we can make our world, our relationships, our very lives more joyful and meaningful if we work together to step over those barriers to freedom that we thought were insurmountable on our own. If everything we need is within us and what is within us is common to all of us, then we are a formidable force indeed.

While we encourage you not to live steeped in unrealistic dreams and expectations for some ideal future, we hope that as individuals, as families, and as communities, we can all move toward the dream of a better world, a higher self, and a greater compassion for each other. If each of us seeks loving kindness on a global scale, then little by little, person by person, town by town, government by government, the world will evolve in a way that can actualize not only human potential, but planetary potential as well. It's our world. We're spinning through space together. Let's all en*joy* the ride.

Joyful Resources

Books That Make Us Happy

Austin, James, M.D. *Zen and the Brain.* Cambridge: MIT Press, 1998.

Beck, Charlotte Joko. *Nothing Special: Living Zen.* San Francisco: HarperSanFrancisco, 1993.

Benson, Herbert, M.D. *The Relaxation Response.* New York: Avon Books, 1975.

Budilovsky, Joan, and Eve Adamson. *The Complete Idiot's Guide to Massage.* Indianapolis: Alpha Books, 1998.

———. *The Complete Idiot's Guide to Meditation, Second Edition.* Indianapolis: Alpha Books, 2002.

———. *The Complete Idiot's Guide to Yoga, Third Edition.* Indianapolis: Alpha Books, 2003.

Cameron, Julia. *The Artist's Way: A Spiritual Path to Higher Creativity.* New York: Jeremy P. Tarcher/Putnam, 1992.

———. *The Vein of Gold: A Journey to Your Creative Heart.* New York: Jeremy P. Tarcher/Putnam, 1996.

Chödrön, Pema. *Awakening Loving-Kindness.* Boston: Shambhala, 1996.

Csikszentmihalyi, Mihaly. *Flow: The Psychology of Optimal Experience.* New York: HarperCollins, 1990.

Dalai Lama, and Howard C. Cutler, M.D. *The Art of Happiness: A Handbook for Living.* New York: Riverhead Books, 1998.

Dalai Lama of Tibet. *Awakening the Mind, Lightening the Heart.* San Francisco: HarperSanFrancisco, 1995.

———. *An Open Heart: Practicing Compassion in Everyday Life.* Boston: Little, Brown and Company, 2001.

———. *Ethics for the New Millennium.* New York: Riverhead Books (reissue), 2001.

Davich, Victor N. *The Best Guide to Meditation.* Los Angeles: Renaissance Books, 1998.

DeMello, Anthony. *Awakenings: Conversations with the Master, Revised Edition.* Chicago: Loyola Press, 1998.

Dominguez, Joe, and Vicki Robin. *Your Money or Your Life, New Edition.* New York: Penguin Books, 1999.

Epstein, Mark, M.D. *Going to Pieces Without Falling Apart: A Buddhist Perspective on Wholeness.* New York: Broadway Books, 1998.

Farhi, Donna. *The Breathing Book.* New York: Henry Holt and Company, 1996.

Feldman, Gail, Ph.D., and Katherine A. Gleason. *Releasing the Goddess Within.* Indianapolis: Alpha Books, 2002.

Fuller, Robert C. *Spiritual, but Not Religious: Understanding Unchurched America.* New York: Oxford University Press, 2002.

Glassner, Barry. *The Culture of Fear: Why Americans Are Afraid of the Wrong Things.* New York: Basic Books, 2000.

Goleman, Daniel. *Emotional Intelligence.* New York: Bantam Books, 1995.

Goleman, Daniel, ed. *Healing Emotions: Conversations with the Dalai Lama on Mindfulness, Emotions, and Health.* Boston: Shambahala, 1997.

Goleman, Daniel, and Joel Gurin, eds. *Mind Body Medicine.* Yonkers, NY: Consumer Reports Books, 1993.

Hanh, Thich Nhat. *Anger: Wisdom for Cooling the Flames.* New York: Riverhead Books, 2001.

———. *Breathe! You Are Alive.* Berkeley: Parallax Press, 1996.

———. *Peace Is Every Step.* New York: Bantam Books, 1991.

Herrigel, Eugen. *Zen in the Art of Archery.* New York: Vintage Books, 1999 (originally published by Pantheon Books in 1953).

Kabat-Zinn, Jon, Ph.D. *Full Catastrophe Living: Using the Wisdom of Your Body and Mind to Face Stress, Pain, and Illness.* New York: Delta, 1990.

Kasl, Charlotte, Ph.D. *If the Buddha Dated: A Handbook for Finding Love on the Spiritual Path.* New York: Penguin USA, 1999.

Katagiri, Dainin. *You Have to Say Something: Manifesting Zen Insight.* Boston: Shambhala, 2000.

Komitor, Jodi M., and Eve Adamson. *The Complete Idiot's Guide to Yoga with Kids.* Indianapolis: Alpha Books, 2000.

Larkin, Geri. *Stumbling Towards Enlightenment.* Berkeley: Celestial Arts, 1997.

LeVert, Suzanne, and Gary McClain, Ph.D. *The Complete Idiot's Guide to Breaking Bad Habits, Second Edition.* Indianapolis: Alpha Books, 2000.

Linn, Denise. *Quest: A Guide for Creating Your Own Vision Quest.* New York: Ballantine Books, 1997.

———. *Sacred Space: Clearing and Enhancing the Energy of Your Home.* New York: Ballantine Books, 1995.

Lockwood, Georgene. *The Complete Idiot's Guide to Simple Living.* Indianapolis: Alpha Books, 2000.

McClain, Gary, Ph.D., and Eve Adamson. *The Complete Idiot's Guide to Zen Living.* Indianapolis: Alpha Books, 2001.

Mitchell, Stephen, ed. *Dropping Ashes on the Buddha: The Teaching of Zen Master Seung Sahn.* New York: Grove Press, 1976.

Reps, Paul, and Nyogen Senzaki, comp. *Zen Flesh Zen Bones: A Collection of Zen and Pre-Zen Writings* (first paperback edition). Boston: Tuttle Publishing, 1998.

Salzberg, Sharon. *Loving-Kindness: The Revolutionary Art of Happiness.* Boston: Shambhala, 1997.

Seligman, Martin, Ph.D. *Authentic Happiness: Using the New Positive Psychology to Realize Your Potential for Lasting Fulfillment.* New York: The Free Press, 2002.

———. *Learned Optimism: How to Change Your Mind and Your Life* (reissue). New York: Pocket Books, 1998.

Siegel, Bernie, M.D. *Prescriptions for Living.* New York: HarperCollins, 1998.

———. *Love, Medicine and Miracles.* New York: Harper Perennial Library, 1990.

Smith, Jean. *365 Zen: Daily Readings.* San Francisco: Harper-SanFrancisco, 1999.

———. *The Beginner's Guide to Zen Buddhism.* New York: Bell Tower, 2000.

Sudo, Philip Toshio. *Zen 24/7.* New York: HarperSanFrancisco, 2001.

Takoma, Geo, and Eve Adamson. *The Complete Idiot's Guide to Power Yoga.* Indianapolis: Alpha Books, 1999.

Weil, Andrew, M.D. *Spontaneous Healing.* New York: Ballantine Books, 1995.

Joy-Inducing Websites

www.beliefnet.com

Beliefnet, a clearinghouse of spiritual beliefs, is filled with interesting information about every major faith from Christianity to Paganism, plus interactive chat boards and quizzes such as "What Religion Are You?" There are hours of fun for the spiritually inclined.

www.wiesenthal.com/mot

The website for the Museum of Tolerance in Los Angeles describes exhibits at this high-tech center for promoting greater humanity and includes information and resources on promoting tolerance in communities.

www.aath.org

The Association for Applied and Therapeutic Humor works to promote healing through humor. According to the website, "Therapeutic humor is defined to be: any intervention that promotes health and wellness by stimulating a playful discovery, expression or appreciation of the absurdity or incongruity of life's situations. This intervention may enhance work performance, support learning, improve health, or be used as a complementary treatment of illness to facilitate healing or coping, whether physical, emotional, cognitive, social, or spiritual." Now there's a cause we can get behind!

www.humor.com
Daily jokes, photo gallery, stand-up resources, this website has it all. Browse and giggle.

www.laughtertherapy.com
Enda Junkins's laughter therapy web page explores the benefits of laughter in relationships and for self-improvement.

www.do-not-zzz.com
This is a fun and enlightening site about Zen practice.

prosperityplace.com/biz/simplify_prosper.html
Joan Sotkin's "Prosperity Place" website offers tips for simplifying your life for greater financial health.

www.simpleliving.net
This network of resources promotes living more simply for greater happiness.

Some Really Great Music

Beethoven's *9th Symphony:* What else would we start with but Beethoven's *9th Symphony?* These four movements of pure genius culminate in Beethoven's most famous masterpiece, "Ode to Joy."

Bach, Johann Sebastian. *Magnificat.* Beautiful orchestra and choral music.

Caesar, Shirley and Rev. James Cleveland. *Gospel Shining Stars.* Liquid 8, 2003. Empowering!

Enya. *Paint the Sky with Stars: The Best of Enya.* Warner Brothers, 1997. Peaceful new age music.

Fisk Jubilee Singers. *In Bright Meadows.* Curb Records, 2003. Excellent gospel music. Don't miss "Rockin' Jerusalem."

Gill, Vince. *Let's Make Sure We Kiss Good-Bye.* MCA Nashville, 2000.

Handel, George Friderik. *Water Music.*

Isaak, Chris. *Baja Sessions.* Warner Brothers, 1996.

Mann, Aimee. *Lost in Space.* Superego, 1997.

Masters of Chant. *Masters of Chant.* Arex Japan, 2000. If you haven't listened to Gregorian Chant, it's time to treat your ears and your soul.

McLachlan, Sarah. *Mirrorball.* Arista, 1999.

Olivor, Jane. *Love Decides.* River Road Entertainment, 2000. Gentle, joyful love songs.

Pachelbel, Johann. *Canon.*

Pendergrass, Teddy. *Joy.* Elektra/Asylum Records, 1988.

Shankar, Ravi. *Vision of Peace.* Deutsche Grammophon/Universal, 2000. George Harrison called Ravi Shankar the "Godfather of World Music."

Taylor, James. *Live.* Sony Music, 1993.

Vivaldi, Antonio. *The Four Seasons.* Any recording of this classic is pure joy!

Index

W–X–Y–Z

The New Age way to get what you want out of life
The *Empowering Your Life* series

Empowering Your Life with Wicca

ISBN: 0-02-864437-9
$14.95 US/$22.99 CAN

Packed with advice and instructions, this book offers New Age Wicca techniques to help you get what you want most out of life, live joyously, and make each day sacred.

Available at all retailers in June 2003.

Empowering Your Life with Dreams

ISBN: 1-59257-092-5
$14.95 US/$22.99 CAN

Provides a window into deeper levels of awareness by exploring the meanings of dreams and giving valuable insights into personal well-being.

Available at all retailers in December 2003.